DOLPH BRISCOE

My Life in Texas Ranching and Politics

T0124036

DOLPH BRISCOE

My Life in Texas Ranching and Politics

By Dolph Briscoe

As told to Don Carleton

BRISCOE CENTER
FOR AMERICAN HISTORY
THE UNIVERSITY OF TEXAS AT AUSTIN

Distributed by the University of Texas Press

Cover: Dolph and Janey Briscoe in front of the Governor's Mansion in Austin. *Briscoe (Dolph) Papers, Briscoe Center for American History, the University of Texas at Austin, di_03921.*

Back cover: Dolph and Janey Briscoe with their children on the Catarina Ranch. *Courtesy of the Briscoe family.*

Frontispiece: Dolph and Janey Briscoe at the Catarina Ranch. *Courtesy of the Briscoe family.*

Book design by David Timmons

CONTENTS

Governor Briscoe was pleased to learn more about his family's history while on a trip to England. *Courtesy of the Briscoe family.*

FOREWORD

By Dolph Briscoe IV

AMONG MY MOST BELOVED MEMORIES are moments spent with my grandfather listening to recollections about his amazing life. From an early age, he regaled me with fascinating stories about my family's ranching heritage and his time in politics. My grandfather's skilled narrating and appreciation for the past helped spark a lifelong love of history in me as a young boy.

I had the great fortune of spending many wonderful years with my grandparents, Dolph and Janey Briscoe. They showered their grandchildren with love and support and continuously encouraged us at each stage of our lives. My grandfather enthusiastically embraced my interest in history and politics. He always answered questions I had about his time in government, notable individuals he had known, and current political controversies. As a senior at Carrizo Springs High School in 1999, I presented an overview of politics past and present through my grandfather's eyes as my major academic project for the year. While completing a master's thesis in history at Baylor University in 2006, my grandfather kindly allowed me to conduct an oral history interview with him about his recollections of Lyndon B. Johnson.

Our close relationship further deepened when I entered the University of Texas at Austin in the fall of 2007 to pursue a doctoral degree in history. He was tremendously supportive of my efforts to become a professional historian. I often have said that if there was any place my grandfather loved as much as our family ranches and the city

Governor Briscoe in 2006 with one of his grandchildren, Dolph Briscoe IV. *Courtesy of the Briscoe family.*

of Uvalde, it was the University of Texas. He took pride in the fact that his Baylor Bear grandson had also become a Longhorn, and I cherish the memories I have with my grandfather wearing the burnt orange at football games and other university events. In 2008, my grandfather helped fund an endowment for the university's Center for American History, and I had the honor of standing by his side when UT graciously named this world-class institution of historical collection, research, and scholarship after him. I benefitted from regularly mining the rich collections of the Briscoe Center as I worked on my dissertation, and I have been privileged to remain actively involved with this outstanding organization since finishing my degree.

This book is a product of the wonderful Briscoe Center for American History. Don Carleton, who has served as a mentor to me in my studies and career in history, did a masterful job interviewing my grandfather and creating this book. As I read the pages of this memoir, I can hear my grandfather's voice, which is a testament to Dr. Carleton's exceptional skills as a historian. Dr. Carleton and the staff of the Briscoe Center have provided my family and me with a gift we always will treasure. Additionally, this book is a fantastic contribution to the historical record of Texas in the twentieth century. In this work readers will find intriguing stories about both ranching and politics over a complex period of time when Texas itself experienced significant change.

Perhaps most importantly, my grandfather concludes his memories with his conviction that Texas's best days await in the future. I frequently heard him mention this belief throughout his later years. Among his many magnificent qualities, this unwavering optimism about life and what lies ahead continues to inspire me. I miss my grandfather every day, and it is one of my life's greatest honors to carry his name and to attempt to live out his spirit of hopefulness. It is my wish that readers will enjoy this memoir by a Texan who revered the past, never forgot the importance of the present, and looked forward with excitement to a grand future.

Governor Briscoe and Don Carleton at the University of Texas at Austin's ceremony honoring his donation to the Center for American History. *Photo by Marsha Miller, the University of Texas at Austin.*

PREFACE TO THE
PAPERBACK EDITION

A s I WRITE THIS, Dolph Briscoe's memoir recalling his life in
Texas ranching and politics approaches the tenth anniversary
of its initial publication, which was in late spring 2008. Governor
Briscoe was deeply pleased by the positive reviews the book received,
and he was honestly surprised by its popularity. His surprise was char-
acteristic of this truly modest and generous man.

Much has happened, both tragic and triumphant, in the more than
ten years since the governor and I finished our work to preserve his
memories for the historical record and to make them available for
the knowledge and enjoyment of the reading public. Sadly, the governor's beloved granddaughter Kate Marmion, who was a freshman
at the University of Texas at Austin, died in an accident just prior to
the publication of his memoir. The governor felt Kate's death deeply,
and he honored her memory by establishing a scholarship fund in her
name at UT Austin's College of Communication.

Late in 2008, in response to an invitation from Bill Powers, then
the president of UT Austin, Governor Briscoe donated $12 million
to be added to his previous gift of $3 million in support of the Cen-
ter for American History. Annual income from the Dolph Briscoe
endowment, which initially totaled $15 million, quickly transformed
the Center for American History, making it possible for it to become
a nationally recognized leader as a history center generating its own
research through its publications, documentary films, and exhibitions,
as well as serving as a significant resource for teaching and scholarly

The John Nance Garner Museum in Uvalde was renamed the Briscoe-Garner Museum in 2011, and the second floor now features an exhibit abut Governor Briscoe's life. *Briscoe Center photograph.*

studies. Accordingly, in 2009 the Board of Regents of the University of Texas System recognized Governor Briscoe's generosity, as well as his widely acknowledged service as a public servant, by naming the center after him. "The history of Texas has long been a passion of mine," Governor Briscoe stated at the time. "Accordingly, I have been an avid fan of the Center for American History, which has the largest collection of Texana in existence. I believe that the outstanding work . . . the center carries out should be continued, enhanced, and expanded." As the center's founding director, I could not have imagined a more fitting and honorable name for our institution.

Governor Dolph Briscoe Jr. died on the evening of June 27, 2010, at his home in Uvalde following complications of heart and kidney failure. He was eighty-seven years old. His funeral service, which was held at the Saint Philip's Episcopal Church in Uvalde on Thursday morning, July 1, 2010, was attended by thousands of mourners, including former governor Mark White, then-governor Rick Perry, dozens of former and current members of the Texas Legislature, several regents of the University of Texas System, executive officers and faculty of UT San Antonio and UT Austin, prominent business leaders, and other local and state officials. Governor Briscoe was buried next to his wife, Janey, at the cemetery on the family's Rio Frio Ranch.

In 2011, the University of Texas at Austin renamed the John Nance Garner Museum in Uvalde, a unit of the Briscoe Center, the Briscoe-Garner Museum. The second floor of the newly renovated former home of Vice President Garner has since been converted into an attractive exhibition space displaying papers, photographs, artifacts, and memorabilia documenting and commemorating Governor Briscoe's life and career and serving as a forum to educate the public about the life and times of Texas's forty-first governor.

The public spaces at the Briscoe Center's research and collections facility on the UT Austin campus reopened in 2017 after an extensive renovation. *Briscoe Center photograph.*

Finally, largely because of Governor Briscoe's transformative gift and his enthusiastic endorsement of the center's work, UT Austin President Greg Fenves and numerous donors made it possible for us to completely renovate the public spaces of the center's research and collections facility on the east side of campus. This beautifully renovated space now features a new and greatly expanded reading room, meeting rooms, and a large exhibition gallery. I only regret that Governor Briscoe did not live to see its completion. I know that it would have made him proud.

I want to thank the University of Texas Press and its talented director, Dave Hamrick, for distributing this new edition of *Dolph Briscoe: My Life in Texas Ranching and Politics*. I also want to acknowledge the skilled work of the Briscoe Center's editor and head of publications, Dr. Holly Taylor, in guiding this project to completion. I am delighted that Governor Briscoe's grandson Dr. Dolph Briscoe IV, an up-and-coming young historian, contributed a foreword to the new edition. Governor Briscoe was extremely proud of all of his grandchildren, but he was especially happy that one of them chose to be a historian, a profession and subject the governor respected and loved. And finally, I want to thank all of the Briscoe Center's friends and generous donors who have joined with Governor Briscoe to help make it possible for the center to contribute to the cause of history.

DON CARLETON

PREFACE TO THE FIRST
EDITION

DOLPH BRISCOE, GOVERNOR OF TEXAS from 1973 until 1979, is the largest individual landowner and rancher in a state famous for its huge ranches. He is one of the most respected businessmen in Texas, with a portfolio that includes banks, agribusinesses, cattle, and oil and gas properties. His philanthropy has provided much-needed support to a wide range of educational, medical, scientific, and cultural institutions. As a hardworking member of the state legislature in the decade following the Second World War, Briscoe was the author of major legislation that vastly improved the daily lives of farmers and ranchers throughout Texas. As an activist leader of the venerable Texas and Southwestern Cattle Raisers Association, Briscoe played a significant role in the successful effort to eliminate an age-old scourge of the livestock industry. As a cattle rancher, he has been a pioneer in the modernization of the industry. As a friend and associate of a number of major American political figures, he has been an eyewitness to history. And as a governor who assumed office following one of the most far-reaching corruption scandals in Texas history, Dolph Briscoe played a crucial role in restoring public confidence in the integrity of state government.

Yet, despite his lifetime of accomplishment enriched with fascinating experiences, Dolph Briscoe is among the most modest and self-effacing public figures that I have ever known. His intense modesty makes it difficult, even painful, for him to talk about himself. Bragging is near the top of his list of unacceptable social behaviors, ranking just below lying. In addition, his strong preference is to spend as much time as possible out on his Catarina Ranch, not behind a desk talking to an intrusive and persistent historian who is invading his well guarded privacy. That is why this "as told to" book has been a long time coming. Dolph Briscoe has been a most reluctant memoirist. It is something that he never intended to do.

Nevertheless, despite his great reluctance, you now hold Dolph Briscoe's autobiography in your hands. What overcame his natural disinclination to—as he said to me so many times during this project—"talk about myself"? The simple answer: his deep and lifelong love of history. This publication represents the victory of Dolph Briscoe's respect for the cause of history over his intense personal modesty. As a child, Dolph Briscoe read and reread *The Raven*, Marquis James's biography of Sam Houston. That book, which has become a classic popular work of Texas history, made Dolph Briscoe a voracious consumer of historical knowledge for the rest of his life. As a result, he has become a lay expert in the fields of American political history, Texas history, and the history of the ranching industry. As an elected official, civic leader, and philanthropist, he has made significant contributions to the cause of history, especially in the areas of historic preservation, historical education, and basic scholarly research in history.

So it was the cause of history, not the need for self-promotion, that persuaded Dolph Briscoe to give us this recollection of a life well lived. And I must stress, as the person to whom he told his story, I know that Dolph Briscoe was not persuaded by any egotistic feelings that HE was important to history. He admitted at one point during our work together that the process of recalling his past made him realize that he had been fortunate in his life to do and see things of importance, and he accepted the need to document these things. That insight cleared the way, but it didn't make it any easier for him to overcome his innate reluctance to "talk about myself."

There is one other person who made this book possible: Dolph Briscoe's beloved wife and partner in everything that he did, the late Janey Slaughter Briscoe. Janey Briscoe believed fervently in this project. I don't think our work would have ever started without her firm and enthusiastic support. Janey Briscoe shared her husband's love of Texas history, and she understood the need for a former governor of Texas to preserve his historical memories in print. This memoir documents the vital role that she played in many of these events. I am profoundly sorry that she did not live to see the results, but I am proud that her hopes for its completion have been fulfilled.

The roots of this project go back to 1992, when Dolph Briscoe donated his personal and gubernatorial papers to the University of Texas Center for American History. I have had the great honor to serve as the director of the center and its predecessor, the Barker Center, since 1979. The Briscoe Papers, which measure more than one thousand linear feet in size, are an essential source for the political history of Texas during Governor Briscoe's years as an elected official. A full description and index of the collection can be found on the internet at www.lib.utexas.edu/taro/utcah/00066/cah-00066.html.

The donation of the Briscoe Papers began my friendship with the man I still address as "Governor." Over the years he became an enthusiastic supporter of the center. In 1993 he and his wife, Janey, provided the funds for us to purchase the oldest datable photograph known to have been taken in Texas. This 1849 photograph is a daguerreotype image of the Alamo. In 1999 Governor Briscoe provided the leadership to make it possible for the John Nance Garner Museum in Uvalde to become a division of the center. In 2007 he provided funds for the center to purchase an important letter written by his hero, Sam Houston, to Gen. Thomas Jefferson Green in 1837. That same year, he donated $3 million to establish the center's Dolph and Janey Briscoe Endowment for Texas History. The Briscoe Endowment is the largest cash gift ever made to the center.

As Governor Briscoe and I got to know each other better, I lobbied him to write an autobiography. Austin attorney and former University of Texas regent Howard Richards, who served as a key aide to Briscoe during his years as governor, helped immeasurably in this effort. Howard and I soon had another valuable ally in Janey Briscoe. Once she came on board, the proposal became a reality. Governor Briscoe agreed to let me interview him in a series of lengthy oral history interviews that occurred over a period of eight years. Events beyond our control frequently interrupted and delayed the project, sometimes for many months. After each interview session, I edited the transcripts to remove my presence as an interviewer and to construct a narrative in the governor's voice. Throughout this process, Governor Briscoe read and revised the text. My only contribution to the final version of the text, other than editing, was to add a few dates and names that Governor Briscoe could not recall at the time of our interviews. Otherwise, this is entirely Dolph Briscoe's personal story in his own words.

Dolph Briscoe and I want to acknowledge and thank those who were helpful to our work. Barbara Woodman, Governor Briscoe's efficient, highly skilled, and personable administrative associate in Uvalde coordinated and facilitated all of the interviews. In addition, Barbara helped gather photographs and transcribed some of the text. Her work has been invaluable. Governor Briscoe's oldest daughter, Janey Briscoe Marmion, provided crucial encouragement as well as practical help with locating photographs. Ron Tyler, director of the Amon Carter Museum and former director of the Texas State Historical Association (TSHA) gave the project an administrative home at the TSHA during its oral history phase. Sheree Scarborough aided me with the research in the early stages. My professional colleagues at the Center for American History, Evan Hocker and Steven D. Williams, found and scanned most of the photographs. Holly Taylor, head of publications at the center, did an outstanding job managing the production of this book. My longtime professional comrades, Kate Adams and Alison Beck, helped me in various ways throughout the project. Governor Briscoe and I thank you all.

DON CARLETON

DOLPH BRISCOE

My Life in Texas Ranching and Politics

Chapter 1

A PRODUCT OF THE LAND

I T WAS MY HONOR AND PRIVILEGE to serve as the governor of
Texas for six wonderful years. As a young World War II veteran, I
served for six years as a member of the Texas State Legislature. My
twelve years of public service gave me deep personal satisfaction, but
my political experiences have not shaped or defined me the way the
land has. I'm a product of the land, and nearly everything that I have
done in my life has had some connection to the land. It seems only
natural to me that this has been so, because the hunger for land has
been a strong Briscoe family trait for many generations.

My earliest known ancestors, the Briscos, were members of the
landed gentry in northern England. The letter "e" was added to our
family name at some point during the eighteeenth century. For cen-
turies, the Brisco ancestral home was Crofton Hall, a grand manor
situated in a beautiful section of Cumberland County near the border
between England and Scotland. The house was demolished in the
1950s, but some of the estate's outbuildings remain. During the mid-
eighteenth century, Sir John and Lady Jane Brisco of Crofton Hall
were influential enough to have commissioned the renowned artist
Thomas Gainsborough to paint their wedding portraits. Sir John's
original portrait, as well as a copy of Lady Jane's portrait, are among
my most treasured possessions.

The first Briscoe to settle in America was Dr. John Brisco, who left
Crofton Hall in 1633 and sailed on the ship *The Ark and the Dove* to
Maryland colony, where he served as personal physician to Lord Bal-

timore. Dr. Brisco settled on the eastern shore of Maryland. His descendents migrated to western Virginia, where they built a distinctive federal-style house called Piedmont. The house, which is now owned by famed public television newsman and native Texan Jim Lehrer, was the centerpoint for Briscoe land holdings in the Shenandoah Valley.

A hunger for land eventually pushed my ancestors farther west. Some settled in Claiborne County, Mississippi, where they established cotton plantations. The most prominent of these Briscoe planters was Gen. Parmenas Briscoe. In 1833, one of Parmenas's sons, Andrew Briscoe, migrated to Anahuac, Texas, and established a mercantile business. Andrew played an important role in the Texas Revolution. He attended the convention at Washington-on-the-Brazos that declared Texas's independence from Mexico. As a captain in the Texan army during the revolution, he participated in the battle of San Jacinto. After the revolution, Sam Houston, the president of the new Republic of Texas, appointed Andrew Briscoe judge of the court in Harrisburg, where he also became a railroad promoter. Briscoe County in the Texas Panhandle is named in his honor.

In 1838, another one of Parmenas Briscoe's sons, James Montgomery Briscoe, settled on a land grant located north of present-day Rosenberg, in Fort Bend County, Texas. His son, William Montgomery Briscoe, was my grandfather. William and his wife, Nora, were the parents of my mother, Georgie, who was born in Fort Bend County on October 1, 1888.

My paternal grandfather, Lee Adolphus Briscoe, owned a farm in Fort Bend County and ran cattle in an area that is now suburban west Houston. His father was Robert Parmenas Briscoe, who served as an officer in the Confederate army under Robert E. Lee. My paternal grandmother, Lucy Wade Briscoe, had her own distinguished family history. She was a granddaughter of Randolph Foster, a native of Mississippi who moved to Texas in 1822. He was a close associate of Stephen F. Austin's during the early years of the Austin Colony. With a family history so deeply rooted in the Anglo settlement of Texas and the subsequent period of revolution and independence, it's easy to understand why I have always had a fascination with Texas history.

My father, Dolph Briscoe Sr., was born on September 1, 1890, in Fulshear, Texas, a little town located on a railroad in Fort Bend County about forty miles west of Houston. His first name was a derivation of his father Lee Adolphus Briscoe's name. Father seemed to have been born with a strong affinity for hard work. He was riding a horse and tending to cattle almost as soon as he could walk. His father taught him the skills he needed for ranch work, including cow roping and culling. My father often told me that when he was a kid he was never happier than when he was on the back of a good horse working cattle. He even delivered the daily morning newspaper, the *Houston Post*, on horseback, usually in the pre-dawn dark, before heading to the cow pastures. As a teenager, my father worked at a livery stable in Fulshear and drove buggies and wagons for hire. Most of his customers were salesmen who came to Fulshear on the train and needed someone to drive them around the area to make their sales.

As a prize for winning a contest for selling subscriptions to the *Houston Post*, my father was awarded a scholarship to attend Peacock Military Academy, a private preparatory boarding school for boys in San Antonio. He graduated in 1907 at the age of sixteen. My grandfather wanted my father to study law at the University of Texas, but Father had no interest in anything that kept him from horse and cow trading and working out on the land. Instead of going to college, he went to work punching cattle on ranches in south Texas.

Father married his second cousin, Georgie Briscoe, on October 1, 1913. His desire for land, to own it and to work on it, attracted him to the town of Uvalde, located on the Southern Pacific Railroad about seventy-five miles west of San Antonio. He and Mother moved there in 1914. My father once told me that he chose Uvalde because he wanted some good land where it didn't rain too much. He was sick of trying to work cattle in the wet Brazos River bottoms in Fort Bend County, only a few miles from the Gulf of Mexico with its subtropical climate. The cattle often got bogged down in the flood plain "goo" of the Brazos. It was a hard, dirty job getting those cows out of the mud.

Father also chose Uvalde for his home because it was a prosperous little town of about four thousand residents that offered some solid business opportunities. The year he and Mother arrived, Uvalde had three banks, a library, a daily newspaper, and eighty businesses. Three years earlier, a railroad had been completed from Uvalde to Crystal City, giving Uvalde an important transportation link to the ranches and farms of one of the most rapidly developing agricultural regions in Texas.

Malcolm Monroe, one of my father's boyhood friends in Fort Bend County, was a kerosene salesman for the Texas Company (Texaco). He arranged for my father to open a bulk oil distributorship in Uvalde. Father drove a little wagon to deliver barrels of kerosene to customers in town and on the ranches around the area. He did well, but he was constantly searching for an opportunity to enter the ranching business. Eventually, Father leased land along the Leona River and ran and traded some cattle, but he lacked the capital necessary to invest in any significant amount of land or cattle. My father did better, however, with a little business in which he took horses and mules from the region around Uvalde and delivered them to the Texas coast to sell to farmers. He soon expanded his operations to Arkansas and Missouri.

During the First World War, my father formed a partnership with J. Patton and Albert Finley to trade cattle. The war caused a big surge in demand for beef, so by the end of 1918 my father and his partners were handling a fairly large number of livestock. Unfortunately, their success was short-lived. In 1921 the cattle market crashed, and my father lost all of the money he had tied up in the business.

Two years prior to the cattle market crash, Father dropped his affiliation with the Texas Company to become an oil distributor for the Humble Oil Company, which had its headquarters in Houston. He made the switch because his friend Malcolm Monroe had become sales manager for Humble. Father's affiliation with this fast-growing oil company proved to be a wise move. In 1911 a group of independent oilmen, including Ross Shaw Sterling, Walter Fondren, Robert Blaffer, and William Stamps Farish, created Humble by consolidating their holdings in the newly discovered oil fields in southeast Texas. By the time my father went with Humble, the company was well on its way to becoming one of the most powerful business enterprises in Texas. My father kept his Humble Oil distributorship for the rest of his life.

Ross Shaw Sterling

During one of Malcolm Monroe's trips to Uvalde in 1923, Father told him that the economic recession that had hurt him so badly two years earlier had created new business opportunities. Good cattle could be purchased for the low price of about twenty-five dollars a head. My father believed that demand for beef would soon increase and drive up the price of cattle. Now was the opportune time, he told Monroe, to buy some cows and get back into the business. If he could just find financial backers, he was certain that he could make money for the investors as well as for himself. Monroe thought that Ross Shaw Sterling, one of the founders of Humble Oil and at that time the company's president, might be interested in helping. Monroe knew that Mr. Sterling, who had plenty of cash available, was interested in the cattle business. Mr. Sterling also had a reputation for helping promising young men wanting to start their own businesses. Monroe noted that Mr. Sterling, who lived in Houston, was an avid hunter. He suggested that my father arrange a deer hunt for Mr. Sterling and serve as his guide. That would give Mr. Sterling an opportunity to know my father and, just maybe, get Mr. Sterling's interest in my father's proposal to start a cattle business. If Father would make all the hunting arrangements, Monroe promised to deliver Mr. Sterling.

Father eagerly accepted Monroe's offer. He persuaded a stockman whose ranch was overrun with deer to allow Mr. Sterling to hunt on his property. Monroe's hunch proved correct. Mr. Sterling accepted the invitation. Father met the Houston oilman at the Uvalde train station in a Model T Ford. The two of them drove alone together over the pastures looking for deer. During the hunt, Dad engaged Mr. Sterling in a detailed and extended discussion about ranching and the condition of the cattle business at that time. My father argued that cattle prices had hit bottom. Now was the time to buy. Father must have been very persuasive as he drove over those dusty ranch roads, because Mr. Sterling agreed to provide him with the funds to purchase about one thousand head of cattle. Mr. Sterling told my father that if he would do all the work, they would split the future profits on a fifty-fifty basis.

My father found one thousand head of cattle at the O-9 Cattle Company, which operated near the town of Barnhart in Irion County, west of San Angelo. Mr. Sterling traveled from Houston and negotiated a deal with W. B. Silliman, manager of the O-9 Cattle Company, to buy the cattle for $25,000. After the deal was made and Mr. Sterling was leaving, Silliman commented that it was too bad that Mr. Sterling didn't have enough money to buy all of his cows. Mr. Sterling had asked my father to find one thousand cows, so that was the arrangement he had made, but Silliman really wanted to sell his entire herd. Mr. Sterling, one of the richest individuals in Texas, took Silliman's statement as a challenge. He asked Silliman how many cows he owned. Silliman replied that he had four thousand in addition to the one thousand he had just sold. His company also owned 640 acres and a lease on several thousand acres of additional land. Silliman was willing to sell the entire operation, land and all.

This unexpected turn of events initiated another round of hard negotiating that eventually reached a point where there was a difference of only one thousand dollars between their offers. Neither man would give in, so they finally agreed to flip a half-dollar coin to determine the price. Mr. Sterling won the toss. He and my father came away with five thousand head of cattle and the land on which to graze them. They formed a partnership and chartered a corporation for their new cattle business. For some reason, my father believed that thirteen was his lucky number, so he and Mr. Sterling agreed to name their company the 13 Ranch.

That was the beginning of a wonderful relationship between Ross Sterling and my father. Born in 1875, Mr. Sterling had grown up near Anahuac, the town where my ancestor Andrew Briscoe had settled in the early 1830s. While in his twenties Mr. Sterling had worked as a farmer and a merchant. He became an independent oil operator in 1903, eventually merging his interests with other operators to form Humble Oil, one of the predecessor companies of today's ExxonMobil Corporation. Mr. Sterling also had branched out into the railroad business by the time he and my father formed their partnership. Later, after serving as chairman of the Texas Highway Commission, he was elected governor in November 1930. He won the Democratic Party's

Governor and Mrs. Sterling in Austin in 1933. *All photographs are courtesy the Center for American History, the University of Texas at Austin, unless otherwise noted; di_02350.*

nomination after a primary battle with ten other candidates, including Miriam "Ma" Ferguson, who he defeated in a runoff.

It's obvious that Mr. Sterling was a gifted entrepreneur and a successful politician, but my family also knew Mr. Sterling to be an extremely kind and generous man. He was a true gentleman. He liked Mother and Father very much, and he appreciated the way my father ran the cattle operation.

As my father predicted, the cattle market improved greatly, and the 13 Ranch thrived and expanded. The lease my father and Mr. Sterling acquired from the O-9 Cattle Company was a small portion of the land the state constitution had set aside as a source of revenue to support the University of Texas. My father and Mr. Sterling had some difficulty because the university changed its leasing policy about the time they acquired their lease, which was a much larger amount of land than the university wanted to lease to any one company. To buy time to develop their business, Father and Mr. Sterling agreed to give up their lease after a couple of years. They subsequently bought the Anacacho Ranch near Brackettville and moved their cattle there, but they kept the O-9 brand.

I was born in our little frame house at the corner of High and Leona streets in Uvalde on April 23, 1923. Two years later, we moved into a two-story frame house that Father built, and that was where I grew up. The year I was born was when my father and Mr. Sterling began their partnership, so Mr. Sterling was a strong presence throughout my childhood. I had the wonderful opportunity to get to know him and his wife, Mrs. Sterling, very well. Her name was Maud, but she was always Mrs. Sterling to me. They treated me like a grandson. Along with my father, Mr. Sterling was one of my most significant role models. He played a strong role in developing my interest in politics and state government. I worshipped the man.

THE CHUPADERA

When I was in grade school, my father learned that the historic Chupadera Ranch, which covered about 50,000 acres bordering the Rio Grande in Maverick and Dimmitt counties, was for sale. Chupadera got its name from a flowing spring on the ranch. One of the first ranches in that area of the country, the Chupadera was blessed with an abundant source of water from several springs that flowed out of the outcrop of the Carrizo sand formation running north and south through the property.

My father told Mr. Sterling that the ranch was one of the finest in Texas and urged him to buy it. Subsequently, Mr. Sterling purchased the ranch from two brothers, John and "Ab" Blocker, who were legendary characters in the history of the cattle industry. The Blocker boys, including their brother Bill, had been trail drivers back in the days when there were no railroads nearby. Ab drove the first herd of cattle from South Texas to the great XIT Ranch in the Texas Panhandle, and he was the one who came up with the XIT brand that gave the ranch its name. John Blocker devised a peculiar but highly effective method of roping cows with a large loop that came to be known as the "Blocker loop." The Chupadera has taken a prominent place in

Here I am on my Shetland pony next to Mr. Sterling in Carrizo Springs. *Briscoe Papers, Box 255; di_04106.*

the historical annals of the ranching industry because of its age and because of the association with the Blocker brothers.

The Chupadera was the ranch of my childhood. It was a very special place for me. For one thing, it looks different from the other ranches in that region. The land is sandy, with a lot of sand rock outcrop, and it is covered with mesquite, huisache, scrub-oak, and cactus. It was full of wildlife: deer, coyotes, javelina, turkey, quail, and doves. There was one road in, and when you got to the ranch headquarters the road ended. As a child, I loved that ranch and everything on it. But some of my warmest memories of the ranch are directly associated with Mr. Sterling.

It was my good fortune as a child to accompany my father when he and Mr. Sterling drove around on the ranch or when they visited some of the towns in the region around the ranch. A trip that especially stands out in my memory was one that we made to Carrizo Springs, the Dimmit County seat, located between the Chupadera and Uvalde.

The town of Carrizo Springs sits on top of the outcrop of the Carrizo sands, from which springs flow. That combination of sand and water makes the area a fine place to grow strawberries. It was such an important crop that the town held a strawberry festival for a period of many years. After Mr. Sterling became governor, he was invited to attend the festival and ride in the parade on a big horse. My father and I went with him. It was a memorable occasion for me because Mr. Sterling asked me to ride along with him on my little Shetland pony. I was about eight years old. You can imagine how thrilled I was.

After the parade through the center of Carrizo Springs, there was a barbecue at the town park. Mr. Sterling had me sit next to him at this barbecue. I guess I got excited at one point and didn't pay attention to what I was doing. I knocked over a full glass of water right onto his lap. My father was sitting at another table nearby and I could see him get red in the face. I knew that I was in trouble. Mr. Sterling stood up and just wiped the water off his lap. Then he smiled and announced to the people sitting around us: "Well, you know fellows, there's one thing about it, a little water never hurt anything in Dimmit County." It didn't bother him at all, but I knew that I was in trouble. So I worked very hard at staying close by Mr. Sterling's side for the rest of the day.

After the barbecue, I went with my parents and Mr. and Mrs. Sterling to the Chupadera Ranch. We drove in Mr. Sterling's limousine with his driver, whose name was Alex. There were a number of gates that we had to drive through on the ranch, so I was designated as the gate opener. Father had always taught me that you open a gate on the double. When you get out of the car you run, you don't walk. You get that gate open and closed as fast as you can. I was trying to get back into my father's good graces, so I was determined to get those gates opened and closed in pronto time. I was really showing off. Everything went fine with the first few gates, but then I moved a little too fast with a gate and caught it on the car bumper as I was closing it. The bumper fell partially away from the car and it pulled the gate off

The Chupadera Ranch was a hunter's paradise. Here I am with my first deer. *Courtesy of the Briscoe family.*

its hinges. Alex stopped the car and everyone got out to survey the damage. It didn't bother Mr. Sterling at all. He actually thought it was funny. I could tell that things were getting worse with my father, however. Alex and my father had to find wire to tie the bumper on the car and to put the gate back up. That was not my best day.

Thank goodness, as soon as we arrived at the Chupadera, Mr. Sterling asked me if I would like to go hunting. "We'll get Alex to take us down to a tank," Mr. Sterling said, "and we'll wait for a deer to come for water." This was a most welcome invitation, because I was happy to do anything to delay the moment of reckoning with my father. We didn't see any deer, but that was okay. Finally that evening, Mr. Sterling went to bed, and I lost my protector. I got a very memorable scolding that night.

As a kid, I liked to spend the summer and weekends on the Chupadera whenever possible. I liked to think that I was working when I was on the ranch, but it is more likely that I was just in the way of the men who were really working. But the ranch workers were always very kind and made me feel as though I was helping them. It made me feel useful and important. Those were wonderful days.

I had learned to ride on a Shetland Paint we called Pinto. When I was on my father's ranch, I was on a horse most of the time, riding with the men as they worked the livestock. Naturally, I liked riding better than working on the fence or on the windmill. We rode most days, usually looking for calves that had been attacked by screwworms. I can still remember enjoying the beautiful wildflowers that would cover the Chupadera like a floral blanket during the spring. That place was like heaven to me. My experience on the ranch was the source of my ambition to be a rancher just like my father, who was my idol. I wanted to be as much like him as I possibly could.

Mr. Sterling was an avid hunter, so the Chupadera also served as his hunting land. I believe Mr. Sterling enjoyed hunting more than owning cattle. Not only did he put my father in charge of the ranch, but also of his hunting parties, which soon became notable events. One of my father's responsibilities was to meet Mr. Sterling when he arrived from Houston in his private railroad car at Carrizo Springs, which is about forty miles from the Chupadera Ranch headquarters. Mr. Sterling often brought a few of his good friends with him to go hunting on the Chupadera. They would leave Mr. Sterling's railroad car on the siding at Carrizo Springs, and my father would drive them to the Chupadera Ranch in a large touring car.

During the Christmas holidays in 1927, Mr. Sterling brought about a dozen of the leading political figures of Texas to hunt on the Chupadera for six days. The party was so successful that they repeated it the next year. Invitations to join Mr. Sterling's holiday deer hunt on the Chupadera became widely coveted. By this time, Mr. Sterling had sold his holdings in the Humble Oil Company to become a land developer and to buy the *Houston Post*. He also was deeply involved in Texas politics. Because of his widespread political and business connections, I got to see some pretty important people who came to the Chupadera for these special hunting parties. They included powerful Houston financier and newspaper publisher Jesse H. Jones, former Texas governors William P. Hobby and Dan Moody, cotton baron M. D. Anderson, Houston land developer and oil man Will C. Hogg, and various railroad executives, bank presidents, federal judges, and other notables. It was exciting stuff for a little kid.

Soon after these hunts began in 1927, a spur rail line was extended from Carrizo Springs to the little village of Catarina, which was much closer to the Chupadera. When these VIPs arrived at Catarina in private rail cars, Mr. Sterling would turn them over to my father. It was his responsibility to drive them to the ranch house, assign everybody a bed, and make certain that they were well fed and properly accommodated. Father also brought in hunting guides and generally supervised every aspect of the hunt.

Mr. Sterling was a teetotaler, so he ran a dry camp. Alcoholic beverages simply were not allowed. That was a strict rule. He would not condone any drinking whatsoever, which was quite a restriction, because some of those guys loved their whiskey. I can imagine that the rules were broken once they got Mr. Sterling safely to bed.

Those Christmas deer hunts on the Chupadera produced many tall tales and playful stunts. Jesse Jones bragged that he shot a squirrel with his pistol as it ran along a path many yards away on the other side of a stream on the Chupadera. He claimed that he had to aim about fifty feet above the squirrel to allow for the bullet's trajectory as it traveled such a great distance and then hit the animal squarely in the head! R. M. Farrar, president of the Union National Bank in Houston, attended every one of the annual hunts and never killed a deer. One year, at the end of yet another failed expedition, Farrar's distinguished companions tied a dead jackrabbit to the hood of his car. They

attached a sign to the rabbit that read, "R. M. Farrar—his deer." Farrar took it well, declaring that he had "hit him running."

My father benefited greatly from Mr. Sterling's patronage. He
made enough money during the late 1920s to branch out and start his
own cattle operation. He leased ranches, including the 30,000-acre
Houston Ranch, east of Uvalde, and one south of Sabinal, on which
he had steers. He also had a separate lease on a portion of the old
Catarina Ranch as well as a lease he shared there with Mr. Sterling.
He also had a one-fourth interest in Mr. Sterling's cattle operation on
the Chupadera.

Unfortunately, in 1931, while he was serving his first term, the
effects of the Great Depression wiped out Governor Sterling financially. He lost his newspaper, the *Houston Post,* and his banks were
closed. A year later, he was defeated in his bid for a second term as
governor, losing to Ma Ferguson by 4,000 votes in a runoff election
that many Sterling supporters believed was stolen by voter fraud. In
addition, the Depression wiped out the cattle business in Texas.
Demand for beef plunged and the severe drought caught the ranges
overpopulated with millions of cattle for which there was no market.
At one point, cows were selling for 2.5 cents a pound, which was not
enough money to pay the freight bill for shipping them to market. As
a result, my father also lost everything he owned in partnership with
Governor Sterling, including his portion of the cattle operation at the
Chupadera and the 13 Ranch. They had to sell all of their cattle to the
only buyer available, the federal government, which needed the beef
for food relief programs.

MY FIRST VISIT TO THE GOVERNOR'S MANSION

One of the most vivid memories I have of my childhood was when my
family went to Austin to visit Governor Sterling in the fall of 1932,
after Governor Sterling lost the Democratic primary race to Ma Ferguson. Governor and Mrs. Sterling insisted that we travel to Austin
and spend the weekend in the Governor's Mansion before he left
office. Father was struggling with his financial problems at that point,
so he felt that he couldn't spare the time. The Sterlings insisted that

we make the trip, however, because they wanted me to have the opportunity to spend the night in the mansion. Father agreed, so we went to Austin. Governor and Mrs. Sterling let me sleep in the bed of my hero, Sam Houston. It was quite a thrill for a young man to know that he was sleeping in the same bed that the great Sam Houston had slept in. From that day forward, I had a burning ambition to get back to the mansion. It was a formative experience.

This was when the country was in the depths of the Depression. I well remember that when my father and I walked with Governor Sterling from the Governor's Mansion to the Capitol we were stopped several times by individuals asking him for a job. I can still see the desperation in their faces. These were men who desperately wanted to work, but there were no jobs. I heard much talk about how President Hoover and the Republicans had done nothing to alleviate this desperate situation. I must say that my memory of those desperate men is one of the reasons that I have remained a Democrat all my life. I have disagreed with many of the positions that my party has taken over the years, but I still believe that the Democratic Party does look after the best interests and basic needs of the common citizen.

After dinner, my father and I and Governor Sterling walked a few blocks to the Paramount Theatre on Congress Avenue in downtown Austin to see a movie. We walked everywhere, and we never had a police escort. I can say honestly that the memory of that weekend was one of the motivating forces that drove me many years later to run for governor.

Although the business partnership between my father and Ross Sterling fell victim to the Depression and was never revived, they remained close friends until Governor Sterling's death in 1949. In the last years of his life, Governor Sterling often visited our home in Uvalde. My father and our family owe so much to him. A couple of years before he passed away, my father told a newspaper reporter that Ross Sterling had "always been and still is my very closest friend. I admire him more than any man I have ever known." That sums up their relationship and Mr. Sterling's importance to my family far better than I can.

Chapter 2

HACIENDA LAS MARGARITAS AND CATARINA

T HE DEPRESSION HIT MY FATHER VERY HARD, but he was not one to give up on anything. He was a shrewd business-man, and he had the kind of personality that made it easy for him to make friends who were loyal and supportive. Even during the great financial crash that cost him the Chupadera, he was able to hold on to the 100,000-acre lease on the Catarina Ranch that he and Mr. Sterling had shared. To help him get back on his feet financially, my father accepted a job from Houston oilman Jim West Sr., who took over the Chupadera after my father lost it. He also retained his Humble Oil Company distributorship, which provided a good and dependable source of income that cushioned us from the worst effects of the Depression. Those two jobs allowed him to accumulate enough cash to hang on to his cattle lease on the Catarina Ranch.

Although my father was a disciplined and hardworking man with a real talent for business, I don't believe that he could have fought his way back to economic success without my mother's love and support. Mother was a southern lady in every positive sense of that term. The culture of Fort Bend County, Texas, where she grew up, was very Old South. The county was settled by transplanted southerners, most of them from Mississippi. Mother was a devout Christian, and she was

My mother and father sometime during the early 1950s. *Courtesy of the Briscoe family.*

kindhearted and generous. In her relations with family and friends, and in her behavior toward everyone she ever met, Mother followed the Golden Rule every day of her life. Her family was the absolute center of her life. And that meant my father and me especially. Mother literally devoted her life to us. We were her life, and that was all she wanted. She was absolutely, completely devoted to my father and to his life and his career. And as far as she was concerned, he could do no wrong. Mother's support was a vital source of strength for my father at all times.

A Ranch in Mexico

In 1932, when I was nine years old, and not long after my father lost everything he had owned with Governor Sterling, he decided to buy a 225,000-acre ranch in the northern part of the Mexican state of Coahuila, about eighty miles north of the town of Musquiz. The ranch, which was owned by the Rosita Livestock Company, was called Hacienda las Margaritas. It was stocked fully with cattle and horses and it had two pine timber mills. It was a beautiful piece of property. My father knew about it because he had leased land in Coahuila and he had traded cattle there for several years. He knew the ranches in the area and he knew how to operate in Mexico, even though his Spanish was not that good. He could understand enough Spanish to get along, but he had trouble speaking it.

Looking back, I now realize that it took a lot of pure nerve, grit, and determination for my father to decide that he would try to buy that property. For one reason, Margaritas had a very cloudy title, which obviously is a risky situation for the buyer of land anyplace, but it is especially risky in Mexico if the buyer is a citizen of the United States. It was mainly for that reason that the Jones and Leary families of Del Rio, the owners of the Rosita Livestock Company, were eager to sell Margaritas. A more obvious and difficult problem, however, was that my father decided to buy Margaritas for $50,000 when he lacked the personal financial resources to pay for it. This also was a period when the Depression was at its worst and $50,000 was a huge amount of money. For most people, the combination of those problems would have been insurmountable.

As I said, my father was a person who easily developed loyal friendships that generally lasted a lifetime. It was to some of the members of that network of loyal old friends, as well as relatives, that he turned to help him acquire Hacienda las Margaritas. My father had childhood friends back in Fulshear, his hometown, who had weathered the Depression well. Those friends included Hunter Harris and Nounes Huggins. They weren't extremely wealthy, but they were out of debt and had saved substantial amounts of cash from their plantation operations. In addition, my mother's older brother, Mason Briscoe, had prospered in the cattle business and had plenty of money in the bank.

My father made this proposition to his friends and his brother-in-law: loan him the money to purchase this ranch in Mexico, and he would pay them back three times the amount of their investment. My father proposed to create a stock company to own Margaritas, and each investor would receive stock. Once the stockholders had earned three times their original investment, they would give their stock to my father. That was the deal. In other words, they would triple their money on the investment and my father would end up with the ranch.

The investors had the ranch as collateral for the loan in case my father failed. He was also given a specific number of years as a deadline to give the investors the total amount of earnings promised. They agreed, and that's the way he bought the ranch. His friends and my Uncle Mason had a lot of faith in my father, obviously, or they wouldn't have invested in anything so risky as a Mexican ranch. My father was a smart businessman with very good judgment, and his friends knew that. But it was a somewhat exotic thing for a Texan to be buying a ranch in Mexico in those days. The investment was about as speculative as you could get for people who hadn't been speculators.

Margaritas was a triangular-shaped piece of property in the Burro Mountains that ran pretty much north and south. The lower elevation was on the south end, which was about 2,500 to 3,000 feet in elevation. The northern end was about 5,000 feet in elevation, with pine trees. It was beautiful country, but there was not a lot of water.

Hacienda las Margaritas proved to be the investment that eventually allowed my father to regain what he lost in the Depression. Margaritas was a critical link in his cattle operation. During the winter, he kept his yearling steers at Margaritas and then drove them across the Rio Grande to his leased acreage in Texas. From there, he would ship them to Kansas, where they would be fattened and then sold. Not too many years after he bought it, the ranch was generating enough money to make it possible for him to pay back his investors.

Father hired a young man named Roberto Spence to operate Margaritas for him. Bob was from England, but he had become a Mexican citizen. His mother was Scottish; her family name was McKeller. They had moved to Mexico when Bob was very young. Bob was working for his uncle, Mr. McKeller, who was running a ranch named La Mariposa for some English owners. My father got him up to the Margaritas. Bob had just gotten married and didn't have any children at the time. He was perfect for the job. On the practical side, he was fluent in Spanish. Even more important, he was utterly dependable, and he was a man of complete integrity. Bob was like an older brother that I never had. My father made him a partner in the Margaritas.

I spent a lot of time at Hacienda las Margaritas during the school breaks each summer when I was a teenager. About this time, I began to assemble the variety of personal items that are needed for ranch work that become an integral part of every rancher's identity. My father gave me a saddle made by a Uvalde saddlemaker named Will Slade, who was a master craftsman. After all of these years, it is still my favorite saddle. I made good use of that saddle whenever I was at Margaritas.

In high school, I also had two pairs of Lucchese boots made in San Antonio. Lucchese boots are still my favorites. The Luccheses I wore at Margaritas had medium heels and were high boots, almost to the knee. One pair had my initials in the design. The other pair carried the O-6 (Open Six) brand, which my father developed during the 1930s. I have continued it as my brand. It's an easy brand to use. The same branding iron for the O-6 can be turned upside down for the O-9 brand that we use for our cattle partnerships. A hat, of course, is as important to a rancher as boots and saddles. I decided early that gray felt was my favorite hat. The brim is wide enough to keep the sun off, but not too big. I have kept some of my gray felt hats for thirty years or more.

The Margaritas ranch house, which was located in the middle of the ranch, was a very comfortable place. It was an adobe structure with a concrete floor and a thatched roof. It even had running water and an indoor bathroom with a shower. The house was built on land just below a hill where a spring called El Fortin flowed year round. The flow from that spring ran down into the house to give us our fresh indoor running water. The water we couldn't use flowed out of the house and down to a big reservoir built out of rock, which is called a *pila* in Mexico. From the *pila*, it would go out to stock water troughs and then run down to a couple of other big *pilas* for storage. There was no need to pump water. It was all gravity flow from the spring down. We had the same water system on the upper end of the ranch.

The *pila* just below the house was good-sized and made a wonderful swimming pool. If we had time in the afternoon after work, we

The *pila* at Las Margaritas that served as my swimming pool on hot summer days. *Courtesy of the Briscoe family.*

went for a swim. That was the first time I'd ever had a swimming pool. And what a nice swimming pool it was: full of clear, cool, spring water. Who could want more?

The ranch house was in a magnificent location, very isolated and quiet. There were no telephones or radios. There was no communication with the outside world. The elevation at the headquarters was about 3,500 feet, so it was quite pleasant in the summertime. Those youthful summers I spent at Hacienda las Margaritas were among the best of my life. The place was my Shangri-la.

My father has been described as indefatigable and I think that is an apt description. He simply would not be defeated. His activities and achievements as a businessman in the face of one of the worst financial decades in U.S. history were remarkable. His energy level was extraordinary. In 1933, while he rebuilt his cattle business and continued to manage his oil distributorship, my father founded the Uvalde Wool and Mohair Company, which became his office when he was not out on his land. He had much success raising goats on his own land as well as on leases, and the wool and mohair business did well enough, even during the Depression. It eventually became a significant source of his income.

During this period, my father also was elected president of the Texas and Southwestern Cattle Raisers Association. At the time, he was the youngest person to have served in that position. The presidency of the Cattle Raisers Association is not just an honor, it is a position that demands a great deal of attention from the holder. My father served two terms as president, from 1932 through 1934. He carried out his duties the way he handled his personal business, with hard work and enthusiasm. He led the association's protest against the weighing of cattle in intrastate shipments, promoted cattle-theft protection, and lobbied for lower commission costs and field inspectors. This level of professional and civic involvement was standard behavior for him. He eventually found time to serve as a director of the Federal Reserve Bank of Dallas, vice president of the National Finance Credit Corporation of Texas, and vice president of the Texas Livestock Marketing Association. All of this activity was in addition to being an involved parishioner of Uvalde's St. Phillips Episcopal Church and an active Mason and Shriner.

CATARINA

By 1939, Hacienda las Margaritas and his wool and mohair operation had generated enough profit to allow my father to purchase 20,000 acres of the grand old Catarina Ranch for six dollars an acre. My father had leased land on the Catarina for many years and he had long wanted to own as much of it as he could afford. That same year he also purchased the Rio Frio Ranch. Through the years, he continued to

This is a portrait of my father that was published in a magazine when he was president of the Cattle Raisers Association in 1932. The Cattleman Magazine, *vol. 39, no. 8, p. 27; di_03943.*

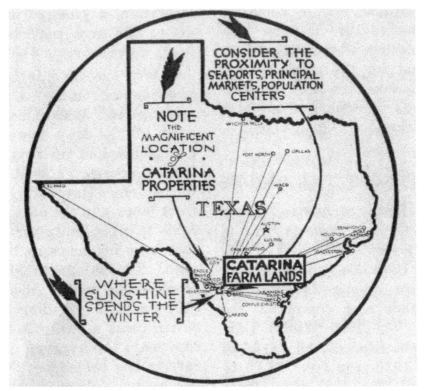

This advertising map is a good example of how Catarina Farm Lands was promoted. Catarina: In the Heart of the Winter Garden District of Southwest Texas *(1927)*; *di_03942.*

purchase additional tracts of land until they totaled 100,000 acres. This was my father's dream come true.

Catarina, which is located in Dimmit and Webb counties, is one of the most famous ranches in the region. The ranch is in the Nueces Strip, the land between the Rio Grande and the Nueces River that Mexico claimed as its territory until the Mexican War settled the dispute. Nevertheless, during the 1860s the strip was the site of numerous skirmishes between Texas Rangers and Mexican raiders. It was also home to Comanche, Kiowa, and Apache Indians, who conducted frequent raids on the small settlements in the area. In the early 1870s, a cavalry regiment of African American buffalo soldiers under the command of Lt. John Bullis finally brought peace to the region.

David Sinton, a native of Ohio and the majority stockholder of the Coleman-Fulton Pasture Company, established Catarina Ranch in the early 1880s. His daughter, Ann, married Charles P. Taft, older half-brother of President William Howard Taft. She and her husband continued to operate the ranch after her father's death. The Tafts expanded the ranch, by then known as the Taft-Catarina, to 235,000 acres in size.

In the early 1900s, the Taft-Catarina Ranch decided to build cattle pens on a site adjacent to the route of a planned railroad line from Artesia Wells to Asherton. After the cattle pens were built, the ranch moved its headquarters and bunkhouse to the site. The ranch soon added a hotel, commissary, one-room school, and a few residential houses. After the Asherton and Gulf railroad line was completed in 1910, the site became known as "Catarina Station." In 1902, Charles Taft decided to build a mansion on the ranch. Known as the Taft House, the three-story mansion soon became a local showplace, although neither Charles Taft nor his younger brother, President Taft, ever lived there.

After the end of World War I, Charles Taft decided to sell the Taft-Catarina ranch to S. W. Forrester, an oilman from Topeka, Kansas. Forrester hoped to find oil on the ranch. When that effort failed, he sold the ranch in 1925 to a land development syndicate in Kansas. The syndicate established a company called Catarina Farms, which subdivided the part of the ranch closest to the ranch headquarters into a large number of small farms. To help promote the area to prospective buyers, the company launched an extensive civic improvement project to turn Catarina Station into a town called Catarina. The developers built a modern two-story brick hotel, a bank, two lumberyards, a waterworks, an electric light generating station, a telephone exchange, and a fourteen-acre park with a concrete swimming pool. The company paved the streets and planted palm trees along both sides.

To serve as the general sales agent, the syndicate hired Charles E. F. Ladd, a razzle-dazzle promoter who previously had great success selling land in the Rio Grande Valley. As a young boy, I met Mr. Ladd when I accompanied my father to a land auction at Catarina. He was a colorful character who wore a ten-gallon hat, jodhpurs, and knee-high English riding boots. I remember so very clearly Mr. Ladd telling my father that he was going to put every acre of land between the Nueces River and the Rio Grande in cultivation, and there would not be anywhere for my father to run cows this side of the Rio Grande. Mr. Ladd was an impressive-looking gentleman, and his prediction certainly scared me, but it didn't seem to bother my father a bit. Of course, it turned out that my father understood the land better than did Mr. Ladd.

Thanks to the promotional talents of Mr. Ladd, however, Catarina Farms seemed to be a major success by the late 1920s. The area was filling up with small middle-class farms with nice little frame houses. Catarina was a small boomtown, with more than one hundred houses, dozens of businesses, and about 2,500 residents at its peak in 1929. The Taft mansion served as the headquarters for the land development company, while Mr. Ladd lived in his own impressive home nearby.

The bubble popped, however, with the coming of the Great Depression. Catarina Farms lost its agricultural markets, banks and investors withdrew their financing, and the region's lack of water became obvious with the onset of the terrible drought that marked most of the early 1930s. Businesses in the town of Catarina closed and their buildings were removed to other locations. Most of the small farms reverted to ranch land. By the time my father purchased his portion of the old ranch, the population of the town of Catarina had dwindled to about four hundred residents. Land prices had plummeted.

BURNING PEAR AT CATARINA

When I was in high school, I often accompanied my father when he supervised work on the Catarina. It was during this period that I first began to gain some rudimentary knowledge about the cattle business and how my father operated. Perhaps my most vivid memories of work on the Catarina in those days were when my father and his men had to carry out an operation to burn the thorns off the prickly pear cactus that grew in great abundance on the ranch, often in large clumps. It's not uncommon to find individual prickly pear plants as

A ranch hand burns the thorns off of a prickly pear cactus with a hand-pumped kerosene torch. *Center for American History Prints and Photographs Collection; di_03953.*

tall as six feet in height. The procedure, which is called "burning pear," is a necessity during periods of inadequate rainfall when there is no grass or other forage for the cattle to eat. And more years than not, the rainfall was inadequate. Cacti are fast growing. They come back fast. You can burn in one place and the cacti usually will be back within three or four years. The term "burning pear" is really a misnomer because the process doesn't actually burn the pear; it just singes the thorns. With the thorns off, you can use prickly pear for feed. Cattle don't gain a lot of weight eating pear, but the flesh is high in moisture content and fiber and, if you mix it with some cottonseed cake for protein, it will keep cattle healthy. Many people have wintered cattle just on pear alone. They won't do quite as well, but they'll survive.

Feeding prickly pear to cattle is an age-old ranching practice in South Texas, dating back to the Spanish colonial era. In the early days, they cut and chopped the pear, hauled it in a wagon, and singed the thorns off by holding the plants over a fire. The livestock would be held in a pen or in a small trap, and they'd feed the pear to the animals that way.

My father planned his pear burning operation carefully to make the work as productive as possible. Every year, he started burning pear the first of December. When I was a kid, ranchers burned pear with miniature flamethrowers called pear burners that used kerosene for fuel. The kerosene was delivered to the ranch in barrels that were scattered throughout the areas on the ranch where the pear was thickest. The ranch hands filled their metal bottles from those barrels and then carried the bottles on their backs. The bottles had little hand pumps that were used to build up pressure to push the kerosene through a hose and then through a burner on the end of the hose that ignited the kerosene to make a torch. The individual carrying the pear burner went from pear bush to pear bush, singeing the thorns off.

Years later, we began to use pickup trucks to carry much larger containers of compressed butane or propane instead of kerosene. A large tank of compressed propane would be placed in the bed of a pickup with two hoses from the tank hanging from each side of the truck. Ranch hands would take both hoses, which had igniters at their ends, and torch the thorns off the plants. That method greatly increased productivity. By the time I was running the ranch, we were using tractors to pull large compressed propane containers on wheels that had burners extending from behind. The burners threw out a hot flame that took off the pear thorns. That method worked best when used on very thick and wide growths of pear. You can burn a wide swath of pear with that method. We still burn pear today, but not on the scale we once did. There has been more planting of new types of grasses and better range management than there was sixty-five or seventy years ago.

After my father got his cattle through the winter, often by feeding them prickly pear, he shipped them from Catarina to Kansas, where he leased grazing land. The shipping date would always be April 13, no matter what. He arranged that date with the railroad and made certain they went out on his schedule. He wanted his cattle to be in Kansas just as that young, tender grass was coming up under their feet. The cattle would eat and fatten up when they were in Kansas. In the latter part of June or early in July, they were shipped to market. Fortunately, the beef market in the late 1930s and throughout most of the 1940s generated good prices, and my father prospered.

Although the early years of the Depression had caused my father much grief, it was the Depression and its impact on Catarina that made it possible ultimately for him to buy the ranch. By the beginning of World War II and the end of the Depression, my father's persistence and hard work had paid off. After "going broke" and starting over twice in his life, he never suffered another devastating financial loss.

Chapter 3

CACTUS JACK

W HEN I WAS A KID growing up in Uvalde, I loved to roller
skate with my best friends, who included George Horner,
Jack Conger, Alex Kincaid, and Needham Cain. One of our favorite
skating places was on the tile porch and the broad walkway in front of
the two-story brick home of John Nance "Cactus Jack" Garner, the
vice president of the United States and Uvalde's most famous citizen.
Mr. Garner's property on Park Street was a wonderful place to skate.
We would skate in circles on that tile front porch and then spin off
and go down his front steps: bumpity, bumpity, bump, bump! We
enjoyed skating around there when no one was home.

But when Mr. Garner was in town, we stayed across the street. We
were scared to death of Mr. Garner. To a kid, he was a ferocious-look-
ing man with wild and bushy eyebrows, red-flushed face, and a fierce
scowl. He seemed always to have a big cigar clenched between his
teeth. We were too young to appreciate it, of course, but the old man
on whose porch and walkway we liked to skate was also the second
most powerful politician in the United States at the time.

Although I would not get to know him personally until a few years
after he had retired from public office, Mr. Garner had an influence on
my family and on me long before that. As a kid living in such close
proximity to one of the most colorful, famous, and powerful men in
the country, I couldn't help but soak up a lot of the political information that his presence naturally generated. I was already politically
aware at a young age because of our family's close relationship with

Left: I used to ride my bicycle on the sidewalk in front of Mr. Garner's house on Park Street in Uvalde. *Briscoe Papers; di_03999.*

Below: The front porch of Mr. Garner's house as it looked after he donated the property to the city of Uvalde in the late 1950s. *Center for American History Prints and Photographs Collection; di_03954.*

Ross Sterling. Having the vice president of the United States as a nearby neighbor just deepened that political awareness.

THE PATRONS

Mr. Garner (we always called him "Mr.") was a dominating presence in Uvalde decades before my birth in 1923. He was elected to Congress in 1902, where he slowly climbed up the ranks of the Democratic Party leadership until 1931, when he became the first Texan to serve as Speaker of the U.S. House of Representatives. Mr. Garner's congressional district was one of the largest in the country, covering all of South Texas below San Antonio. As the congressman from South Texas, he forged a close alliance with the political bosses, or *patrons*, who ran their counties like feudal fiefdoms. Among those *patrons*, his strongest supporter probably was Judge James B. Wells, an attorney and longtime power broker in Brownsville.

In later years, after I got to know Mr. Garner, I was invited occasionally to the afternoon sessions out on his porch when he liked to have his bourbon (he called it "striking a blow for liberty"), chew a cigar, and tell one of his many political stories. Naturally, he had his favorites that he repeated often, and one of them was about how he conducted his congressional campaigns during the days of the political bosses. He usually told this story whenever the subject of political campaign costs came up. Mr. Garner would frown and complain that the world had gone crazy. Back in the old days, whenever he had to stand for reelection to Congress, he got the "boys" from South Texas together at his place for a little barbecue. He never said who the boys were, but undoubtedly they were the *patrons*, including Judge Jim Wells, Judge Manuel Raymond in Webb County, Archie Parr in Duval County, and Manuel Guerra in Starr County. He would call them together, along with the Klebergs of the King Ranch, and they would have a barbecue in his backyard. They would enjoy a few drinks, eat their barbecue, and tell stories and jokes. Everyone would have a great time, according to Mr. Garner. Finally, Mr. Garner would stand up and ask a question: "Well, boys, it's time for reelection. Do y'all want me to run again?" And the boys would all shout, "Yeah,

John, we want you to run again." And then Mr. Garner would say, "Okay, boys, it's up to you. The campaign is over!" And with that, the campaign and the election *were* over. He was reelected fifteen times.

Under the *patron* system, those who worked for the *patron*, and that usually included a significant portion of a county's voters, looked to the *patron* for everything from jobs to social welfare, and that included instructions on how to vote. And they would follow the *patron*'s request. That was the political system and the way of life in most of South Texas until the 1920s. A couple of the bosses even held power until after World War II.

Of course, the main reason why Mr. Garner stayed in Congress long after the boss system ended was that he took care of his district, especially after he gained enough seniority to have real influence. One of the projects that he pushed very strongly was the dredging of the intracoastal canal from Corpus Christi to Brownsville along the lower Gulf Coast of Texas. Mr. Garner almost single-handedly made it possible for Corpus Christi and Brownsville to have deepwater ports. He served his district well. And he believed strongly in the idea that for every dollar one of those "Yankees" (as he would say) got for his district, Mr. Garner would get two for his. He was very successful in doing that, and that made him popular back home.

"Not Worth a Bucket of Spit"

In 1932, newspaper and motion picture tycoon William Randolph Hearst initiated and orchestrated an effort to make Mr. Garner the Democratic Party's candidate for president. As House Speaker during the second half of Herbert Hoover's presidency, Mr. Garner was the symbolic head of the Democratic Party. Mr. Garner later told us that he wasn't interested in the presidency. He had wanted to remain Speaker of the House, but he did nothing to discourage Hearst and his other supporters.

At the Democratic National Convention, Mr. Garner's delegate strength kept Franklin Roosevelt from winning the first three ballots against his main opponent, Al Smith, the party's unsuccessful presidential nominee in 1928. After the third ballot, Mr. Garner agreed to transfer his delegates to FDR to avoid a deadlocked convention that might result in the nomination of a weak candidate, who might be beaten so badly that the Democrats could lose control of the House. After his nomination, Roosevelt decided to make Mr. Garner his running mate in order to have a balanced ticket representing both the North and the South. I should add that Texas Congressman Sam Rayburn served as Mr. Garner's agent at the convention. He negotiated the deal that brought Mr. Garner to the ticket.

Mr. Garner thus became the first Texan to serve as vice president of the United States. His decision to throw the nomination to FDR placed him in an especially influential position with the new president, and Mr. Garner took every advantage of that debt. To the horror of the liberal and progressive members of his administration, Roosevelt made Mr. Garner a full-fledged member of his cabinet, the first vice president to have that privilege.

Mr. Garner variously described the position of vice president as "the spare tire on the national automobile," a "no man's land somewhere between the legislative and executive branches," and, most famously, "an office not worth a bucket of warm spit." Despite Mr. Garner's sarcastic public characterizations of the job, it is clear that he flourished as vice president and that he loved the opportunity it gave him to serve as the dominant figure in the legislative domain during the New Deal. During his eight years as vice president, Mr. Garner maintained his influence in the House, especially with the members of the Texas delegation, most of whom he had mentored. In addition to that, Mr. Garner had built his contacts on both sides of the aisle, with the Republicans as well as the Democrats. He had done favors for most of them, and he had his political chits out everywhere. When he wanted to pass legislation, he knew what to do.

Mr. Garner's continuing influence over the Texas delegation was one of the critical reasons for his legislative power because no fewer than nine Texans held chairmanships in the House. The Texas delegation was the most powerful of all the state delegations during the Roosevelt years. Very little New Deal legislation could pass Congress without going through one of these Texan-chaired committees. In the Senate, Mr. Garner quickly renewed his close ties with twenty former

Vice President Garner and President Roosevelt enjoying a meal in the White House shortly after their inauguration. *Garner (John Nance) Papers, Center for American History; di_01408.*

House members with whom he had served who were now influential senators, including Alben Barkley, Millard Tydings, Joe Robinson, Pat Harrison, Jimmy Byrnes, and Carter Glass. Mr. Garner's long-standing friendships with these men in both houses of Congress, some of whom chaired powerful committees, paid huge political dividends to Roosevelt's legislative agenda.

During the critical first one hundred days of the Roosevelt administration, Mr. Garner rammed much of FDR's emergency legislation through Congress, playing an especially significant role in the passage of the Federal Deposit Insurance Corporation, the Farm Credit Administration, the Federal Relief Administration, and the Public Utility Holding Company Bill. And he did it even though he was philosophically much more conservative than Roosevelt. But he thought, and I think history has proven him to be correct, that the country was in a real crisis, and that something had to be done because there was a real danger of a revolt. He believed that there were plenty of people during the early 1930s who would be happy to serve as an American dictator. Mr. Garner told me many times that the man who scared him the most was Sen. Huey "Kingfish" Long of Louisiana. He believed that Long had been capable of leading a revolt. According to Mr. Garner, President Roosevelt had felt the same way. Long's assassination in 1935 had ended that threat.

I always thought it was interesting that the Roosevelt-Garner ticket was composed of two men who were the products of political boss systems. Franklin Roosevelt came from the Tammany Hall urban boss system in New York City, the same system that produced Al Smith. Mr. Garner, of course, came from the South Texas political boss system. It made an interesting combination. They had those political connections in common, but they were starkly different in background, style, and outlook. A graduate of Harvard, Franklin Roosevelt was from one of the oldest and wealthiest of the landowning aristocratic Dutch families in New York, while John Nance Garner was a product of the rough-and-tumble country of South Texas. He was raised on a very small and poor farm in North Texas, and he studied law in a law office, not at a prestigious university.

The relationship between FDR and Mr. Garner was a fascinating combination of two men who really understood politics and how our national government works. They knew how to make government work to their will. And the two of them together made an effective team the first two terms of Roosevelt's presidency. Roosevelt could play to the northeastern elite, and Mr. Garner could play to the masses of the South and West because he was one of them.

My Father and Mr. Garner

My father had always supported Mr. Garner politically, and he had much respect for him, but they were never close. Naturally, Mr. Garner had people who were in business in Uvalde who were his cronies and who were subservient to him in some way or would do his will whenever he asked. Of course, Mr. Garner's influence in Uvalde was helped considerably by his owning the First State Bank, which was the only bank in town. Nevertheless, my father was an extremely independent person and kowtowing to Mr. Garner didn't appeal to him. My father was redheaded, and he had one of those independent streaks in him that one often associates with redheads. That independent streak occasionally put him at odds with Mr. Garner.

Just before the Depression hit, my father bought some stock in Mr. Garner's bank, which he mortgaged to Mr. Garner's other bank in Crystal City. When Mr. Garner built a new building for the First State Bank in Uvalde, my father opened an office in it. As I have said before, the Depression hit my father very hard. When he hit bottom, Mr. Garner foreclosed on my father's stock, and he had to move his office out of the First State Bank.

At one point, Mr. Garner and my father also were in a contest for control of the Uvalde Livestock Loan Company. I'm not exactly sure how this was done, but Mr. Garner made my father a buy-or-sell offer on the company. One of them had to buy or sell the other's stock at a very low price by a certain time in a period of two or three days. My father accepted the challenge. Mr. Garner didn't think he could do it, but Father worked out a plan. He had a friend, Dred Smith, who owned and ran the bank in Eagle Pass where Father had done a lot of business. My father called Mr. Smith and said, "You'll get a call from Mr. Garner by seven o'clock to find out if a check that I have given him for $10,000 is good. I'll be there by the time you open at nine o'clock with another check to cover it. If you'll tell Mr. Garner that the check is good, I'll cover it. But I'm asking you to have faith in me and to believe me."

My father had done lots of business with Mr. Smith, so he decided to take the risk that my father would honor the check. Father met Mr. Garner at six o'clock and gave him a check on the bank at Eagle Pass for $10,000. He had arranged with the directors of the Uvalde Livestock Loan Company that they would meet immediately at six o'clock and that they would lend him $10,000 with his livestock as collateral. Father took the check to Eagle Pass before Mr. Smith's bank opened. That made it possible for my father to buy the Uvalde Livestock Loan Company from Mr. Garner. Father later told me that before he actually took control of the company, Mr. Garner transferred all of the bad livestock loans in the First State Bank and put them in the Uvalde

Sam Rayburn, right, when he was chairman of the House Committee on Interstate Commerce. He and Secretary of the Treasury William H. Woodin flank President Roosevelt. *Rayburn (Sam) Papers, Center for American History; di_03285.*

Livestock Loan Company. When Father finally had control of the company, he discovered that he had a lot of bad loans.

After Father's unhappy business experiences with Mr. Garner, he decided that if he ever got in a financial position to do it, he would open a new bank in Uvalde in competition with Mr. Garner's First State Bank. Cattle prices were so good during the war that by 1945 my father had accumulated enough capital to seek that bank charter. He and a small group of investors bought the property opposite Mr. Garner's bank to serve as the location for their proposed bank, and then they submitted an application for a national charter. My father was quite optimistic that the application would be approved. He did not know, however, that Mr. Garner was working quietly behind the scenes to have it denied in Washington.

A few years ago, I discovered a letter at the University of Texas

Center for American History that Mr. Garner wrote to Sam Rayburn, who was Speaker of the House of Representatives. The letter is in Rayburn's papers at the center. Mr. Garner had been Rayburn's mentor when they were both in the Congress, and they had maintained a close relationship over the years. Rayburn was indebted to Mr. Garner for helping him climb up the ranks to a position in the House leadership, ultimately rising to the top.

In his letter to Sam Rayburn, which is dated March 30, 1945, Mr. Garner asked him to intervene with the Comptroller of the Currency to stop Father's bank application. By this time, Mr. Garner had retired from public life and had returned to live in Uvalde. "My friend, Dolph Briscoe, et al," Garner wrote to Rayburn, "are trying to organize a National Bank in the town of Uvalde. There is absolutely no excuse for another bank here." Mr. Garner concluded his letter by saying that he would "always be grateful for this favor."

Mr. Garner also called on his good friend Jesse H. Jones, who was FDR's Secretary of Commerce and head of the federal government's Reconstruction Finance Corporation (RFC), which had enormous power over all aspects of the government's finances, including banking matters. Jones owed his position in Washington to Mr. Garner, who had made his appointment to the RFC possible. It was Jones who gave my father the news that his bank application was dead. In the spring of 1945, my father was in Washington, D.C., with Judge Joe Montague, who was the attorney for the Cattle Raisers Association. He had not yet heard anything about the status of his bank application. Late one afternoon during their trip, my father and Judge Montague paid Jones a courtesy visit. Jones had been a frequent visitor to the Chupadera Ranch back in the 1920s, so he and my father were friends. They had a nice visit, and as they were leaving Jones said to my father, "Say, Dolph, you're going back to Uvalde, aren't you?"

Father said, "Yes."

And Jones said, "Well, would you do me a favor? Please tell John Garner that I took care of that little bank matter that he called me about."

My father replied, "I certainly, will, Mr. Jones. I'll personally deliver the message to him." Of course, as soon as they closed the door to Jesse Jones's office, Father and Judge Montague agreed that the message from Jesse Jones was that the bank charter was dead—and that was that.

So, my father went back to Uvalde and paid a visit to Mr. Garner late in the afternoon when Mr. Garner was on his porch striking a blow for liberty. Father told him that he had been to Washington, that he had seen Jesse Jones, and that Jones had asked him to deliver a message to Mr. Garner in person that Jones had taken care of that little bank matter for him. Then my father and Mr. Garner poured some bourbon, and they struck a blow for liberty. That was the end of the matter. There was no point in fighting it. That's just the way it was, no bitterness at all.

That episode shows how business was done and how effectively. The charter was turned down. Father really thought it was sort of funny, that he had met his match. Mr. Garner had beaten him. I have to say that Mr. Garner always came at you straightforward. There was never any mystery about how he felt about anything. But I also must say that the episode didn't exactly make their friendship any stronger. Father later said, "You know, that was the best thing that ever happened to me. I took the money that I was going to put in that bank and I bought some more land to add to Catarina." That turned out to be a much better investment to him than if he had put his money in that bank, which would have had to struggle to compete with Mr. Garner's bank.

I don't want it to seem that my father and Mr. Garner always had a contentious relationship. Mr. Garner was a big help to Father on several occasions. Before Mr. Garner became vice president, for example, when he was still in Congress, he helped Father with a cattle problem. Father had about four thousand steers on the Hacienda las Margaritas in Mexico that he needed to move to the Chupadera in Texas. The two ranches were across the Rio Grande from each other, although separated by a wide strip of land on the Mexican side of the border. The Mexican government prohibited foreign ownership of borderland. Obviously, cattle from Mexico had to be inspected by U.S. federal agents before they could enter Texas. The nearest inspection center was in Eagle Pass, about seventy miles from the Hacienda

Secretary of Commerce Jesse H. Jones, center, showing a document to President Roosevelt in the Oval Office during the early 1940s. *Center for American History Prints and Photographs Collection; di_03955.*

las Margaritas, and then another seventy miles from the Chupadera.

To save my father from having to drive those cattle that far, Mr. Garner arranged for the customs agents and the animal health inspectors to go down to the Chupadera to meet the cattle as they came across the Rio Grande. In those days, there were no weighing scales at Eagle Pass. The duty was per pound and the agents just guessed the weight of cattle for the customs duty. The federal agents didn't need to have the cattle in Eagle Pass to weigh them. They could estimate the cattle weight on the Chupadera. They had fever ticks on both sides of the river, so they didn't have to worry about fever ticks coming with the cattle; they were already here.

On another occasion, someone circulated some counterfeit currency in Uvalde. When the Treasury Department agents came to town to investigate, they discovered that my father was one of the individuals who had spent one of those counterfeit bills. They discussed their investigation with Mr. Garner, and they mentioned that Father was on the list of people who had possessed some of the counterfeit money. "Well, I'll tell you one thing about Dolph Briscoe," Mr. Garner responded. "He's as honest and honorable as they come. I can personally assure you that he had nothing to do with that counterfeit money."

It was unfortunate that Mr. Garner and President Roosevelt eventually had a falling out, but I suppose it was inevitable, given the differences in their political philosophies. Mr. Garner was very conservative, and he was rigidly opposed to Roosevelt's plan to add judges to the Supreme Court. The final blow to their partnership, of course, was Roosevelt's decision to run for a third term in 1940. That was the end of the Garner–Roosevelt partnership. Mr. Garner left Washington after his second term as vice president ended. He announced that he would never again cross the Potomac, and he never did. Mr. and Mrs. Garner left Washington to return to private life in their two-story brick home in Uvalde.

Eventually, I would have the opportunity to become Mr. Garner's friend and to learn some valuable political lessons from him during late afternoon visits on the front porch that I had so loved to skate on as a child. But I'm getting ahead of my story.

Chapter 4

JANEY, THE UNIVERSITY, AND THE WAR

D URING THE SUMMER OF 1939, after my graduation from high school, I went to Hacienda las Margaritas thinking that I was going there to stay. My fervent wish was to work on that ranch for the rest of my life. I couldn't imagine any life better than the one I could live on that beautiful ranch. I was young, happy, and full of energy. It was one of the best summers ever.

Our manager, Bob Spence, had the ranch in great shape, and his wife ran a very efficient and comfortable household. I must say that I had it made. I had my own cook, Joaquin, and my own maid, Doña Maria. Joaquin was an outstanding cook who prepared delicious meals. Doña Maria kept everything neat and clean. Every morning Joaquin brought me coffee to wake me up and to get me ready for the day. After a hearty Mexican-style breakfast, one of the ranch hands brought my saddled horse up to the front porch, ready to go. All I had to do was get off the front porch, step up, get on my horse, and away I would go. I was pampered in every way, and I loved it! A person could get used to that way of life. I know that I did.

I may have been pampered back at the hacienda, but out on the range there was more than enough hard work for me to tackle. For most of the summer, I worked on horseback with the cattle, trying to control our fever tick problem, which was serious. We had Hereford cattle, which are more susceptible to fever ticks than the Brahma breed. We started working with the cattle at the south end of the ranch. We dipped them in arsenic, which was the only effective weapon that we had in those days. It had no residual effects, however. It killed the ticks effectively, but other ticks would get right back on the cattle. By the time we finished on the north end of the ranch, we had to turn around and start over on the south end. The effort to keep ticks off our cattle was an endless project, but that didn't bother me one bit. I was riding horseback and working cattle every day, and that was just as perfect as it could be. It was just what I wanted to do.

I spent the entire summer of 1939 at Hacienda las Margaritas. My life there was pretty close to perfect, and I had no intention of leaving it to attend college. My father, however, had a very different plan. He was keenly aware of the fact that I was living a pampered life, even if I was working hard with the cattle. He had no intention of letting me stay there and ignore my education. Late that August, my father showed up at the ranch and explained that he was taking me to Austin to attend college. He had enrolled me at the University of Texas and had me assigned to a dormitory room in Roberts Hall. I was less than thrilled. My fantasy about spending my life on an idyllic ranch in Coahuila was shattered. It seemed as though the next thing I knew my father was dropping my bags and me off at the dorm room on campus. I remember him looking me in the eye before he returned home and saying, "Now, son, I brought you here and I intend for you to stay here. Don't you flunk out." The only thing I could say was, "Yes sir!" When my father gave me instructions I knew it was futile to argue. I knew he was serious. He didn't joke around about things like that. I knew I had to stay in school whether I wanted to or not.

Janey and the University

With my father's instructions ringing in my ears, I resolved to work as hard as possible on my studies that first year. The fear that I might fail and disappoint my father was all the motivation I needed. I had been valedictorian of my graduating class in high school, but I wasn't that impressed with myself, because my senior class only had fifty members. When I arrived at the university, I was amazed at the number of students. I believe there were about nine or ten thousand students at the time, more people than I had ever seen in one place before. I was sixteen years old, and I was scared and a little disoriented. But I soon discovered that I had a lot of company. My anxieties were shared by many of my new classmates, who were from towns as small or smaller than Uvalde and who were living away from home for the first time in their lives.

I have few memories of my first year at the university. Obviously, time has played its tricks on my memory, but I also believe that I was so focused on my studies and so serious about making a place for myself that there isn't much to remember, other than I worked as hard as I could. I decided to go on pre-law track with a major in business administration. Fear can be a great motivator. Somehow, I managed to earn good grades. I even made Phi Eta Sigma, the freshman honor society. I was doing so well that I actually dreamed about being a Phi Beta Kappa at some point. Although I was shy, I gradually came out of my shell and got involved in student organizations and activities, including the newly organized Pre-Law Association, the honorary scouting service fraternity Alpha Phi Omega, and the Friars. I also joined the staff of *The Cactus*, which is the school yearbook.

By my sophomore year I finally felt at home on campus and, like most University of Texas students, I fell in love with Austin. I joined the Chi Phi fraternity, where I made some wonderful friends, including a young man from Goliad named D. B. Hardeman. D. B. was a brilliant guy who had been in school several years. He liked studying so much that he just kept taking classes. The Chi Phi house was a beautiful Victorian mansion located at 1704 West Avenue. It had been the residence of Col. E. M. House, who had been a behind-the-scenes power in Texas political circles and was President Woodrow Wilson's confidant and political advisor. The old structure made an outstanding fraternity house.

In the spring of 1942, I was able to join the Texas Cowboys, a student service organization with a great campus tradition. At special events such as football games, the Cowboys wear distinctive outfits that include riding chaps, boots with spurs, bandanas, and hats. My fellow inductees that spring included future U.S. senator Lloyd M.

Bentsen. Famed Houston heart surgeon Denton Cooley was an upper classman member. The group that joined the Cowboys with me was the last that had to endure the organization's special initiation rite, which was to have the letters "UT" branded on our chests with a hot iron.

Of course, that practice is called hazing today, and it is prohibited. Dick Kleberg, a leading member of the family that owned the famous King Ranch, was the person who branded me. Dick was gentle and didn't brand me too deeply. He certainly knew how to handle a branding iron, of course. As a result, I was fortunate, and my brand didn't get infected as some of them did. Dick was a good friend of mine and he remained so all his life. The Cowboys' old branding iron is hanging in a room at the Ex-Students Association building on campus.

As a member of the Texas Cowboys, I was able to benefit from the wise counsel of Arno "Shorty" Nowotny, the assistant dean of stu-

Displaying my University of Texas Cowboys brand to the camera. Janey, my mother, and my university roommate, Ray Keck, look on. *Courtesy of the Briscoe family.*

Riding in a parade in Austin as a member of the UT Cowboys. *Briscoe Papers.*

dents, who served as the faculty advisor to the Cowboys. Dean Nowotny was one of the finest men I have ever known. Of the faculty I knew on campus, he had the greatest influence on me as a student. Dean Nowotny taught me how to conduct myself properly in public, and he encouraged me to be involved actively in campus activities. He was a small man in terms of physical stature, but he was a giant in his

47

ability to inspire and encourage the young people—and there were many—who were fortunate enough to be associated with him. He was a gifted educator. I'll never forget him. Dean Nowotny is the person who gave me the confidence during my last two years at the university to become a student leader. I was elected to the Interfraternity Council, the Student Publications Board, and, during my senior year, the editorship of *The Cactus*.

My roommate at Roberts Dorm was Ray Keck, who was from Cotulla, which is about thirty miles east of Catarina. His father owned the bank at Cotulla. Being from my part of Texas, he and I had a lot in common. In my sophomore year, Ray and I moved out of the dorm to an apartment house next to the old Pig Stand Drive-In restaurant on the north side of the campus. D. B. Hardeman roomed with Ray and me in that apartment.

Not long after our move to the apartment, Ray and I managed to make "blind" dates with two girls who lived in a house on Oldham Street on the east side of campus in a beautiful, hilly neighborhood full of huge oak trees. It is the area where the LBJ Library and Sid Richardson Hall are now located. The house, the street, and the entire neighborhood are now gone. I don't even remember with whom I had a date. But I certainly remember Ray's date; she was the most beautiful girl I had ever seen. Ray's date was a petite, dark-haired beauty wearing this big, but quite fashionable, hat. Her name was Betty Jane Slaughter, a freshman from Austin who was one of the campus beauties. It was love at first sight for me. I knew right then and there that she was the one for me. I thought, Ray, my friend, I don't know what I'm going to do about you, but I'm going to get you out of the way. Lucky for me, Ray had a girlfriend back home.

We took the girls to the Chi Phi fraternity house for lunch. And from that point on, winning Betty Jane Slaughter became my full-time project. I forgot all about studying, and my grades went down real fast. I lost all interest in my course work, except to make certain that I was not going to flunk out. After meeting Janey, I never came close to being an honor student again, much less a Phi Beta Kappa.

Janey was born in Columbia, Missouri, on November 30, 1923, when her mother, Lucille Slaughter, was visiting relatives. Janey's par-

This is a portrait of Janey Slaughter as she looked
when I met her. It was taken for *The Cactus*, the
university's yearbook. The Cactus *(1941); di_03956*.

ents, Lucille and Sam Slaughter, lived in Austin, and that is where she
grew up. Her father was in the grocery business. After Janey graduated
from Austin High School, she went straight into the university, where
she excelled in the classroom and made a splash on the campus social
scene. I worked very hard to win her over. I had to, because I had tough
competition from some very rich boys from Dallas who also were
courting her. I was just a country boy, and these boys from the big city
were more socially sophisticated than me in every way. For example,
they were good dancers. Janey was also a wonderful dancer, probably
the best jitterbugger on the university campus. I could barely walk
much less jitterbug. If I were to try, I'd have looked as big a fool as there

ever was, but I didn't even try. I took Janey to school dances, and she would jitterbug with some of my competition. The more she would jitterbug, the madder I got. The madder I would get, the more she would jitterbug. It was touch and go for a while, but I never gave up.

One of the things I did to impress Janey was to run for election as editor-in-chief of *The Cactus*. I might not be able to dance, but I knew how to put out a yearbook, and being editor of *The Cactus* was a high-profile position on campus. My chief political rival in student politics was Jack Brooks, a brash kid from the Beaumont–Port Arthur area of Texas, who later served for many years as the powerful chairman of the Operations Committee of the U.S. House of Representatives and, later, as the chairman of the House Judiciary Committee.

Jack Brooks had the energy of three men. He also had an unfair advantage over me because he wrote for the student newspaper, *The Daily Texan*, which gave him an excellent campus forum. In campus politics, Jack was what we called an independent, which meant he was not a representative of the fraternity system. I was a fraternity man, but there were more students who were independents than there were fraternity members, which gave Jack another advantage. Jack and I competed in everything. At one point, we were going to run against each other for student body president, but the war came along and forced many of us, Jack and me included, to alter our plans.

Fortunately for me, Jack Brooks didn't run for editor of *The Cactus*. He probably would have beaten me if he had. Instead, Jack was elected associate editor of *The Daily Texan*, the student newspaper. To my delight, I won the election. The staffs of *The Daily Texan* and *The Cactus* worked in the same area of the old journalism building, which was located to the west of the university's Main Building, where the Peter Flawn Academic Center is now located. After I became editor, I asked Jack to be our publications editor. I figured that if Jack was nearby anyway, we might as well make use of his considerable energy and talent. Jack and I eventually became close friends, but I have never let him forget that he had some unfair advantages over me when we were campus political rivals.

I loved being editor-in-chief of *The Cactus*. I had an enthusiastic staff, and we all worked well together. Because we worked next to the students who put out *The Daily Texan*, there was always a lot of excitement in the air. For much of its existence, *The Daily Texan* has been the center of controversy on campus, and it was fun being in the middle of the action, even if we weren't on the newspaper staff.

I was on a roll in the fall of 1942. I had become editor of *The Cactus* and I finally made some progress with Janey. The United States had been at war with the Axis powers for nearly one year. I had to face the reality of going into the military as soon as I graduated in February 1943. Many of my former classmates were already on the battlefront. With this in mind, I launched my final campaign to win Janey. I explained that I would soon have to go away to the war and that there was a reasonable chance that I would not return. I poured it on as thick as anybody could and still get away with it. I kept reminding her that once I went to the front, we might not ever see each other again.

When it did finally become obvious that I was going to have to go into the army, she accepted my marriage proposal. I won the battle, either through persistence, luck, or both. We were only nineteen years old, but we somehow talked our parents into letting us get married. We were married on December 12, 1942. My former roommate, D. B. Hardeman, who was already in the army by this time but was on leave, was my best man at our wedding. If I had it to do over again, I'd certainly do the same thing. I don't know that a Phi Beta Kappa key would do me much good, but I wasn't about to get one. But I'll tell you what, having Janey by my side meant all the difference in the world to me. The day we were married was the best day of my life.

I had only a couple of months after our wedding to get as much done on the yearbook as I could before my graduation. The school year 1942-1943 was the first full year of the war and the mood on campus had changed accordingly. We decided that the theme of the 1943 *Cactus* should be patriotic and that we should set aside a large amount of space to serve as a tribute to the ex-students as well as the faculty and staff of the University who were serving in the military. We had the names of 120 of our former classmates who had been killed and nineteen who were missing in action, so we dedicated the entire yearbook to those who had already given their lives for our freedom. We

My father congratulating Janey and me on our wedding day. *Courtesy of the Briscoe family.*

were able to get the military pictures of some of these young men, so we placed those throughout our publication. The end of the war in Europe was still a distant two years away and the end of the war against Japan was even further away. The Italian campaign, the landings at Normandy, the Battle of the Bulge, and most of the assaults on Japanese-held islands in the Pacific remained in the future. The university's casualty figures were fated to climb much higher.

Of course, the campus environment had changed considerably as a result of the war, so we made a special effort to reflect that change in the images that illustrated the yearbook. Along with the traditional pictures of sporting events and campus beauties (one of whom was my beautiful Janey), we added photographs of war-related activities. Those included pictures of All-American football player Stan Mauldin being given a blood test on campus by an army medic prior to his induction into the service, special events to sell war bonds, and student service organizations conducting scrap metal collection drives. I was unable to complete the editing of *The Cactus* yearbook because I graduated in the middle of the regular school year, so Janey stepped in and finished the job for me.

After the United States entered the war in December 1941, I was not drafted immediately into the military because the local draft boards automatically granted a deferment to any college student who was close to finishing a degree. I was in an accelerated academic program in business administration, with a minor in law, which allowed me to graduate in February instead of June 1943. I had planned to enter law school, but I realized that I would have to put that off until I fulfilled my military obligation.

After my graduation, however, I learned that I didn't have to go through the draft after all. I was eligible for an agricultural deferment because my family was engaged in farming and ranching on a large scale. Agriculture was considered absolutely essential to the war effort and deferments were made almost without exception. My father urged me to take the deferment, and I can understand why, because if it were my son today, I'd want the same thing. But there was never any question in my mind about my going into the military. Everyone that I knew at the University of Texas felt strongly that this was a war we had to win and that each one of us had to do our part. I don't remember anybody taking a deferment, and there were a number who could have had one. I do remember some students who were turned down by the military because of health reasons, but that's entirely different. If you can't get in, you can't get in. But those individuals did other work in support of the war effort.

So, despite my father's wishes, I applied for admission into the Naval Air Corps. While attending the university, I had taken flying lessons from Bobby Ragsdale at the Austin Municipal Airport. Ragsdale taught several generations of university students and Austin residents how to fly. He and his wife offered a preparatory course for anyone who wanted to be a pilot in the military.

I had wanted to learn how to fly ever since my father had taken me on a ride in a big old Ford Tri-Motor airplane when I was a kid. A "barnstorming" pilot came to Uvalde and offered anyone a brief ride for a couple of bucks. That was the only time I had flown in an airplane before I took lessons. I learned how to fly in a Taylor Craft, a little two-seater that you piloted with a stick rather than a wheel. Before World War II, the Austin airport was a rudimentary affair with grass runways. The terminal was an old two-story frame house.

I enjoyed the lessons, and I did well, but there was one thing we had to do that I disliked. It was a lesson called the "stall and spin." In those days, your instructor would get you to a high altitude and then you had to pull the nose up until the aircraft stalled and went into a spin. You had to spin the airplane straight down several times, and then you had to pull the nose up and take it out of the spin. I never was very good at doing the stall and spin, but I managed to pass the course, anyway. I had my license by the time I met Janey. Occasionally, she would go flying with me, which was either a very brave or foolish thing for her to do.

Working for Uncle Sam

I enjoyed flying, and I looked forward to serving in the Naval Air Corps, but it was not to be. I went to Houston for the physical exam and promptly failed because of my poor eyesight. Of course, if you couldn't fly for the navy you couldn't fly for the army, either. That ended my dream. I returned to Uvalde and entered the regular draft. I was drafted into the army as a private and sent to Fort Sam Houston in San Antonio for induction. I was at Fort Sam for just a few days, and then the army shipped me out to Fort Frances E. Warren at Cheyenne, Wyoming, for basic training. This was in March, but it was still very cold when I arrived. The north wind blew hard and without end. And of course, the barracks in which we were housed had been built very quickly and weren't insulated. The icy wind just blew right through the walls. I did not expect basic training to be fun, but that cold, hard, constant wind in Wyoming made it an even more unpleasant experience than I had anticipated.

After basic training, I spent a few months at an ordnance depot near Olympia, Washington, until I was accepted for officers' candidacy training at Aberdeen Proving Ground in Maryland. Janey came with me to Olympia, and we spent the weekends together. And then we made the cross-country train trip to Maryland together. I had a pass for a few days' leave, so we traveled to New York City and did some sightseeing before I had to report to officers' school.

This was in the winter of 1943-1944, and it got pretty cold in Maryland, too. I remember that very well. Janey rented a place to stay on the Chesapeake Bay estate of Sen. Millard Tydings. She lived in one of their servant's houses, which was a very nice little place. I remember that the servant's quarters had a coal furnace, which was a real mystery to me. I didn't know how to operate it. I always kept the house either too hot or too cold. It was a wonderful experience, because the house was next door to the Tydings' mansion and had a beautiful view of Chesapeake Bay. We got to know Senator and Mrs. Tydings, who were extremely nice to us. Janey and I had some happy days there.

In the school at Aberdeen, I was assigned primarily to mechanics, for which I had absolutely no aptitude. I don't know why I got that particular assignment, but that is one of the traditional challenges of life in the military. Decisions are made without any rationale that is apparent to the soldier whose life they impact. But whatever job the army wanted me to have was okay with me. You really had no choice but to try to do whatever you could in whatever field you were assigned.

After I finished officers' school, I was commissioned as a lieutenant, and the army sent me to a camp on Lake Erie. Janey came with me, and she rented a room in a little old frame hotel located between the railroad track and Lake Erie. Of course, the trains all used coal in those days, and the coal dust was several inches deep everywhere. The entire town was black with coal dust. Even the snow was black in this town. It was just a horrible, wretched little place. It was Christmastime, and Janey was determined to make the best out of the situation, which she was always quite good at doing. She found a little Christmas tree that she somehow persuaded a storekeeper to let her have. We put that little tree up in our room, and we had a Christmas party there for just the two of us.

A few days after Christmas, the army sent me as a replacement to Indian Gap in the northern part of Pennsylvania, not far from Hershey. Janey came with me, and we got a room at the Hershey Hotel.

When I got off on the weekends, I stayed at the hotel with her. I was in Indian Gap for only a short time when the word spread that we were bound for Europe. This was in January 1945. The Battle of the Bulge had been raging for a month, and everyone assumed we would be sent to the front as replacements. We were warned to be ready to move out rapidly when the orders finally came in.

Being in Hershey, Janey bought a lot of chocolate, and she knitted some thick socks for me, which I stuffed in my footlockers with my other winter clothes. I was able to get a couple of days off to stay with Janey at the Hershey Hotel. It was a grand, wonderful hotel. It was wintertime and there were very few people around. It was really a great place to be. Janey and I savored the brief time we had there, knowing that I was bound for northwest Europe, which was experiencing one of the coldest winters on record and was the site of a ferocious struggle between the Allies and the Nazis.

As we anticipated, we soon received an urgent alert to report back to barracks immediately. Janey drove me to Indian Gap. As soon as I entered the camp, we were ordered to board the trucks immediately. Janey was in the civilian area outside the military compound itself, waiting for me to tell her where we were headed. I had no time to go back and tell her. I tried to wave to her as the trucks drove out of the camp, but she was too far away. She couldn't tell who was waving at her. She thought it was someone flirting with her. That was my last chance to say goodbye, and I was heartsick.

When we arrived at the train station, we were shocked to learn that the train was going to the West Coast, not to Europe. I was assigned responsibility for two hundred African American soldiers who were being sent to various places in the Pacific as replacements. The entire U.S. military was racially segregated, so African Americans served in all-black units, but their officers were white. That assignment was not a problem for me, because I had been around African Americans all my life. My family had employed black maids, and we had black workers at some of our ranches. I had no difficulty getting along with these men or understanding their fears.

We traveled across the United States on a relatively slow train. My main job was to keep the men on the train wherever we stopped, which was not as easy as it may sound. This wasn't an organized unit. Most of the men hadn't known each other before this trip, and they had never laid eyes on me. We had never been together, and we wouldn't stay together when we arrived at our final destination overseas. They knew they were just replacements and that eventually everyone would be scattered to many different units, so there was no group loyalty whatsoever. We stopped in St. Louis for almost a full day. It was an impossible task to keep everybody on that train. The army had military police around the train station, of course, but that didn't do much good. I lost some of my men at that point; they just jumped the train and went absent without leave (AWOL). To be honest, I could understand why so many of them were ready to jump off. I remember wishing that I could just jump off myself, so I could surely understand why they wanted to leave.

Of course, I was chewed out and reprimanded when we arrived in Los Angeles and it was discovered that I had lost some of my men. I deserved a reprimand, but my sympathies were with the men who went AWOL, I have to admit. Anyway, we remained together and were sent to a base south of Los Angeles, where we stayed for several weeks. While en route to California, I got word to Janey about our destination and that we would be staying there for a while. She took a train to Los Angeles, and we were reunited. We had a good time, but we knew that sooner or later I would ship out and be gone for several months at the least.

Off to India

The order to leave came sooner rather than later. To my surprise, I boarded a troop ship with the same group of men I had been in charge of on the train. We embarked for India, ultimate assignment unknown. India was a mystery to me. I might as well have been on the way to another planet. I didn't know anything about the place. We had studied very little about India in school. About all I knew about India was that it was part of the British Empire.

One of my most vivid memories is that once we were at sea, I soon noticed that the ship was steaming in a very obvious zigzag course.

That was a constant reminder that we could be the target for a torpedo from a Japanese submarine. You soon realized, however, that was one of the many things you could not do anything about, so you tried not to think about it.

Our first stop was Hawaii, but they wouldn't let us get off the ship, of course. That was extremely disappointing, but those who were in charge were wise not to let us off that ship. I'm certain that I would have lost some of my men. After we docked in Hawaii for a couple of days, we headed southwest across the Pacific to the island of Tasmania, south of Australia.

It was a long trip, but as a junior officer I had plenty of work to keep me occupied. The ship was crowded. It wasn't too bad up where the officers stayed, but down below it was extremely crowded. We brought the men up on deck every day to get fresh air and to exercise. The conditions were terrible down there. Sanitation was a major problem. It was very difficult to keep the latrines clean. And of course, the junior officers drew sanitation duty, which was an unpleasant and difficult duty to carry out. We understood fully, however, that it was a critical duty.

We finally reached Tasmania, where we refueled. We didn't get off the ship there either. The army was taking no chances. From Tasmania, we went around Australia and then into the Indian Ocean. When the ship reached India, it steamed up a river to a dock thirty or forty miles south of Calcutta. After several weeks on board that ship, my men and I were more than ready to get off. We were soon trucked to a replacement camp near Calcutta. At that point I was separated from the men I had commanded since leaving Pennsylvania on that troop train. By this time I had become very good friends with many of them. Unfortunately, I never ran across any of them again. They were scattered to many different units just the same as the officers who were on the ship were scattered. I never saw any of the officers again either. The army scattered us all over India and Burma.

If the British had not been there, I think I would have felt as though we had landed on the dark side of the moon. This was a long way from home for a boy from Southwest Texas. The British, however, had succeeded in laying a thin veneer of polished English culture

You can see that Janey wasn't far from my mind even when I was in India during the war. *Courtesy of the Briscoe family.*

over Indian society. The infrastructure was entirely British. They had built the railroads, which ran on time, and they had imposed the English legal system on the country. Of course, English was the dominant language in the cities and among the educated. The British presence and influence made it much easier for us to operate. Nevertheless, it was apparent to me that the British had never really conquered the Indian people. It was obvious that they were just barely hanging on to this crown jewel of the empire.

When I arrived at the camp, I opened the footlocker that I had packed back in Pennsylvania and found my clothes soaked in chocolate. All of the Hershey's chocolate that Janey had given me had melted in the tropical heat as we sailed in the South Pacific. It was a mess. But that's not all—I had the wrong clothing. I had packed for winter conditions in northwest Europe, not for the tropics.

I was assigned to an ordnance unit in Calcutta that operated the automotive supply depot for jeeps and trucks. We received the new transportation equipment when it arrived from overseas, and then we delivered that equipment to the army units, wherever they might be. We also served as the maintenance base for jeeps and trucks. Our unit was commanded by a Major Schwartz, an older gentleman who had volunteered to join the army. He was over age at the time. The major was a skilled manager who ran the entire operation like a business.

We lived at Camp Hialeah, which was a temporary army camp that had been built at the Hialeah Race Track. It was very close to downtown Calcutta, near the Queen Victoria Memorial. Then the army moved me to Camp Braeburn, an ordnance depot that had been a British girls' school before the war. The living quarters were much improved over Hialeah. I was appointed commander of the camp, which was a nice duty to have. The officers had a separate house where the faculty of the school used to live.

We acquired a habit from the British officers. Each one of us had a bearer, which was a Hindu who served as your personal valet. The bearer would arrive before it was time to get up in the morning. He would wake you up, have a pot of hot coffee ready, and have all your clothes put out for you. He also prepared your bath, shined your shoes, made up the bed, and cleaned your room. Fees for bearer service were very low. The American officers, of course, fell for that service pretty fast.

I had an outstanding bearer named Mike, who was up in years. He had been with the British all of his life, so he was excellent. When it came time for me to leave India, he wanted to go with me. It was obvious that the British would soon be leaving, too, of course, and he didn't want to stay there in India. He feared that his life was going to be miserable after that because he had been such a close collaborator with the British colonial authorities. I tried to find a way for Mike to come home with me, but I wasn't successful. He was forced to stay in India. I had numerous letters from him after I got home. But I could never make arrangements for him to come to the United States. I finally lost touch with Mike.

The army had a "rest and recreation" (R&R) program that provided two weeks of vacation at one of the camps it had established for that purpose. A group of us was selected to drive a large number of vehicles in a convoy from Calcutta to New Delhi. During that trip, we had an opportunity to visit the Taj Mahal and other ancient sites of Indian civilization in the area. From New Delhi, we went up to Kashmir Province, where the army maintained an R&R camp. Four of my army buddies and I got a houseboat on Lake Shalimar. The houseboat was at a beautiful spot, but the lake was badly polluted. Nevertheless, it was an enjoyable break away from the routine of army life. We had some spectacular views of the Himalayas.

The truth is that we saw a lot that I really didn't care about seeing. I was very homesick, and I missed Janey terribly, so I wasn't in a touring mood. I was so homesick that it just killed any curiosity I might have had under different circumstances. As a result, I didn't take advantage of the opportunities to see more of the country. Travel was just one way to pass time until I could get home. That is all it meant to me then.

Thank goodness that we had dependable mail service. That helped me a great deal. It was dependable but not timely. Janey had moved back to Austin and returned to school. She wrote regularly, but her letters usually took a month to reach me. It didn't matter, just so long as they came regularly. Reading her letters was the high point of my day.

I was stationed at Camp Braeburn until a few months after the end of the war. There was quite a bit to do to close the camp, especially because of all the vehicles that had to be disposed of. I believe that most of them were turned over to the British instead of being sent home. I don't think they were worth sending home. The time went fairly fast because we were so busy, and we knew that we would soon be on our way home. We finally completed our job, moved out of camp, and boarded the troop ship near Calcutta. We sailed back to the United States on a different route than we had taken to get to India. We went on the Red Sea and up through the Suez Canal to Alexandria, Egypt, where we docked. We couldn't get off the ship, however, which was a real inconvenience because of the crowded conditions on board. The ship was packed to capacity with soldiers going home. A number of the American officers had married Indian women during their tour of duty, and they brought their brides home with them. From Egypt, we went on through the Mediterranean, past Gibraltar, and then across the Atlantic to New York City.

I had traveled around the world. I had departed from the West Coast of the United States, and I returned to the East Coast. I hadn't planned it, of course, but I have been around the world, for whatever that's worth. To me it wasn't worth very much at the time, nor is it now. But it was worth more than I can say to get home.

I took a train from New York to San Antonio and mustered out of the army at Fort Sam Houston. I had a chance to stay in the active reserves, but I declined the offer. When I had a chance to get loose from the army completely, I got loose. Janey met me in San Antonio. It was absolutely one of the happiest days of my entire life. As was the case with millions of other young men and women immediately after the war, we were desperately eager to get on with our lives together.

Chapter 5

LIFE ON THE DRY FRIO AND A PUSH INTO POLITICS

W HEN I GOT OUT OF THE ARMY, Janey was in graduate
school taking classes for her master's degree in education, so I
joined her in Austin. I took some agriculture and advanced business
classes, but I didn't stay in school very long. My heart simply wasn't in
it. The entire time I had been in the army, all I had thought about was
moving with Janey to the Rio Frio Ranch north of Uvalde that my
father had given us as a wedding present while I was still in the service.

At the time, the Rio Frio Ranch was a 13,000-acre sheep and goat
operation located on the Dry Frio River. My father had acquired the
ranch in 1939 from the Bernard and Chapman ranching operation. He
was attending a cattle raisers meeting at the Saint Anthony Hotel in
San Antonio when he learned that the ranch was on the market. He
sought out Mr. Bernard, who was a good friend of his, and asked him
what he wanted for the ranch. Mr. Bernard said six dollars an acre. My
father asked him if he would pay a 5 percent commission to sell it, and
Mr. Bernard said yes. My father replied, "All right, I'll tell you what. I'll
sell it for you. I'll just buy it myself and you can pay me the commission." Mr. Bernard agreed and sold it to my father for $5.70 an acre.

My father operated the Rio Frio Ranch as a sheep and goat operation before he gave it to us. It was a very generous gift that included a
large number of sheep and goats that my father had stocked the ranch
with. The only cattle on the property were a few milk cows. In addi-

tion, the ranch was debt free, and it came with cash in the bank. We also took over my father's lease on 7,000 acres of grazing land on the Vanham Ranch over in the Nueces River canyon. Altogether, we had about 20,000 acres for our sheep and Angora goats. My father essentially gave us his entire sheep and goat operation, and he gave it to us debt free. It was a great time to be in the business because wool, mohair, and lamb prices were high. That was a very nice way to start out. I have to admit that not many people have that kind of opportunity. My father had set Janey and me up pretty strong. One could not have gotten a better start in any business.

My father was crazy about Janey, and he always looked after her interests. When he gave us the ranch, he instructed his attorney, Darwin Suttle, that Janey's name had to go on the title. There was never any doubt in my father's mind that Janey and I were full partners in everything, and that was just fine with him.

I was itching to get to that ranch and to make my mark with it. After a few months in Austin, Janey, who could tell that I was restless, agreed to move to our new ranch. By this time Janey had completed her course requirements for her master's degree, but she had not written her thesis. She didn't have to be in Austin to complete her thesis, but our lives soon became too complicated for her to return to that task as soon as she would have liked. Janey always finished every project she started, although this particular project took more than twenty years. She eventually wrote her thesis on the life of Richard Coke, governor of Texas from 1874 to 1876. Coke was a pioneer in developing the state's educational system. Janey was awarded her degree from the University of Texas in 1972, the same year our eldest daughter, also named Janey, received her undergraduate degree.

LIFE ON THE DRY RIO FRIO

We left Austin and moved into a small frame house on the Rio Frio Ranch. The house had served as a hunting camp, so it was a very modest structure without electricity or a telephone. The Rural Electrification Authority had planned to bring electricity to the area, but the war started before they could get the lines up. All of the copper needed for

Janey and me with Willie Caraway, who was my nanny when I was a child, on our place on the Dry Rio Frio not long after the war. *Courtesy of the Briscoe family.*

the delivery wires was redirected to the war effort. It seems amazing to me now, but Janey and I lived there for almost two years without electricity.

You might think that it was a terrible situation without electricity. But the truth is that we enjoyed it very much. We sat out on the front porch in the evening until dark, and then we lit kerosene lamps for light. My father gave us a little Delco generator that used gasoline to generate electricity. We started that generator, and we had enough electricity for one light in the kitchen! To get the Delco generator to start, I had to go out and kick it real hard. And then to turn it off at night, I had to go out and kick it again. Turning it on wasn't any problem, but going outside at night during the spring and summer wasn't that much fun because you had to be a little concerned about stepping on a rattlesnake in the dark. That is snake country.

We did get a telephone, but we had to string the one-wire line to

Uvalde ourselves. No telephone company would service the rural area in those days. They wouldn't even string you a wire a mile out of town. The electric company wouldn't either. They would serve you in town, but if you lived out of town, you didn't have electricity. Of course, we got all of our water out of a well. We had a gasoline pump on the well, so we did have running water.

Janey and I were deeply grateful to my father for his support and his faith in us. As a result, we were determined to work hard to keep the ranch in good shape and to take care of our animals. We both wanted to prove that we deserved his trust. I really tried to make myself something of a ranch hand, and I enjoyed it. Janey had grown up strictly as a city kid who had never dreamed that she would be a ranch woman, but she accepted the challenge. We had a milk cow, some hogs, and chickens. Janey churned butter and took the butter and eggs to Uvalde to sell at the Schwartz Grocery store. She worked as hard as I did to make the ranch a success, quite often right by my side, and occasionally in difficult and unpleasant situations.

Perhaps the most difficult situation we faced together on the ranch was dealing with screwworms. We were plagued with screwworms on that ranch, as were all the ranches in the region, particularly in the summertime. Flies lay their screwworm eggs in any wound in an animal, no matter how small or where it is located. Male sheep fight, which often results in open wounds on their bodies, usually on their heads. Another problem is sheep eating prickly pear, which leaves wounds on their lips and around their mouths. The flies go right to the bloody lips and deposit their eggs, which become worms that live on the flesh of the infected animal. It makes a terrible wound. The larvae turn into flies, and the life cycle of the screwworm starts over.

I worked a pasture every morning to locate the screwworm cases. Janey often helped me. We had to separate the animals with worms from those that were worm free and put them in the worm trap. During the noon hour, we doctored the wounds on the animals in the worm trap. That afternoon we worked another pasture. To get the worms off the animals, we had to doctor them with what we called tacoli. When this medicine was applied in large amounts to the wound, the worms dropped off. I'll never forget the smell of that medicine; it was foul stuff. You ended up smelling just like it, of course. And the dead flesh where the worms had been had quite a terrible odor of its own. It was difficult, literally stinking, work. One difficult problem was treating mouth wounds. The problem with doctoring the mouth was that the animal would go to a water trough for a drink and wash the medicine off. Curing a case of worms in the lip was quite a difficult problem. We also had to be extremely careful when shearing the animals. It is easy to cut a sheep or a goat by accident when you are shearing them. We had to treat every cut with the medicine to prevent flies from laying their eggs. That worked to some extent, but when it rained or if the animal got into a water trough it would wash the medicine off, and then you would have a problem.

Janey and I weren't the only people who had to struggle with this plague. It was what everybody in the sheep and goat business had to do. Screwworms were also a problem with cattle, especially in the navel of young calves. With sheep and goats, it was more of a problem than with cattle because it is easier for the worms to kill a smaller animal. Because of their habits, sheep and goats also have more ways to get worms.

If untended, it didn't take long for an animal to die, particularly if the worms were somewhere in the head. We had to be vigilant at all times, because the worms could work their way deep into the flesh of the animal and kill it fast if ignored. So it was a necessity to work six, sometimes seven, days a week to stay on top of the problem. I worked all day long and got home about dark, smelling of screwworm medicine and dead animal flesh.

I did that for about two and a half years. I know it sounds pretty difficult, but the truth is that I enjoyed the work and the life we led in that little house without electricity. We didn't have children, so that certainly made it easier. We were in our early twenties in age. That's the time to have an adventure anyway. And it was a wonderful adventure. We finally got electricity, which improved things because then we had a radio that we listened to every evening. And we had wonderful neighbors up in the hills who we enjoyed visiting.

Janey was eager, however, for us to be more involved in the community and to have an opportunity to do something more broadly meaningful. Janey, who was always more of a social person than I, also tired of the isolation she had to endure by living full time on the Rio Frio Ranch. She loved the ranch, but not as a seven days a week, twelve months a year, residence. One time I forgot that I had the keys to Janey's car in my pocket when I went over to the Vanham Ranch, which is a drive of about one hundred miles round trip from our place on the Rio Frio. When I got home that night, I heard about my mistake. Janey said: "You go off and leave me on this rock pile again and I'll not stay here another day." From that day on I called the house at Rio Frio the rock pile. Janey was trapped for a full day on that rock pile. Actually, rock pile was an accurate description because that's exactly what the place was.

A Push into Politics

So, Janey and I began to look for something else to do. Several of our former classmates and friends from the university had been elected to the state legislature after they had returned from military service. My old friend Jack Brooks was one of them. The fact that Jack was in the state legislature along with many of our other friends gave us the idea that I might also make a bid for the legislature in the 1948 election. The more Janey and I talked about it, the more it sounded like a good idea. Janey had grown up in Austin, and she favored the idea that we could live part of the year there. And of course, I had dreamed of being in politics ever since that wonderful night I slept in the Governor's Mansion as a child.

Although I thought we were still in the thinking and talking stage, Janey concluded that I had decided to be a candidate. Janey drove to San Antonio for some reason, and on her way back to Uvalde she stopped at the Medina County Courthouse in Hondo. She visited our friend Jim Duncan, the county clerk. While she was there, Janey filed the papers declaring me a candidate for the legislature. She thought she was doing me a great favor. When she got home and told me she had filed my candidacy, I nearly fell out of my chair. I thought we hadn't quite made up our minds. But I knew then that it was too late. I didn't sleep much that night for quite a few reasons. The main reason was that I had never been a candidate for political office, and I had some doubts about my ability to run a campaign. Another reason was that I dreaded delivering this news to my mother and father.

I was very aware that Mother did not hold politicians in very high regard. And I assumed that my father wanted me to work on the ranch and that he felt that I didn't have any business running off and getting into politics. My father also thought that being a member of the legislature didn't amount to much. Some of the sorriest people he'd ever known had been members of the legislature and some of them were from our part of the state. He didn't think that being in the legislature was a very lofty ambition. I had heard his opinions on the matter many times earlier.

It was a traumatic event when Janey and I gave Mother and Father the news about my political aspirations. As I had expected, Mother didn't take it well at all. She tried not to show it, but she just couldn't help it. Mother said, "Well, I just can't imagine a son of mine in politics." Her younger brother had run for county commissioner and had lost. That had hurt badly. All she thought about politics was rejection and hurt. In addition, politicians did not enjoy very high moral reputations, probably with justification, then as well as now. Mother thought running for office was a dirty, nasty business in which moral, Christian people shouldn't engage. The political life meant to her that you associated with a lot of people with low moral standards. It was like running off and joining the circus. She just couldn't hold back the tears. She tried, but it was a pretty sad experience.

My father also made it clear that he didn't want me to run. He had been around politicians a lot because of his relationship with Mr. Sterling. My father and mother had seen the Sterling family go from being one of the wealthiest families in Texas to being broke, largely, they felt, because of politics. They believed that if Mr. Sterling had not been governor, he would have paid closer attention to his business, and he wouldn't have lost it. I think they were right about that.

Despite such intense opposition from my parents, I filed my candidacy in all of the counties in the legislative district. Once my father understood that I really was in the race, he resolved to do everything he could to see that I won. Mother was a little slower in getting

=ELECT=

DOLPH

BRISCOE, JR.

State Representative
77th District

Subject to Democratic Primary July 24th

YOUR VOTE AND SUPPORT APPRECIATED

This was my campaign poster when I first ran for the state legislature. It wasn't fancy, but it made the point. *Briscoe Papers; di_03952.*

adjusted to it. But she did adjust, and then she gave the effort her total support. Their support meant everything to me.

My campaign platform was pretty safe. It called for good roads, good schools, and conservation of our water resources. It was difficult for anyone to be against those positions. I convinced myself that those were ideas that nobody else in the county had ever thought of. Good roads meant that I was going to have rural roads paved. That was needed and it was a hot issue at the time. I said I was going to have to get it done because our current representative in the legislature hadn't done it. So, I tried to make an issue out of the need for rural roads. I was going to make the schools better by raising teacher pay. We were going to take action to help conserve our water, but I was against any legislation that would take control away from individual property owners. I supported plans to conserve water by storing it on the surface behind dams. But I was not going to let the state tell a farmer how much water he could pump out of the ground.

This was during the era when a Republican wouldn't have dared to run for public office in my part of Texas, so the only contest was in the Democratic Party primary. The incumbent in the race was Brittan T. Edwards, a young veteran from La Pryor who was serving his first term in the legislature. To be honest, there was no great issue between us. He was a good young man. We later became close friends. As a legislator, however, Edwards had supported a bill to give the state authority to limit the amount of water that each farmer in our part of Texas could pump. That was a sensitive issue with the farmers. During the campaign, I made a point of emphasizing my strong opposition to the water conservation law that Representative Edwards had supported. I took the position that if we captured a major portion of the surface water flowing down our streams with dams, we would have a sufficient supply of water. We would not have to limit the pumping of underground water on private property.

A Visit with Mr. Garner

Before I started my campaign, my father urged me to visit Mr. Garner to pay my respects and to get the benefit of his advice. I really didn't want to make that visit. Obviously, I knew much about Mr. Garner, and, as I have already discussed, he knew my father. But Mr. Garner did not know me. He had a well-earned reputation as a pretty tough old curmudgeon who had a low tolerance for foolishness. He was a formidable and intimidating character. I really didn't want to go see Mr. Garner, but I knew my father was right. I might not get any good out of visiting him, but if I ignored him, I risked insulting him to the point where he might work against me. When he was displeased about something going on in the community, he let people know it.

For example, two years earlier, in 1946, Mr. Garner had fought against the creation of our local junior college. He strongly opposed the proposition simply because he was against any new taxes, even though this tax would be very small. Mr. Garner believed, correctly I should add, that while taxes might start out very small, they would increase through the years. Mr. Garner therefore led a vigorous fight against the college. If Harry Hornby Jr., owner and publisher of the *Uvalde Leader-News*, had not succeeded in pulling together enough of the community to pass it—just barely—Garner's opposition would have killed it. It was one of the rare examples of anyone prevailing against Mr. Garner in Uvalde County.

Interestingly, a few years after the college was established, it was threatened with closure because of its financial woes. Mr. Garner shocked everyone by suddenly coming forward to help save it. He had convinced himself that the school, which is named Southwest Texas Junior College, was doing a great job. He gave them money for a building in honor of Mrs. Garner. Then he gave them some more money, and then he gave them some more. And it started adding up. Then he gave them his bank in Crystal City, where he owned the majority of the stock in the bank. His family was very pleased that he had seen the light. There was no resentment on their part for what he was doing. But when Mr. Garner instructed his attorney to draw up the papers to give the college everything he had, the family had to intervene. Mr. Garner needed money for his own care, but he was giving it all away. The family had to go to court and stop him. When Mr. Garner changed his mind about something, he changed it all the way.

I realized that I could not delay paying Mr. Garner a courtesy visit, so I told Janey, "Now look, you got me into this thing, you've got to go with me to see Mr. Garner. Maybe if you go with me he'll be more of a gentleman."

Aware of her complicity in my predicament, Janey consented to go with me. We went to Mr. Garner's house about three o'clock one afternoon, and I knocked on the front door. When the maid opened the door, I announced: "I'm Dolph Briscoe, Junior, and this is my wife, Janey, and we would like to see Mr. Garner." And she said, "Well, he's out on the sun porch." She sent us in the right direction, but we noticed that she didn't go out there with us.

We found Mr. Garner dressed in the khaki pants and shirt that he always wore. He was playing solitaire. Janey and I stood there a little while, but Mr. Garner didn't acknowledge our presence. He seemed too wrapped up his game. After a few moments, I said, "Mr. Garner, I'm Dolph Briscoe, Junior. I'm running for the legislature. And I wanted to come by and ask you for your advice and your help." He finally looked up, gripped his chewed-up cigar between his teeth, and said, "Young man, there are 40,000 voters in this district. If you go out, shake the hands, and ask for the vote of over half of them, you might get elected." With that Mr. Garner got up, put his arm around me, and sort of gave me a little shove toward the back door. He never noticed Janey standing there, never said a word to her. After I said, "Thank you, sir," we were out the door. That was the end of the conversation and the visit. Mr. Garner was a man of few words most of the time, and besides that, I was interfering with his card game. When he was ready for you to leave, he would gently but firmly get you by the shoulder and steer you toward the door. There was no doubt about what he had in mind when he did that. He had a lot of practice doing it. He was an expert. As we went around the corner from the back of the house to return to our car, Janey expressed some strong thoughts about Mr. Garner's rudeness. I'm glad he didn't hear them. That would not have helped our relationship.

Learning How to Campaign

I didn't see Mr. Garner again for quite some time, but as I thought more about what he had said, I realized that he had given me the best advice a young man in politics could have. He had told me everything I needed to know in a few short words. It just had to soak in. That is when Janey and I decided to take Mr. Garner's advice. We divided up the counties and started campaigning on foot, personally meeting as many voters as possible. Janey spent most of her time working in Medina County. She literally went from house to house, knocking on doors, asking people to vote for me. I concentrated on Zavala and Dimmitt counties, where I also went from house to house. Janey and I both worked in Uvalde County. We had cards printed with my name on them and my platform. If the residents weren't at home, we wrote: "Sorry to have missed you—sure would appreciate your vote" on the back of the card and left it on the front door.

I was new to politics. When we started campaigning, I found it difficult to introduce myself to people. I remember that the first place we campaigned was in a little village called Quihi, which consisted of a small church and a community building. It's northeast of Hondo, the county seat of Medina County. They were having a turkey shoot. Janey and I arrived just a little early and there were just four or five men standing around. Janey urged me to introduce myself. But I said: "Oh no, I'd better wait and do that a little later, when more people are here." Janey said, "You go do that now!" I realized then that I had the choice of overcoming my shyness or incurring the wrath of my wife. Given those options, I walked over and I said, rather lamely and almost in a whisper, "I'm Dolph Briscoe and I'm running for the legislature."

One of the men walked up and introduced himself as Judge Rothe, the Medina County judge. I replied, "Well, I'm certainly glad to meet you, Judge *Rotty*." I mispronounced his name. And he said, "The name is Rothe." And I thought, good night, I've blown this one. The Rothes were one of the pioneer families of Medina County. They had founded a ranching community on Hondo Creek in the northwest part of the county, and they were one of the most respected families in the area. And there were a lot of them. I thought, "Man, I blew this." But he took it well. He thought it was funny that I couldn't say the German pronunciation correctly. I also met the other men, and I told them I was running for the legislature. One of them said, "Boy! Why are you running for the legislature?" I replied, "Well, I believe we ought to have better schools and I think we ought to pave some of your roads here." He said, "Well, that's a damn good idea." That gave me some courage to talk up my candidacy with them. Judge Rothe finally said, "Young fellow, I think you're all right. You may not know how to pronounce my name but I think I'm going to be for you."

Judge Rothe's comments made my day. And he did support me. He was a tremendous help. He had been county judge for quite a while, and he was highly respected. His relatives were spread all over Medina County, so that was a major boost. It was a great start for my campaign. After that positive experience, I found that I had a little more courage to go out and meet people. Of course, it didn't go that well with everyone I met. After I introduced myself, some of the voters would say, "Well, boy, you're running against a good man. Why are you doing that?" I'd reply that my opponent was indeed a good man, but that he hadn't done much in the legislature to benefit the district.

One of my strongest supporters in Uvalde was Judge Ross Doughty, who had been district attorney but at the time of my campaign was the district judge. Ross was born and raised in Uvalde, so he knew the area very well. All the years that he served as district attorney and district judge he never had an opponent. Judge Doughty was blessed with much common sense and good judgment. He was an important source of advice and counsel throughout my political career.

I also had good advocates in the other counties beyond Uvalde. I received strong support from all the cattle raisers in my district. In Medina County, the management of the local electric cooperative gave me significant help. Sam Lanham, the head of the Medina Electric Cooperative, was a key supporter. Sam was a direct descendent of former Texas governor S. W. Lanham. He took a keen interest in politics and in the political affairs of the Rural Electrical Cooperative statewide organization. I could always count on Sam's backing.

As time went by and I got more experience, I found it easier to campaign. It got to where I didn't mind going up to strangers and holding out my hand. To my surprise, I discovered that most people were receptive to my greeting. Whether they were going to vote for me or not, they were ladies and gentlemen. Of course, every now and then I met a disagreeable person. I learned that the best thing to do in that case was just to move on as quickly as I could. There was no point in getting into an argument. I would try to say something nice, smile, and just move on. I had to figure that person was a lost cause. That was just part of the learning experience. I soon discovered that if you didn't master the face-to-face part of political campaigning, you didn't survive.

I believe that a campaign at the local or grassroots level is something that every citizen involved in his or her community ought to go through. I highly recommend it. A campaign for the school board or the water district board or any other elected public service position is an experience that you can't get out of a book or out of class in school. One can find out more about human nature by running for elected office at the local level than almost any other way. It can be a great experience. It can also be a humbling one, even when you win. I can almost guarantee that if you enter a local political campaign with an over-inflated ego, you will come out of it with a much smaller one. And that's good. It will bring you down to earth, which is where you ought to be.

Unfortunately, candidates for statewide and national offices are too insulated and protected by their campaign professionals to have the kind of character-building experience that a local campaign can provide. They have people telling them exactly what to do and when to do it. They don't have the opportunity to have a dialogue with the average person in any meaningful way.

Janey was an outstanding campaigner, much better than I was. She just seemed to be a natural-born politician. And the election results clearly showed which one of us was the better campaigner. Janey spent most of her time in Medina County. She worked hard there. I carried Medina County by a large margin, and I know it was because of Janey. I lost Zavala County because that was my opponent's home county. I carried Dimmitt and Uvalde counties, but barely. It was close, but I won the primary.

Victory in the Democratic Party primary meant that I would be going to Austin in January 1949 to serve in the legislature. I had no opponent in the general election in November. That gave me several months to get things in order at our Rio Frio Ranch and to prepare for the life of being a legislator. Although the general election was irrelevant for state offices, the national presidential campaign was another matter. I followed that very closely, and I was fortunate enough to take part in one of the campaign's most interesting events.

GETTING DEWEY'S GOAT

Harry Truman was running as the underdog Democratic candidate against the Republican nominee, New York Gov. Thomas Dewey. Despite Mr. Truman's status as the non-elected incumbent who had

Janey was my best vote-getter. Here she is campaigning with constituents at a barbecue in my district. *Briscoe Papers.*

assumed the presidency after the death of FDR three years earlier, the press and most of the leadership in the Democratic Party believed that he could not beat Dewey. The Democrats had split into three parts: the pro-segregationist Dixiecrats led by Strom Thurmond on the far right, the Progressives led by Henry A. Wallace on the far left, and the Truman supporters in the broad middle. Dewey led a unified Republican Party, and he appeared to be unbeatable.

In Texas, the Democratic Party leadership decided to do as little as possible to help Mr. Truman's campaign. Aware of his problems in Texas, President Truman scheduled a trip across the state in his campaign train. One of his stops was Uvalde, which is located on the main rail line between El Paso and San Antonio. Obviously, Uvalde's voting population was too small to warrant such a stop. What President Truman wanted was the public endorsement of the grand old man of the Texas Democrats: Cactus Jack Garner.

The president and Mr. Garner were old and close friends from Mr. Truman's years in the U.S. Senate. When Mr. Truman was a freshman senator, Mr. Garner was vice president, which made him the presiding officer of the Senate. Mr. Garner liked Mr. Truman very early on and helped him adjust to the ways of the Senate. He often asked Mr. Truman to take the vice president's chair and preside in his absence. Mr. Garner also invited Mr. Truman to a private lunch in the Capitol with Will Rogers, who was a good friend of Mr. Garner's. That was a personal favor that Mr. Truman never forgot. Mr. Garner also included Mr. Truman in his late afternoon private get-togethers to talk politics, play cards, and enjoy good bourbon. There were very few people, including Sam Rayburn, who could call Mr. Garner "John." Mr. Truman called him John, and Mr. Garner called him Harry.

When we received word that the president would be stopping in Uvalde to visit Mr. Garner, Janey decided to host a reception at the Kincaid Hotel for Mrs. Truman and her daughter, Margaret. I remember Janey worrying about what she should charge people to attend the reception. When she told my father that she needed to charge admission to pay for the cost of the reception, he protested. "Now, that won't do," Father said. "You can't charge people to come to a political reception like that." When she asked Father how she was supposed to pay for it, he told her to stop worrying, he would pick up the tab.

While Janey was busy planning the reception, I was persuaded to take part in a publicity stunt to bring attention to the severe problems we were having with the low market price of mohair. Jack Richardson, a mohair producer here in the area, was also quite a promoter. Jack got an idea that we ought to drive a herd of goats up to meet the president's train. He was certain that the stunt would inspire the reporters traveling with the president to write a story about the bad condition of the mohair market. Mohair producers needed help from the government in the form of price support, and that was going to be the message we would be sending to President Truman. But then Jack, bless his heart, got the idea that he would take a little kid goat and paint it up with a mustache to look like Governor Dewey. He planned to hand it to President Truman and to announce that Mr. Truman was going to get Dewey's goat in the election. I don't know how Jack talked me into helping him with this crazy scheme, but he did.

The president's campaign train arrived at the little Southern Pacific depot in North Uvalde at 6:50 in the morning on Sunday, September 26. The train, which had come from El Paso, pulled into a siding by the depot platform. This was a major event for Uvalde. It is hard to remember now, but we had no television and the world was a much larger place then. We weren't as jaded as we are today about the presidency. Hardly anyone in Uvalde had ever seen a president of the United States in person. The president was someone you saw only in photographs in the newspaper or in newsreels at the movie theater. It was an exciting moment for us. Ten thousand people and the high school band showed up at that very early time in the morning to greet the president. You could tell by the big grin on President Truman's face that he was surprised and delighted by the welcome.

Mr. Garner was standing on the platform to greet the president. Mr. Garner had borrowed a car, a convertible, and the top was down. He had one of my good friends, Duke Bryson, as his driver. Another car was there for Mrs. Truman and the Trumans' daughter, Margaret.

Jack Richardson and I had put this herd of goats behind a little fence out by the train platform in clear sight of the president and his entourage. President Truman glanced at the goats with a puzzled look on his face. He didn't know why they were there, and I'm sure he didn't care, either. When the president got into the backseat of the car with Mr. Garner, Jack Richardson and I walked up carrying this little goat that Jack had painted to look like Tom Dewey. The goat was dressed in a gold blanket with the words "DEWEY'S GOAT" printed across it. Mr. Truman didn't quite know what to make of this business. But Mr. Garner assured him, "It's all right, Harry. These are good boys. They're just trying to do something for the goat business down here. They're good boys. It's okay." He asked Mr. Truman to just go along with us. So, the president went along with it. I'm certain that there were Secret Service agents around the car, but they didn't give us any problems. I can't imagine that being allowed today. But Jack Richardson handed Mr. Truman this goat that really did look like Tom Dewey. Jack announced as loudly as he could: "President Tru-

Jack Richardson showing "Dewey's goat" to President Truman and Mr. Garner in Uvalde in 1948. *Courtesy of the* Uvalde Leader-News *Collection, El Progresso Memorial Library Archives.*

man, you're going to get Dewey's goat in November." The president laughed and declared, "I'm going to clip it and make a rug, then I'm going to let it graze on the White House lawn for the next four years."

Of course, reporters from the national press were traveling with President Truman. They got some good pictures, naturally. It even made the movie newsreels. And that's exactly what Jack wanted. I had pulled back a bit from the car, because I wasn't particularly interested in being in those pictures. I guess I felt embarrassed about being involved in giving the president of the United States a goat. But it didn't embarrass Jack a bit. Jack was the kind of fellow that you couldn't embarrass. Mr. Truman held the goat long enough to have the pictures taken, and, thank goodness, the goat behaved well. I guess it was a slow news day, but they sent the picture of President Truman getting Dewey's goat to the *New York Times*, which printed it on the front page the next morning. It was such a long shot that something like that would end up from Uvalde on the front page of the *New York Times* of all places. Jack Richardson was delighted that his scheme had worked so well.

We quickly reclaimed our goat, and President Truman rode with Mr. Garner to Mr. Garner's house on Park Street. Mrs. Truman and Margaret followed in another car. The other members of the president's entourage went to the Kincaid Hotel, where Janey was hosting the reception. After they arrived at his house, the Garners fed the Trumans an enormous breakfast. We found out later that they served large portions of fried chicken, white-wing dove, ham, bacon, scrambled eggs, rice in gravy, hot biscuits, Uvalde honey, peach preserves, grape jelly, and coffee. Only the Garners and the Trumans were in attendance, no one else was allowed in the house. I was not on Mr. Garner's "gofer" staff yet, so I didn't get inside. Margaret Truman later stated in her memoir of her father that at the breakfast he gave Mr. Garner a present of Kentucky bourbon concealed in small black satchel. President Truman told him that it was "medicine" that should be used only in case of snakebites.

After breakfast, the Garners and the Trumans were joined by Texas Gov. Beauford Jester and Sam Rayburn, both who had just arrived. Mr. Rayburn, another old friend of both Truman and Garner, had been expected, but some of us were surprised to see Governor Jester. He had been very critical of President Truman, especially about the president's civil rights program. They all came out in the backyard, under the trees where Mr. Garner had held his political meetings, and met the press. I was among a large group of town people who were allowed to watch the press conference. Mr. Garner gave Mr. Truman a strong endorsement. Mr. Garner was at his very best. He declared that his "old and very good friend" Harry Truman was a man of integrity who deserved another term and who should have the support of all Texans. At that time, Mr. Garner was held in great respect by the conservative element of the Texas Democratic Party. Many Texans considered Truman to be a liberal. It took an endorsement from Mr. Garner, who was an absolutely staunch conservative, to help turn the situation around. I have no doubt that his support had an extremely positive effect on Truman's vote in Texas. Mrs. Truman was so moved by Mr. Garner's warm words and hospitality that she stepped forward and thanked everyone for being there at such an early time on a Sunday morning. It was unusual event for her to speak in public. Margaret Truman has claimed that Mr. Garner's endorsement that morning was the turning point for the campaign in Texas. Truman subsequently carried the state, despite little help from the state's Democratic leadership, including Lyndon B. Johnson.

As President Truman was leaving for San Antonio, accompanied by Sam Rayburn and Governor Jester, he announced to the press and the crowd that he would come back to Uvalde in ten years, which would be 1958, for Mr. Garner's ninetieth birthday. "I fished around for another invitation and got it," Truman proclaimed. It was a promise he kept.

When the breakfast was over and prior to the press conference, Margaret and Bess Truman went to Janey's reception at the Kincaid Hotel to visit briefly with the guests. The reception was a great success. Mrs. Truman and her daughter were warm and unpretentious, lovely people.

CACTUS JACK'S NINETIETH BIRTHDAY PARTY

True to his word, a few months before Mr. Garner's ninetieth birthday, on November 22, 1958, Mr. Truman called Mr. Garner and told him that he would come to Uvalde as he had promised to help celebrate Mr. Garner's ninetieth birthday. When he heard about Truman's upcoming visit, Harry Hornby, editor of the *Uvalde Leader-News*, who was my dear friend, talked me into being chairman of the event. We created a planning committee and decided to try and make it into as big an event as possible and attract as much publicity for our town as we could. When Mother learned of the planned visit and event, she told Janey and me that we could stay in her house in town because it would be more convenient than our ranch on the Rio Frio. My father had passed away a few years before. Mother said that she would go to

Fort Bend County to visit her family. She wanted nothing to do with politicians or a political event.

We took several cars to the airport to meet Mr. Truman. Mr. Garner rode out with his son, Tully. Mr. Truman's plane had some mechanical difficulty, and he arrived a couple of hours late. Mr. Garner, who was a man of little patience, had lost practically all of it by the time Mr. Truman got here. Still, he greeted him warmly and they rode together to Mr. Garner's house. At the time, Mr. Garner was living in the small white ranch house behind his large main house. He had given his two-story brick house to the city of Uvalde for a public library. As soon as we got to the cabin, Mr. Garner announced, "I'm going to bed. Dolph, you take care of Harry." With that, he walked away.

That was the first time I had a former president of the United States entrusted to my care. I quietly asked Tully Garner if he wanted Mr. Truman, but he said, "No, Dolph, you take him." So I turned to Mr. Truman and said, "Mr. President, we have a room reserved for you at the Kincaid Hotel. My wife, Janey, and my children are around the corner at my mother's house. Will you please join us for dinner?" He readily accepted the invitation.

We went to Mother's house and Janey and the children were there. My mother's cook was there and had something for everyone to eat. I remember our five-year-old son, Chip, was not the least impressed by Mr. Truman. He wanted to watch *Bonanza*, the popular western series, on television and insisted on eating on his television tray instead of at the table with the former president. During dinner, Janey asked Mr. Truman if he would like to spend the night there at my mother's home. He replied that he certainly would like to stay there because he didn't like staying at hotels.

When Mr. Truman excused himself to go to bed, he wrote a telephone number on a piece of paper and gave it to Janey. He asked her to telephone Mrs. Truman, who he called "the boss," and tell her where he was and that he was in good hands. I wondered at the time why he didn't want to call Mrs. Truman himself. It occurred to me later that, since he had struck several blows for liberty, he thought best if Janey called. Janey called Mrs. Truman, and she had a very nice visit with her.

The next morning, after breakfast, I had an opportunity to have a private visit with Mr. Truman. I asked him how it was that he had been able to make decisions so momentous as the decision to drop the atomic bomb on Japan. In my opinion, that was one of the most difficult decisions ever made in the history of the world. "It was very simple," Mr. Truman replied. "I got all the information that I could get from my advisors and others whose opinions I respected. I weighed the arguments and the facts. I made the decision and I never thought about it again." I thought that was a great lesson for anyone who has to make difficult decisions.

The remainder of the day turned out to be memorable. Mr. Garner was in great spirits again. The governor of Texas, Price Daniel Sr., attended, as did the majority leader of the U.S. Senate, future president Lyndon Johnson. Speaker Sam Rayburn also came. All the schools turned out and the businesses closed. The entire town came out to honor our number one citizen and his celebrated guests.

Although Speaker Rayburn attended the birthday celebration, it wasn't easy to recruit him. When I called the Speaker to invite him, there was a lengthy pause on his end of the line. Finally, Mr. Rayburn said, "All right, Dolph. I'll come. But under these conditions: You meet me at the airport, you stay with me, and when I say go, we go." He didn't want to be left alone with Mr. Garner, who never passed up an opportunity to lecture Mr. Rayburn about his failings as Speaker. Mr. Garner didn't think he was tough enough.

I should mention that Mother was pleased that she had missed this celebration. And she never regretted not being present when President Truman stayed in her home. Instead, she was happy that she had the foresight to be with her family in Fort Bend County. Politics and politicians she could always do without. Happily, she made an exception for her son, who served eight years in the Texas State Legislature while she was still living.

It is to those years that I will turn next.

Chapter 6

THE TEXAS LEGISLATURE

Aᴛᴛᴇʀ ᴍʏ ᴠɪᴄᴛᴏʀʏ in the Democratic Party primary in the spring of 1948, Janey and I decided to rent an apartment in Austin in which we could live during the weekdays while the legislature was in session from January until May 1949. We planned to spend our weekends at the Rio Frio Ranch. Janey's mother and father, as well as her brother, lived in Austin, and many of our former classmates at the university were still in town. We were excited about moving back to Austin and getting involved in the action at the Capitol.

Tʜᴇ Sɴᴏʀᴛɪɴɢ Pᴏʟᴇ ᴀɴᴅ ᴀ Hᴏᴜꜱᴇ Fᴜʟʟ ᴏꜰ Vᴇᴛᴇʀᴀɴꜱ

My first legislative session, the fifty-first since Texas became a state in the union, began in January 1949. As I mentioned before, my old campus political rival Jack Brooks was in his second term in the legislature. Jack and I arranged to have our desks next to each other on the House floor. I had much to learn about the ways of the legislature, and I knew Jack would educate me. Preston Smith, who at that time was a thirty-six-year-old state representative from Lubbock, sat right behind Jack. Preston, of course, later served two terms as governor of Texas, and his career and mine would intersect in significant ways in the future. This was the first time I'd met Preston, who was beginning his third term in the House. Preston remained my good friend until his death in 2003. G. P. "Pink" Pearson from Navasota sat right behind me. G. P. also was a freshman in the legislature. He liked to thrust his hand out and introduce himself in a dramatic manner, declaring loudly that you were now in the presence of "G. P. 'Pink' Pearson, Junior." He was wonderful man who became a lifelong friend.

The members of the House did not have offices in those days. We had to do our work at our desks on the floor of the House, which meant that we had to dictate to our secretaries while sitting there on the floor. You couldn't dictate when the House was in session, of course. But when we weren't in session, usually early in the morning or at night, I worked at my desk. There was nowhere else to go. Because we all worked there on the floor of the House, the members got to know each other well. You knew who was doing what because there was no privacy. Quite a few of my colleagues in that first session, however, enrolled in the university to finish their undergraduate degrees or to work on their law degrees, so they didn't spend a lot of time working at their legislative desks.

Preston, Jack, G. P., and I were in a little area next to the so-called "snorting pole," which was right across from Jack's desk. The snorting pole was a podium where the members of the legislature would go to get the attention of the Speaker during the period in the morning when time was set aside for personal privilege remarks. The representatives would walk over to it and yell "Mr. Speaker, I rise to make a point of order," or, "I want to speak on a motion," or whatever.

The members produced a lot of hot air and engaged in much grandstanding at the snorting pole during the time for personal privilege speeches. The pole was right by Preston's desk, and every morning Preston would stand up and make a personal privilege speech denouncing Gov. Beauford Jester because he had vetoed an appropriation for the Texas Tech University Library. Preston, a Tech graduate, was the school's chief advocate in the legislature. And, of course, that played well to the folks back in Lubbock. In one of his more memorable speeches, Preston declared that the only thing Governor Jester had ever done was to "ponder, piddle, and mess up everything in general." He often referred to Jester as "our so-called governor." The capitol reporters sat at a long table in front of the snorting pole. Preston always made certain that the Lubbock reporter heard his speech, and then he'd sit down and be just as happy as he could be for the rest of the day.

The freshman class in 1949 was not as large as the freshman class of 1947, which had included many war veterans. There had been a huge turnover in membership in the legislature in 1947 as a result of these veterans running against incumbents. That was an unusual election in 1946 because incumbents were at a disadvantage running against military veterans who had just come home from World War II. Nearly every veteran came home a hero just for taking part in that war. That gave veterans a decided advantage in a political race against anyone who had stayed home, no matter how honorable their reason for not having served.

Swapping Votes with Jack Brooks

As a rookie legislator, I had the good fortune of having Jack Brooks around to show me the ropes. He really took me under his wing that first year. We may have seemed the odd couple to outsiders. We were close friends, but our constituencies gave us different political agendas. Jack represented the heavily industrialized Beaumont–Port Arthur area, which had the largest concentration of labor unions in Texas. Labor was more influential there than they were anywhere else in the state. I represented a rural, conservative district dominated by agriculture. Jack was pro-labor in a quite vocal manner, while labor unions were anathema to a vast majority of my constituents. These political differences, however, caused no problems between us. We helped each other out in any way we could.

In those days, there was no rule in the House against voting somebody else's machine. If I went home on a Friday and the legislature was going to stay in session, Jack would vote for me. And he always voted for me the opposite way from how he voted. I knew I could go and leave my machine open and that Jack would cast my votes the way I would have cast them. And I voted for him when he was away. We trusted each other completely and never had a problem. Of course, there were some bills that we both voted for and some that we both voted against. A good example was my support for upgrading Lamar

College in Beaumont into a four-year, state-supported school named Lamar Tech, which Jack was promoting actively. Jack had gone to school at Lamar before transferring to the University of Texas. I voted for that bill without having to worry about negative reactions back home.

The Lamar Tech bill is a good example of how Jack and I would trade votes. I voted for his Lamar Tech bill, and, in turn, he agreed to vote for my rural roads bill. Usually, that's all either one of us would have to do, just vote for the other's bill. The Lamar Tech bill, however, didn't work out that way. When the legislature passed Jack's Lamar Tech bill in 1949, Governor Jester let it be known that he might not sign it because it would create a new continuing expenditure for the state. There were a number of lobbyists then as now whose mission was to kill any legislation that might increase corporate taxes anywhere in the state, no matter how small the increase. Jack asked me to meet with the governor to urge him to sign that bill. I reminded Jack that Lamar College is about four hundred miles from my district. When I asked him what I was supposed to tell the governor, Jack replied that he didn't give a "blankety-blank," he just wanted me to do it. Jack had been in the Marine Corps during the war, and he'd experienced almost every island battle in the Pacific. When he returned home, Jack's language was exactly like what you would expect from a battle-hardened "leatherneck." When he finished telling me—in Marine language—why I had to do it, I understood a little better.

But I still didn't know what to say to Governor Jester. I pleaded, "Jack, he's going to ask why I am so interested in a school in Beaumont." Jack replied that I should tell him that I'm for the citizens in that part of the state to have an opportunity to get a good education. Then he reminded me that he was going to support my rural roads bill, which he didn't give "a two-bit hoot about," so I could do this favor for him. He had me where he wanted me, so I made an appointment with Governor Jester.

I had met the governor in Uvalde when President Truman had paid his visit to Mr. Garner just a few months earlier, but I did not know him well. When I walked into the governor's office, he greeted me warmly. He seemed to be quite a nice fellow. I wish I'd had a

Gov. Beauford Jester speaks at the dedication of a memorial on the Capitol grounds. He was puzzled about why I supported the Lamar College bill. *Center for American History Prints and Photographs Collection; di_03957.*

chance to get to know him better, but he died of a heart attack a month after our meeting. During our only meeting, he wasn't as hard on me as I thought he would be. I said, "Governor Jester, I'm sure interested in this bill on Lamar Tech. I think it would do a lot of good." Just as I had feared, he replied, "Dolph, if my geography is correct, it's unlikely that many students from your district will go to Lamar." I replied, rather uncomfortably, "Yes, sir, that might be right, but I'd sure like for them to have the opportunity if they wanted to go." With a big grin, Governor Jester replied that he could appreciate that I was concerned about the various college opportunities for my constituents. "But you know it's going to cost us some money," he said, "and since it's so far from your district, I just can't understand what your real interest is in it." And I responded, very lamely, "Well, Governor, I'm just interested in better education for all Texans." That's all I could think of to say. I was getting more nervous by the second. But the governor said, "You know, Dolph, that sounds pretty doggone good, whether you mean it or not."

We ended the meeting with some nice small talk. I don't think I had any affect on him, but he did sign the bill, mainly because of the tremendous pressure on him from Lamar supporters in the Beaumont–Port Arthur region. Jack Brooks wasn't just depending on me. And of course, Allan Shivers, the powerful lieutenant governor, was from Port Arthur, and he was strong for the bill. Shivers had promised the people of that area that if Jack Brooks could pass the bill in the House, Shivers would get it passed in the Senate and then persuade the governor to sign it. He stuck his neck out a little too far by saying he would get Governor Jester to sign it, because he was absolutely convinced that Jack could never get it passed by the House. But Shivers underestimated Jack Brooks. Jack attracted the support of his fellow war veterans in the House by emphasizing how most of the school's students would be former GIs. I don't know what all he promised them, but whatever it took, he did it.

The bill went to the Senate, so Allan Shivers had no choice. He had to get it passed in the Senate. And then he had to go to work on Governor Jester. I don't know what he did for Governor Jester to get it signed, but I'm sure he did something. Governor Jester undoubtedly had Shivers somewhat indebted to him after that. Lamar Tech actually served a great purpose and it still does. As the school, which is now called Lamar University, expanded and established a good record, I was very proud of the little part I played in its history.

"Foolishness and Monkey Business"

The great turnover of the previous session when of all the veterans had been elected destroyed the seniority system in the legislature to a great extent. Indeed, one hundred and twenty of the one hundred and fifty members were serving either their first or their second terms. Many of the chairmen were new members of the legislature. The old guard had lost much of its power. Young military veterans who didn't know what they couldn't do or shouldn't do dominated the House. For example, the chairman of the Appropriations Committee, Ray Kirkpatrick, was twenty-six years old. Joe Fleming, the chair of the Revenue and Taxation Committee, was twenty-seven. Pierce Johnson, chairman of the State Affairs Committee, was a ripe old thirty-one. I was twenty-six. Few of us knew or understood the old rules, and, in many cases, we didn't care. It was a pretty unruly situation because we all thought we were sent there personally to run the state government, and we proceeded to try to do just that. The power structure was pretty fluid and changed from day to day, depending on the issue. Things were so chaotic that it took us three weeks just to organize the House into committees and to elect a Speaker.

While we were trying to organize the House, Lamar Zivley of Temple introduced a resolution to ask Texans to arm themselves with baseball bats to keep groundhogs in the ground. After much arguing and shouting, the resolution was finally defeated. Then a Texas A&M graduate went to the snort pole and asked that every representative who had gone to school at A&M register their presence by lighting their voting machine. He wanted to take them all to dinner. That inspired someone else to get up and ask for all of the Baylor University graduates to do the same. Suddenly, members were standing in line to have the graduates of several schools indicate their presence. Finally, someone shouted from the floor that this was foolishness and "monkey business" that was wasting everyone's time and the taxpayer's money. Those particular shenanigans, which weren't unusual, took up most of a morning. Most of the sessions were so chaotic and noisy that the Speaker frequently had to order the sergeant at arms to seat the members and to clear the floor of everyone except the members themselves.

We finally got things together enough to elect a war veteran, Durwood Manford, as Speaker of the House. At the time, Durwood was a thirty-one-year-old rancher and attorney from Gonzales County. He was one of the youngest persons ever to be elected Speaker of the Texas House of Representatives. Durwood defeated Joe Kilgore, another young war veteran, for the speakership. Kilgore, who became a good friend of mine, later served with distinction in the U.S. Congress.

As fellow ranchers, Durwood and I had much in common, and we became very close, social friends. His wife, Joyce, and Janey also were good friends. Durwood was a man of absolute integrity and honesty who wanted to do the very best he could. He served only one term as Speaker. In those days, it was the tradition in Texas for the Speaker of the House to serve one term only. I think the system the state has today, where the Speaker typically serves more than one term, is much better. It guarantees leadership continuity and allows the House to organize more quickly at the beginning of the session. A Speaker being able to serve more than one term makes it more likely that the House will run more effectively and efficiently.

In 1961 Gov. Price Daniel appointed Durwood Manford to the State Board of Insurance. He was still on the board when I became governor in 1973. I was delighted to be able to reappoint Durwood to a six-year term in 1978. I was extremely fortunate that Durwood was Speaker during my first session for many reasons, but the most important was his key support of my effort to have the state's rural roads paved. I had promised my constituents that I would get those roads paved. It was a hot issue in Texas at the time. We had a surplus in the state treasury because the state couldn't spend money on improvements to the infrastructure during the war. Paving the rural roads was my biggest issue, so I was pleased to be appointed to the Highway and Roads Committee and selected to serve as its vice-chairman. I. B.

Durwood Manford being sworn in as Speaker of the Texas House of Representatives in 1949. *Center for American History Vertical File; di_03941*

Holt, from the small town of Olton, was the chairman. As a second termer, Jack Brooks succeeded in grabbing the chairmanship of the Banks and Banking Committee.

Janey and I did not have children when I first entered the legislature. Our first child, Janey, would not come along until 1950. With no children at home, Janey was eager to be involved in the action at the Capitol. She was an excellent typist, so she worked as my unpaid secretary. In those days, each member was allocated just enough money to fill one full-time position and one half-time position for a staff. That was the entire staff, so Janey was a big help to me. There was a typing pool in the large hallway behind the Speaker's podium where typewriters were available to staff on a first-come, first-served basis. Because Janey often used the typewriters there, she learned much from the secretaries about what was going on behind the scenes. Of course, the ladies' room was another source of news and gossip. As a result, Janey gave me an additional pair of eyes and ears with which to gather useful information about the legislative maneuvering and intentions of some of my colleagues.

During that first session, Janey also ghost-wrote articles for our hometown newspaper, the *Uvalde Leader-News*, and the other weeklies in our four-county district about what was going on in the legislature and what I was doing for my constituents. Naturally, the articles stressed what a dynamic leader I was! Harry Hornby Jr., the owner of the *Uvalde Leader-News*, was among my most important supporters back home. Born and raised in Uvalde, Harry knew people from every section of town and every walk of life, and he knew everything that was going on. Harry was one of my closest, dearest friends. I could depend on him to let me know how people in the district were feeling about any issue. Of course, his strong support gave me the luxury of having favorable articles in the paper about my work in the legislature. Actually, I enjoyed the support of every newspaper in my district.

Harry published Janey's articles under someone else's byline. The small newspapers in the district were starved for something to put in the paper, so it worked real well. A lot of those papers outside of Uvalde ran Janey's articles word for word, without identifying the author. The readers of those articles thought that I was running the legislature and that the only issues of importance were those with which I was involved.

John Nance Garner, Legislative Constituent

A few weeks after the beginning of my first legislative session, Mr. Garner sent word to me that he wanted to receive copies of the official House journal. Mr. Garner rarely ever contacted anyone directly, his style was to use a third party to deliver a message when he wanted something. Each member was allowed to send a dozen or so House journals to constituents. Naturally, I put him on the mailing list immediately and thought that would be the end of the matter. I hadn't had many requests for the journal because it's dull reading, even for a member of the House.

A few weeks went by and then I got another message that Mr. Garner wanted me to come see him. Janey and I returned to Uvalde just about every weekend, so I made a point to go by Mr. Garner's place during the next weekend trip. When I arrived at his house, he went straight to the point. I had cast a vote, I don't remember now what it was on, which Mr. Garner thought was terribly wrong. He proceeded, of course, to tell me how big a mistake I had made. He had found my vote by reading the House journal, which came as a big surprise to me. Naively, I had thought that he wouldn't read the journal that closely. But he was monitoring my votes in the legislature very closely. I was flattered by his attention, of course, but it made me nervous as well. We had a very interesting discussion. Actually, it wasn't a discussion; it was a lecture. By the time he got through, he had absolutely convinced me that he was right. After he had said all that he wanted to say, he made it clear that I would be welcome to come back. He didn't actually invite me back. That wasn't his style either. But I could tell that I was welcome to return. I took advantage of that unspoken invitation on a regular basis.

I went to Mr. Garner's house almost every weekend during legislative sessions. At first, we met on the screened back porch of his house, where he liked to sit in the late afternoon. Later, after he donated his big two-story brick house to the city of Uvalde for use as a public library, he moved to the small frame house in back and we visited there. I enjoyed those visits immensely. Mr. Garner talked to me about what was going on in the legislature and how I was doing and what I should be doing. He told some of his stories about what happened when he was in the legislature and when he was in Congress. I might hear the same story several times, but it was always interesting. It was a great experience for me to have a chance to really get to know Mr. Garner. One thing about it, if you were going to get along with Mr. Garner, you didn't go talk to him about something he didn't want to hear. You had to give a lot of thought to what subject you might bring up or you'd find yourself on the "not welcome" list.

Unfortunately, Janey never had the opportunity to sit in on these talks. Mr. Garner wasn't interested in discussing politics with women present. Mr. Garner was very "old school" in that way. Generally in the afternoon he would take a siesta after lunch and then maybe play solitaire or something like that. Then along about four o'clock some of his old friends would come by, such as his lawyer Darwin Suttle, who later became a federal district judge; or Josh Ashby, who ran his bank in Uvalde; or Owen Williams, who ran his bank in Crystal City. And then at five o'clock sharp he'd strike a blow for liberty, and he would invite everyone there to join him. If you didn't want to take a drink, he would never ask the reason, he would just say, "Well, I've saved my manners." He had some connection with the people at the Jack Daniels Distillery. Every now and then they would send him a case of the highest quality Jack Daniels bourbon, and he would share that. He also always had a cigar with him, which he usually just chewed, but he would smoke it sometimes. He could blow big smoke rings with that cigar. Whiskey and a cigar in the late afternoon, that was Mr. Garner's steadfast ritual.

I also saw Mr. Garner frequently when the legislature wasn't in session. If he knew that someone important was coming by to see him, he would ask me to come over. My job was to be there to do what he wanted done and to be seen but not heard. I got to meet a lot of interesting people that way, including President Truman, Sam Rayburn, and President Roosevelt's former political manager Jim Farley.

Mr. Garner only had one child, Tully, who in turn had a daughter, Genevieve, who was my age. Genevieve had married and was living in Amarillo by this time. Tully was not much of a political person, so to some extent Mr. Garner sort of adopted me. That may be putting it too strongly. But I was the only young politician around, and he was interested, of course, in politics. He took an interest in my political activities as a result.

Mr. Garner became my most important legislative tutor, which was very fortunate for me. He talked about what I should do to get along with my colleagues in the legislature, especially those who held completely opposite views from me. He emphasized how important it was to build and maintain friendly personal relations with as many members as possible, even with those who voted against my bills. It was very good advice. He also talked about the importance of hard

Mr. Garner in the backyard of his house in Uvalde in the early 1950s. *Briscoe Papers.*

work, that being in the legislature required my constant attention. I shouldn't just drift along. It was critical for me to know what was going on at all times. Mr. Garner stressed the importance of knowing the House rules and not to depend on anyone else to know them for me. He told me to study the rules to know what I could do and what I couldn't do and when and how. Mr. Garner also urged me to be vigilant about counting my votes before I tried to do anything. "You've got to know where your votes are," he would say. And if you have your votes, move quickly to get the bill to a vote and don't talk about it. Most important of all, he warned, don't engage in grandstanding. Mr. Garner's theory was that the more you "ran your mouth," as he would say, the more likely you are to lose a vote. After you know you have the votes, the less you say about it, the better. It was his belief that you're not going to influence much in the legislature by giving public speeches. That is excellent advice for any member of a legislative body. It was the same advice that he gave his protégé, Sam Rayburn, when he was coming up the ranks in the U.S. House of Representatives. And Rayburn passed the same advice on to his own protégés.

Mr. Garner, by the way, judged Sam Rayburn at all times by the standard of what Mr. Garner would have done. Mr. Garner frequently gave Mr. Rayburn low grades after he became Speaker of the House. But Mr. Rayburn told me once that Mr. Garner would never have lasted as Speaker. He behaved very differently as Speaker than he had as a regular member. He was too much of a tyrant. Mr. Rayburn believed that there would have been a revolt by the members eventually. I think Sam Rayburn was absolutely correct about that. Mr. Garner could never have served as Speaker for many years like Mr. Rayburn did. Mr. Garner's models for Speaker were old Joe Cannon and Nicholas Longworth, and he ran things the way they had, which was dictatorial. You either lined up with him as the leader, or you might as well go home. You were with him, or you were against him. There wasn't any middle ground, and no excuses were allowed.

Of course, Mr. Garner's style of leadership did work well during his days of power and it reaped great benefits for Texas. He always told the Texas congressional delegation that if they all voted alike they would be better able to defend their votes with their constituents because they could say that the rest of the delegation also voted that way. He insisted on strict solidarity in the Texas delegation, and woe to those who didn't go along. He built a high degree of solidarity in the Texas delegation. His constant admonition about the members of the delegation was "pick 'em young, pick 'em bright, send 'em there, and keep 'em there." And that's what Texas did. That's why Texas had so many chairmanships and why we were the envy of other states. Texas's influence was so great for so many years in Congress because of seniority. In those days, seniority meant everything in Congress. It was the whole basis of power.

A Productive First Session

I had my ups and downs, of course, but overall I had a great first session. We met for 177 days, which made it the longest continuous session in state history. Despite the chaos of the early days of the session, by the time we adjourned in July, we had accomplished much. We created the Legislative Budget Board and the Texas Legislative Council. We also passed reform legislation for state hospitals, medical education, prisons, and state educational systems.

Perhaps the most significant accomplishment was passage of the three Gilmer-Aikin bills, which reorganized the public schools. I served on the House committee that handled the Gilmer-Aikin bills. After they passed in the Senate, I served on the House-Senate conference committee that worked out the final provisions of the bills. Those bills created the state board of education, required nine-month school terms, set minimum standards for teachers, improved facilities, and raised teacher salaries. Claud Gilmer, the state representative from Rocksprings, was the sponsor of the education reform bills in the House. Claud was one of the outstanding members of the legislature. His name on the legislation gave considerable weight to what was considered at that time a revolutionary proposal for change in the financing of our public education.

Revolutionary is a strong word, but I don't know any other term that so accurately fits that time and place in our education history. Opponents worked hard to prevent passage, even labeling the bills "communistic." Claud Gilmer, however, was undaunted. He fought hard for those bills. He personally took each member aside to answer his or her individual questions and to stress the critical need for education reform. Claud's leadership and strong advocacy got the job done. Claud did the work, but he never asked for the credit. The Gilmer-Aikin laws made public schools more efficient and better funded, which improved the educational opportunities for Texas children. The laws have passed the test of time, with only minor reforms within the original framework.

I was able to play a small role in the other accomplishments of the 1949 legislative session by sponsoring the House version of the bill to provide funds for an extensive statewide farm-to-market road system. The federal and state highways in Texas were in decent shape, thanks to the work of the Texas Highway Commission during the 1930s, especially under the leadership of Ross Sterling. The rural road system, however, was a scandal. Only a tiny percentage of the state's county roads were paved, which severely hampered the ability of our farmers and ranchers to get their products to market. The terrible condition of these unpaved roads had a negative effect on a wide range of critical local services, including law enforcement, school bus routes, and the postal service.

The most important promise I made during my campaign for the legislature was to get a rural roads bill passed that would pull Texas farmers and ranchers "out of the mud." I knew that, because the state had been unable to appropriate money for major construction projects during the war, the treasury was full, and money would not be a problem. Of course, there is always someone who will oppose anything that requires state funding. In those days, however, rural interests dominated the state, and the proposal to improve rural roads was popular in the rural areas, so I expected little opposition.

I soon learned that there was major opposition, but not against the appropriation. The controversy was over who controlled the money, the State Highway Commission in Austin or the county judges and commissioners in each of the state's 254 counties. A bill was intro-

Taking my turn at the legislative podium. *Briscoe Papers.*

duced to send the money to the counties and leave it to them to build the roads. This bill was strongly supported by the county governments and the Farm Bureau. I was against it because the counties generally had a poor record in the area of road planning and construction. There was no doubt in my mind that the quality of the roads would vary greatly from county to county. And to be candid, there were a couple of places in the state where you didn't want the money to be handed over to local officials, who might be tempted to misplace some of it. I also feared that because the counties had such a poor record when it came to cooperating with each other, it was likely that many roads would simply end at the county line instead of linking properly with the adjacent county's road system.

Dewitt Greer, the talented state highway engineer, shared my feelings on this subject. Dewitt was a brilliant man who was totally dedicated to the public good. Dewitt's plan was to have the state highway department plan, construct, and maintain the rural roads project as a single statewide system. This would make certain that the roads in every county would be consistent in quality and would not be restricted by county lines.

Greer also was politically astute. He quietly sold his plan to Gov. Beauford Jester, Lt. Gov. Allan Shivers, and Speaker Durwood Manford before it was submitted as a bill. Greer actually drafted the text of the bill. Speaker Manford asked me to lead the fight to pass it in the House. Behind the scenes, the Speaker and I worked closely with Greer to develop strategy. While the battle over who would control the money was raging in the legislature, Greer quietly drew plans for a number of the most critical roads. He put in place a system that would allow him to move quickly to get bids and to initiate construction as soon as the bill passed. Greer knew that if his plan passed, it would only cover the next two years, which was plenty of time for the opposition to find problems with it. His plan was to move quickly to demonstrate the soundness of his approach and to impress the voters with the quality of his roads.

I worked hard to get the bill through the House. I soon learned, however, that my leadership in this fight was not appreciated back home. The Farm Bureau and the commissioners' courts in my four-county district strongly opposed me on this issue. Some of my friends let me know that I was in serious political trouble. When I returned home and attended some Farm Bureau meetings, I discovered that I was the most unpopular fellow at the meetings. It became clear to me that there was an excellent chance I was going to be a one-term state representative.

The House eventually passed the Greer plan, and it went to the Senate, where Neveille Colson, an interesting woman from Grimes County, sponsored the bill. After serving in the House from 1939 until 1947, Ms. Colson had been elected to the Senate in 1949. She also played a key role in the passage of the Gilmer-Aikin public school reform bills. Ms. Colson remained a senator until Bill Moore, the formidable "bull of the Brazos," defeated her in 1966. Our bills were combined and passed as the Colson-Briscoe Act. The legislation made it possible, with the help of federal funds, to double the number of paved rural roads in the state within two years. The bill appropriated $15 million a year to the Highway Department to be used to pave local roads that did not have sufficient traffic to pay for their construction and maintenance. With his carefully drawn plans ready to go, Dewitt Greer went to work immediately. His new roads were so well and efficiently built and planned that the opposition evaporated within a few months. The program was so popular that succeeding legislatures increased funding, resulting in more than 15,000 miles of paved rural roads. It wasn't long before the county commissioners' courts and the Farm Bureau began to take credit for the program they had fought against. Texas now has the most extensive network of secondary roads in the world. I am very proud of the part I played with Ms. Colson in making this incredible road system possible.

I am proud of the success of the rural roads program, but it did have one result that I hadn't intended. One of my purposes in getting it passed was to encourage families to continue to reside on their farms and ranches. When I shared that goal with my father, however, he responded that the program would accomplish just the opposite. "That's not about to happen," he said. "If they have a good road that will make it easy for them to go back and forth, they are going to move to town because the wife will insist on it. She's not going to stay isolated out in the country." He pointed out that the kids could go to the school in town, the church would be nearby, and social activities would be more available. And of course, he was right. The program didn't slow the movement from farm to town; it actually accelerated it. It was a good example of the law of unintended consequences.

A SPECIAL SESSION

Although we accomplished a great deal in the 1949 session, some business remained unfinished, including the problem of lack of telephone service in the rural areas, an issue of special interest to my constituents. Early in 1950, Allan Shivers, now the governor of Texas after Jester's death, called a special session of the legislature to tackle some of that unfinished business. Under the Texas state constitution, only the governor can call special sessions and only the governor can decide what kind of bills can be considered during those special sessions. One of the bills the governor's call allowed was one related to rural telephone service. The major telephone companies, claiming they couldn't make a profit serving isolated rural farms and ranches, generally refused to string telephone wire to them. As I have mentioned in a previous chapter, I had personal experience with this problem back on my ranch. I was able to string my own wire, but many farmers and ranchers were not able to do it themselves.

Accordingly, in February 1950 I sponsored a rural telephone-enabling bill in the House to allow rural telephone cooperatives to organize and apply for federal support. The bill was strongly supported by the Rural Electric Cooperative, but the telephone monopoly vigorously opposed it. When the House considered my bill early the next afternoon it initiated a fierce legislative struggle, resulting in a continuous session that lasted more than twenty-three hours. The problem was that many of my colleagues in the House were indebted to the Bell Telephone companies for campaign funding, but it was difficult politically for most of them to be on record opposing extending telephone service to rural residents. One of the traditional strategies in the legislature for killing legislation while avoiding a vote on the record was to make certain that not enough members would be present to make a quorum. The Speaker has to adjourn the House in that situation, and the vote is delayed and often never enacted.

That tactic can be defeated, however, when two-thirds of the members present vote for the Speaker to put a call on the House, which prohibits any member from leaving. It also compels those who are absent to attend. The sergeant at arms and his staff are required to go out after the members who are not there. And they are supposed to get the help of the Texas Department of Public Safety, whose officers are sent out to round up absent members from wherever they might happen to be at that time. A call on the House is rarely made. But those of us who felt strongly about the rural telephone issue forced the vote, and we won.

This may have been the most unusual day I ever spent in the legislature. The doors of the House were locked by the sergeant at arms and guarded by armed officers of the Texas Department of Public Safety. The sergeant at arms issued arrest warrants to bring absent members back to the House to obtain a quorum. Some of the members tried to escape. Several climbed out windows during the night and catwalked around the two-foot-wide granite ledge twenty feet above the ground, trying to find an open window in some other part of the Capitol. That was a very foolish thing to do, but some of them tried it. Many of my colleagues slept on the floor during the night while the highway patrol searched for absentee members. James Norton of Nacogdoches was found at home and hauled 240 miles back to the Capitol. Representatives Douglas Bergman and George Parkhouse of Dallas led the opposition. We finally had an opportunity to vote, and the bill passed easily. We had convened at 1 p.m. on a Friday and adjourned at 1:06 on Saturday morning. The result was the installation of thousands of rural telephones that would not have been installed by Bell Telephone.

The irony of this legislative battle was that Bell Telephone had no intention of serving the rural areas. Bell's opposition was very short-sighted. The cooperatives were no threat to anything Bell wanted to do, and the rural cooperatives never gave them a problem. In those days, the Bell Telephone system enjoyed the benefits of being a monopoly, and they vigorously opposed any legislation that might hint of the possibility of market competition.

TEXAS VETERANS LAND PROGRAM SCANDAL

My performance in that first session and later sessions must have satisfied the constituents of my district, because I ran unopposed the next

My legislative colleague from San Antonio, Maury Maverick Jr., in a contemplative mood. *Maverick (Maury, Jr.) Papers, Center for American History, photograph by Russell Lee; di_03959.*

three elections, from 1950 until 1954. As I said earlier, I made a real effort to keep in close touch with the voters in my district and to keep them informed about my work in Austin. I never took my supporters for granted. None of the other three sessions I served in the legislature were as fun, exciting, and eventful for me as the first, which is natural. Nevertheless, I found each session challenging, and most of our actions were satisfying.

In my second term, I was joined by two new members who became close associates for the remainder of my days as a legislator: Maury Maverick Jr. and D. B. Hardeman. Maury was a young attorney from San Antonio and a Marine Corps war veteran. He was a brilliant guy, really one of the most interesting people I've ever known. Maury was quite an agitator who was always stirring up the legislative pot. He was just like his father, Maury Maverick Sr., who had been mayor of San Antonio and a very liberal congressman back in the 1930s. Maury Jr., who died in 2003, had a gruff exterior that might make you believe that he was tough and mean, but he wasn't. Maury had a great sense of humor and he was always a real gentleman with it. He was an extremely likable fellow. I really enjoyed serving in the legislature with him. Maury was a great friend, but he was such an overwhelming liberal that he could never support me when I ran for statewide office.

Of course, D. B. Hardeman had been one of my roommates in college, and he was the best man at my wedding. D. B. was a real intellectual. He had grown up on a ranch near Goliad, and his family had ranched in the Texas coastal bend region for many generations, but he represented a district in North Texas in the legislature. I greatly admired the quality of his mind and his outstanding abilities as a public servant. He had high ethical standards and a true compassion for others. When D. B. passed away in 1981, I gave the eulogy at his funeral. Janey and I actually persuaded D. B. to run for the legislature. We had maintained a close relationship with D. B. ever since our marriage in 1942. D. B. frequently joined us for dinner in San Antonio during the Christmas holidays. During our holiday visit in 1949, Janey and I urged D. B. to be a candidate for the legislature in the next election. We knew that he had always wanted to be in the legislature. He had moved recently to Sherman, in North Texas, and it looked as though he might have a good chance of being elected from that district. He thought it was a crazy idea at first, mainly because he was new to the area and unknown to the voters. D. B. agreed finally to look into it. As it turned out, he had no opposition for the seat! He made an outstanding legislator.

Although we had a lot of "ups and downs" in the legislature during my last three terms in office, most of the "downs" were minor. There was one major exception, however, and that occurred during the last session that I was a member of the House.

Back in the 1949 session, we had passed legislation to create the Texas Veterans Land Program whereby the state could purchase land for resale to veterans at a low interest rate for a forty-year period. The program was contingent on voters approving a constitutional amendment to allow its establishment. The legislature authorized $100 million to fund the program. The amendment subsequently passed and the Texas Veterans Land Board, composed of the governor, attorney general, and the land commissioner, was created in 1950 to oversee the program. Under the legislated rules, a veteran could select land that he wanted to purchase and then notify the Land Board, which would buy the land from the owner at the fair market value and then resell it to the veteran.

It was certainly a well-meaning program to give every veteran a chance to own some land. There was a limit on the amount of money that could be borrowed. I think it was something like $7,500. Of course, land at that time was much cheaper than it is now. That was enough money to buy a couple of hundred acres in most places. I didn't sponsor the bill, but I voted for it, and I was proud of it. I thought we had really done something very good. I remember my father telling me, however, that it was a dangerous program. He said, "Dolph Junior, that's going to turn out like all government programs. There's too much money lying around in that program and that is going to attract some of the wrong people. There's going to be a scandal." Of course, I thought that he was wrong.

I didn't pay any attention to the program after it began. Sometime near the end of 1954, I was the speaker at an American Legion meeting in Uvalde. While visiting with some of the members at the little reception before my speech, I overheard some of the veterans talking about how they had gone to Crystal City and picked up their one hundred dollars in cash for being a veteran. Of course, some of the other veterans asked how they could get their money. "Well, I don't know how I did it," someone answered, "I just went down there and they gave me some papers to sign waiving my rights to some kind of state land program. I signed them and they gave me a hundred dol-

I enjoyed my visits with the folks I represented back in my legislative district. I always learned more on those visits at home than I could ever learn in Austin.
Briscoe Papers

lars." I realized that something wasn't right. I asked them what kind of document they had signed in Crystal City, and they all replied that they didn't really know. They had gone to some little office, signed the papers, and were given one hundred dollars in cash.

The more questions I asked the more concerned I became. I realized that it had to have something to do with the Veterans Land Program because there wasn't any other state land program. I made a few calls and verified that veterans were being paid to waive their rights in the program, but no one seemed to know why. It was clear that something was very wrong. A few weeks later, in January 1955, when the legislature convened, I submitted a resolution asking the Speaker, Jim Lindsey, to create a special five-member House committee to investigate the Texas Veterans Land Program.

I didn't think there would be any opposition to my resolution. I thought, you know, who wouldn't want it investigated? It turned out, however, to be a real hot political potato. The major problem was that the Veterans Land Board only had three members: Governor Shivers, Attorney General John Ben Sheppard, and Land Commissioner Bascom Giles. So the resolution was sent to a committee, where it just sat for a while. I then found that there was a tremendous amount of opposition to my proposal. The Shivers administration wanted to stop it. I don't remember any pressure put on me to back off. I think that Shivers's people put the pressure on other members. I kept hearing from some of my colleagues that an investigation wasn't needed, I didn't know what I was talking about, and this was a great program that was being well managed.

During the middle of this struggle to get the resolution passed, the major urban newspapers in Texas reprinted an expose of the land program by a journalist named Kenneth Towery, who had first reported it in the *Cuero Record*. Towery's story broke the scandal open because it was very specific about what was happening. As it turned out, Bascom Giles had conspired with a group of crooked appraisers and real estate developers to buy large tracts of land at regular market prices. This land was subdivided into small tracts, which would then be "selected" by veterans, without their knowledge, as the land they wanted to purchase. The real estate developers would give small amounts of cash to veterans to sign papers asking the Land Board for the land. The veterans would sign additional papers forfeiting their rights to the land they were supposedly buying from the state. The Land Board's appraisers were bribed to inflate the land's market value. The real estate developers would then sell these small tracts at the highly inflated prices to the Land Board and pocket the windfall, which they shared with Giles and some of his assistants.

When that news broke, the House suddenly passed my resolution on February 6, 1955. Nobody could stop it, even though, of course, they wanted to stop it. Normally, it had always been the tradition that if someone introduced a resolution like that, they would be appointed chairman of the committee. But I wasn't even appointed to that committee. If they thought they were going to get a whitewash, however, they made a big mistake, because they put Joe Burkett from Kerrville in as chairman. Burkett was as straight and honest a man as there ever was. There wasn't going to be any cover-up with him as chairman. He was a very capable lawyer, who made a much better chairman than I would have.

I knew Bascom Giles. I had the highest regard for him, but I guess I didn't know him that well, as things turned out. It never entered my mind that he was involved in any of it. He eventually pleaded guilty of committing fraud and served almost three years in prison. Some people have claimed that Bascom Giles was the fall guy for Governor Shivers, but I don't believe that is true. Both the governor and the attorney general, John Ben Sheppard, had left the program to the land commissioner to manage. After all, it was a land program. Commissioner Giles was one of the most respected men in Texas, highly thought of, with an excellent reputation. It was natural for them to leave it up to Giles to run because they had plenty of other things to do. Obviously, it was the wrong way to set up a program because the governor and the attorney general don't have the time to pay close attention to the details of a program like that. They have to depend on somebody else to do it, which is exactly what they did. I know that's all they did. I think anyone in that position would have done the same thing. Giles knew that they wouldn't be looking over his shoulder while he manipulated the program for his financial benefit. It was a pathetic affair, all in all, and, unhappily, it would not be the last time that a serious scandal in state government would intersect with my political career. That affair was the Sharpstown scandal in 1971 and 1972, the aftershocks of which would play a major role in electing me governor of Texas.

I had the opportunity to work closely with John Ben Sheppard during the Veterans Land Program investigation. John Ben was one of the finest public servants I have ever known. If it had not been for this scandal in which he had no personal involvement, he would have been governor. And I think he would have been a great governor.

I was deeply honored that the voters in my district agreed to return me to Austin every time I ran for reelection. I loved my four terms in the House. I would have run for reelection in 1956, but a personal tragedy intervened, and I had to turn my attention to the family business.

Chapter 7

RED NUNLEY

M Y FATHER DIED SUDDENLY of a massive heart attack at his home at seven o'clock in the morning on July 17, 1954. He was sixty-four when he passed away. My father had experienced a bit of heart trouble for several years, and his overall health had declined gradually. Nevertheless, he seemed to be improving at the time when he was struck down, so his death was a deep shock. I was devastated by his loss.

My father had a number of characteristics that stand out in my mind after all of these years since his death. One was his ability to get things done, no matter how difficult the task might be. He was very disciplined. My father always was much better organized than I am. He would set a goal, develop a strategy to meet that goal, and persist until he had carried it out. He wouldn't deviate from his plan. My father decided what he wanted to accomplish, and then he would get it done. He was a better businessman and a more knowledgeable rancher than I am. He certainly knew more about cattle than I ever will. I believe that I have inherited some of his positive traits, but not nearly enough. I do know that I acquired my love and respect for the land from him. My father had an intensely strong bond with the land. He sincerely believed in the old adage that if we take care of the land, the land will take care of us. That's a simple but meaningful philosophy that my father followed his entire life.

My father also was a deeply caring and loving father. He and I had a close relationship. We never had any serious arguments or difficul-

My father near the end of his life. *Briscoe Papers.*

ties getting along. Although my father didn't always agree with the votes I cast in the legislature, most of our political differences, which weren't serious, were simply the differences that normally exist between generations. As I got older, gained more experience in business, and assumed more responsibilities, my political views evolved to a point where they more nearly matched his.

I guess it's obvious how much I both admired and loved my father.

A HEAVY BURDEN, A HARD DECISION

With my father's passing, responsibility for his various business endeavors fell on my shoulders. With Mother alone, it became clear that managing my father's enterprises would require my full-time attention. By then, Janey and I had two children. Our oldest daughter,

Janey, had been born in 1950. Our son, Dolph Briscoe III, who we nicknamed "Chip," was born in 1953. Our youngest child, Cele, would be born two years later, in 1956. With a growing family and the added responsibilities of my father's business, I realized that I faced a difficult decision about running for reelection to the legislature in the 1956 Democratic primary. Janey and I had several talks about what I should do. As she always did, Janey made it clear that it was my decision to make. Whatever I decided, she would support it completely.

Eventually I concluded that if I returned to the legislature, I would not be able to take proper care of the ranching businesses that my father had entrusted to me. Accordingly, in April 1956 I announced that I would not be a candidate for reelection. It was not an easy decision. I really had enjoyed the eight years I served as a state representative. The voters in my district had given me strong support. I never had another opponent after my first election to the House in 1948, and that certainly made my experience even more enjoyable. Although Janey and I discussed my decision thoroughly, I'm really not certain that she truly agreed with it. She backed me all the way, but I always suspected that Janey believed that I could operate our business and stay in the legislature. In hindsight, I think that is what I could and should have done. I valued the camaraderie with my colleagues, the feeling that we were all working for the benefit of our fellow Texans, and the simple thrill of being in the center of the action. I missed all of that later, much more than I anticipated at the time.

The Inheritance

At the time of his death, my father owned 190,000 acres of South Texas ranch land plus the beautiful ranch in Mexico, Hacienda las Margaritas. I kept that ranch and Roberto Spence continued to manage it. We had to divide and sell the ranch in the 1960s because of its cloudy title and pressure from the Mexican government. That was a very sad day when we did that. Roberto had acquired a quarter interest, so he kept his share of the ranch for his children. Because he and his children were Mexican citizens, their title was good. To this day, his children continue to hold on to their part of the ranch.

Father's largest ranch in Texas was Catarina, but he also owned the 45,000-acre Fowlerton Ranch in McMullen County that he had purchased from the South Texas Syndicate in 1949. That same year, my father also acquired a 30,000-acre section of the old Callahan Land Company, which was located in northern Webb County and southern LaSalle County. All four of his ranches were stocked with cattle and they were debt free, which was quite an accomplishment. In addition, my father still owned the wool and mohair warehouse as well as a feed and ranch supply business in Uvalde. Suddenly, this all became my responsibility.

My father often said that it is much easier to build a cattle business than it is to hold on to it. He told me about the families who had lost their ranch holdings after the father or grandfather who had built it had passed away. The heirs did not have the same instincts and knowledge, or maybe just the grit that the founder had. My father's observations made a strong impression on me. After his death, I was determined to preserve what he had created. It was a daunting task, however. I had raised sheep and goats exclusively on my Dry Frio Ranch, so I was afraid that I lacked the experience to manage a cattle and ranching business as extensive as the one my father had assembled. It was that fear that drove my decision to leave the legislature.

By the end of his life, my father had enough cash on hand to pay our inheritance tax without having to sell any of the land. He understood the tax system well, and he estimated what the inheritance tax would be eventually. I wondered sometimes that maybe my father had feared that I couldn't hold on to our land unless he had everything in such outstanding condition that it would be hard for me to mess it up. But, as I said, he had seen too many examples of heirs who couldn't hold on to what they were fortunate enough to inherit. I was extremely fortunate that my father left his affairs in that kind of shape.

RED NUNLEY

Much of the success that I enjoyed in ranching was the direct result of the work of my partnership with R. J. "Red" Nunley, an extremely capable rancher. Red had been my father's dear friend and business partner. After my father passed away, he took me under his wing, and he made certain that I didn't lose what my father had left me. Red became the older brother that I never had.

Red was raised on a ranch north of the town of Sabinal, which is about twenty miles east of Uvalde. His father lost the ranch during the Depression. In the early 1930s Red attended Southern Methodist University on a football scholarship and then returned to Sabinal, where he entered the cattle business. I don't think he had but a few dollars at the beginning. Red actually started out in the business by trading one steer at a time. He literally hitched rides to the stockyards in San Antonio on a cattle truck and then hitched rides back.

Father liked to help young men who were trying to make their way in the business. He never forgot how important Ross Sterling's help had been to him when he was starting out. When my father first met Red, he was impressed with his eagerness and his strong determination to be a cattleman. Father agreed to make Red a partner in a trading deal. That first deal between them turned out well, so my father included Red in more deals. They bought cattle together, with my father providing the money. They sent the cattle to pasture with someone, or placed them on a leased ranch. Red actually did the work in the field. He bought the cattle, sold them, took care of them, and then he and my father split the profit. That's how my father helped him get started, and Red was extremely appreciative.

The Nunley–Briscoe Partnership

In the fall of 1954, Red and I drew up a one-year contract that made us equal partners in a cattle business, which we called the Nunley-Briscoe Partnership. I leased the Fowlerton Ranch to our partnership, and that was how we started. As the years went by, we leased other ranches, but we never wrote another contract. We just had an oral agreement to keep working as partners.

Red's business rule was to operate debt free as much as possible. I put up the money for the steers on the Fowlerton Ranch. I financed the ranch and Red was the operator at no cost to the partnership. Through the years, we leased other ranches on the same basis and the profit we

Red Nunley and I are talking business. Red was one of the best ranch managers and cattle operators in the country. *Briscoe Papers.*

made went into our partnership. Red never drew any money out of the partnership. Red just continued to build up his stake. Usually, we had an equal amount of money invested, but sometimes Red had more than half of the money in the partnership. In 1959 we had a very profitable year at our Fowlerton Ranch. Red and I had stocked the ranch with steers in the summer, and we had enough prickly pear to keep those steers well fed during the winter. By spring, the market price had jumped up considerably. We were fortunate enough to make a good profit on the herd, which made it possible for us to lease more land.

THE WEST ESTATE: CHUPADERA AND THE LONGFELLOW RANCHES

Soon thereafter, Red and I used some of the profit from the Fowlerton Ranch to lease the 140,000-acre Chupadera Ranch, which is near the Catarina on the western edge of Webb and Dimmitt counties. The Chupadera Ranch was part of the estate of Jim West Jr., the son of the independent oilman from Houston for whom my father had worked during the Depression. Jim West Jr. had died, and his estate sold the cattle that he had on his ranches. That gave us the opportunity to lease the land and put our cows on it.

When we leased the Chupadera Ranch, Red decided that it was time for us to get out of the steer business and start raising cows. The market for heifers was much less volatile than for steers. When you buy steers, you are gambling that the price is not going to fall by the time you have them fat and ready to sell. Too many times the price for steers fell, and we suffered a loss. To my knowledge, just about everyone in South Texas who stayed with the steer business eventually went broke. If you can hold on to your cows, producing and raising their calves is a much safer business than a steer operation. Following that plan, we invested in Santa Gertrudis cows and stocked the Chupadera Ranch with them.

Shortly after we leased their Chupadera Ranch, the West estate announced that its 225,000-acre Longfellow Ranch, which is about twenty miles west of Sanderson, was available for lease. The estate's lawyers wrote a very thick and complicated lease contract and sent it to a number of operators. The contract had some unusual provisions, including one that restricted the entire lease to no more than 2,000 cows. The ranch had been running more than 4,000 head of cattle, and it was badly overgrazed. The West family wanted to give the grass a chance to come back. Another problem with the lease was that the heirs of the West family were engaged in some serious legal disputes among themselves. There was a real possibility that anyone who wound up with that lease might be pulled inadvertently into the middle of a lawsuit.

Red and I got a copy of the Longfellow contract just before we were to attend an annual meeting of the Cattle Raisers Association in Fort Worth. Whenever we traveled within the state, Red and I liked to get there by flying our own little airplane, so we planned to look at the contract on the way to the meeting. We were interested in the Longfellow Ranch, but the contract was so lengthy and difficult that we weren't sure we wanted to get involved. Janey came out to the airport to see us off. As we were getting into the plane, she noticed that

Janey and me with the kids on the Catarina Ranch. *Courtesy of the Briscoe family.*

we were taking the contract with us. Janey said, "You boys ought to bid on that ranch."

I waved the thick contract at her and said, "Janey, look at this thing, it's awfully complicated."

Janey challenged us to go on and bid on it. She said, "Well, what's the matter with you. You ought to go ahead and bid anyway."

Janey was good at giving you a challenge. The tone of her remarks made it clear that she was asking if we had enough nerve and the backbone to take the risk. She didn't put it that way exactly, but that's the way we heard it. So, Red and I discussed the deal as we flew to Fort Worth. Actually, we argued about it. Red and I liked to argue a lot when we were driving or flying somewhere because it helped us to keep awake. We finally decided that we would make a bid and just see what happened. I think more than any other reason, we decided to do it because Janey had challenged us so firmly.

We made what we thought was a low bid. We decided that if we were going to get the lease, it had to be a very good deal from our point of view. We weren't going to expose ourselves too much. After we sent in the bid, I didn't give it another thought, because I didn't think we could win. It turned out to be the only bid. The potential problems scared everyone else away. To our great surprise, we ended up with the lease on the Longfellow Ranch.

I suppose the biggest problem for everyone else was the requirement that you could only put 2,000 cows on the 225,000 acres. It turned out to be a blessing for us, however. We were fortunate because we got a decent amount of rain, which grew enough grass for our cows to have plenty to eat. And they had a lot of room. We never had to provide extra feed.

The Longfellow was an interesting ranch. It actually had one pasture that was 180,000 acres in size, with no cross-fencing. I believe it was the largest single pasture on private land in the United States. There's no pasture like that left in Texas today. And not on that ranch either, because it's been divided among the West heirs.

By the third year of the lease, our Santa Gertrudis calves weighed like lead. We were producing calves in the weight range of 700 pounds. At one point we sold a lot of cattle to Bob Cage, who was one of the best ranchers and one of the finest men I've ever known. He went out to the Longfellow Ranch to look at the cows when they were small, and we sold them to him. He thought they were going to weigh about 450 or 500 pounds by the time we delivered them, but they all weighed over 700 pounds, with some weighing up to 800 pounds, which for a calf is just unbelievable. The cattle had been on the lease long enough to get well acclimated. Bob couldn't believe it. He was just absolutely dumbfounded, because he had looked at them, and they hadn't been on anything but grass.

We had the Longfellow for only five years, but it turned out to be an outstanding deal for us. We also developed and maintained an excellent relationship with the West family. We never had a problem with them. As far as I know, no one ever had to consult the terms of the lease agreement while we were there. Red had the theory that if you leased a ranch, you tried to do what was right, and you treated it just like you owned it. And if you did that, everything would work out okay. The West estate was very happy with the results, because the grass came back like they wanted. After five years we tried to renew the lease, but that didn't work out. The West heirs had agreed to divide the ranch among family members. They also wanted to go into the cattle business themselves, so we sold them our herd.

While we were still on the Longfellow, we were getting along so well with the West heirs that we leased another ranch from the estate: the 135,000-acre Corn Ranch north of Van Horn, in far West Texas. That's arid and hard country out there, so we only ran 1,000 cows on the ranch. That deal also worked out for us, because the cattle had a lot of room, and the calves wound up with a good weight.

The Partnership Expands

Red was a great partner because he never had enough to do. A lot of people complain about how busy they are and how much work they have to do. That was never the case with Red. He was never satisfied. All he ever wanted to do was work. He always wanted another ranch to lease. As a result, we were always looking for more acreage. Our leases eventually included the 33,000-acre Saner Ranch in Maverick County; the 275,000-acre Lykes Brothers Ranch, south of Alpine; the 100,000-acre Leoncita Ranch, which is the east half of the old Kokernot Ranch, northeast of Alpine; the 50,000-acre Kincaid Ranch south of Uvalde; the 35,000-acre Harris Ranch west of Uvalde; the 20,000 acre Ball Ranch between the King and Armstrong ranches in Kenedy County; and the old Dobie Ranch, which was 50,000 acres of land in Webb County. The latter ranch had once belonged to the uncle of J. Frank Dobie, the famed Texas author and University of Texas professor. The Nueces River runs through that ranch. The farthest north Red and I ever operated was the 26,000-acre ranch we leased west of Plainview, in Cochran County, which had once been part of the great XIT Ranch. At the peak of our partnership in the 1970s, Red and I were operating about 850,000 acres, and we were running about 13,000 to 14,000 cows.

We also leased the Chaparosa Ranch, 75,000 acres southwest of Uvalde. It's a good ranch with numerous creeks running through it and good water right under it. Later, I tried to buy the Chaparosa from a family in Shreveport. I offered fifteen dollars an acre, which was close to the market price at the time. I could have bought it for twenty-five dollars an acre, but I wouldn't go that high. That ranch today is worth five or six hundred dollars an acre. That's where I made a mistake. It was a ranch that I should have bought. I made a bust on a lot of other deals, but that one was a real bust, because it is truly one of the best ranches in South Texas. I had it in my hands, and I let it slip out. I realized a long time ago, however, that I just can't let myself get down about what might have happened if I had only done this or that.

Red was a much more conservative operator than I would have been by myself. Once we got our partnership out of debt he wouldn't let us go back into debt to buy cattle. Red bought our cattle with cash. And because we were continually leasing other ranches, most of our cash was needed to buy the cattle to stock our leases. As a result, we never had a lot of cash on hand.

I was much more inclined to invest our cash in land. Red took a more conservative short-term view. He didn't want to speculate. Red often said that we were in the cattle business, not the real estate business. But he was never afraid of leasing a ranch because he knew he could make that work. I have to admit that my way would have been highly risky. In the long term, carrying a lot of debt would have broken us during economic downturns. Cattle businesses that operate on leased land with cattle acquired with loans get into serious trouble sooner or later. Red and I would have gone broke in that situation because there were years that we didn't make enough money to pay the interest on the cattle loans. When you don't owe any money, however, it's pretty hard for something to break you. You may get pretty well bent, and you may get hurt, and you may not be worth as much at the end of the year as you were at the beginning, but you're going to be able to hang on. That was Red's theory: let's stay in a debt-free position that will allow us to hold on in the worst of times.

There were a few times, however, when Red agreed to buy land, but in every case they were ranches that we had leased for many years, had done extremely well with, and knew every inch of the property. For example, the Leoncita northeast of Alpine was an outstanding ranch that we leased for fifteen years. It was in some of the better country in the Fort Davis–Marfa area. We were there long enough that we almost felt like it was ours. When our lease expired, we didn't want to leave. We tried hard to buy that ranch from the heirs, and at one point thought we had the deal completed. Eventually, however, the family decided to keep it. I didn't blame them a bit. That is a great ranch.

Eventually, Red and I did buy two ranches together. First, we bought the 40,000-acre Nicholson Ranch east of Laredo in Webb County. And then later we bought the 30,000-acre Gato Creek Ranch between Uvalde and Eagle Pass. We operated both of those ranches through our partnership.

We leased the Nicholson Ranch for several years before we bought it, so we knew it as well as we knew the Leoncita. The Nicholson was in very hard country with little grass, but it was loaded with prickly pear, which appealed to us. The ranch belonged to an oilman who had made his fortune in the great East Texas field. We purchased 17,000 acres of the ranch, and then Mr. Nicholson donated the southern part of the ranch, which was 23,000 acres in size, to Southern Methodist University (SMU). We retained our lease on SMU's portion. Naturally, SMU didn't want to operate a cattle ranch, so they decided eventually to put their acreage on the market. By accident, I learned that the ranch was for sale before it was publicly listed. The real estate agent in Corpus Christi called to tell me that he would need to show SMU's portion of our lease to prospective buyers and that he would appreciate our cooperation.

This was exciting news, because Red and I were eager to reassemble the original 40,000-acre ranch. We didn't have the cash to buy a ranch, but I knew that Red felt good about borrowing the money because we had leased the ranch and he knew what it was like. I knew the ranch would have a number of prospective buyers, however, so I got off the telephone as fast as I could without being rude. I called Red immediately. We agreed that we needed to move as quickly as possible if we were going to have a chance to make the deal. I knew that the trust department at the First National Bank in Dallas was handling SMU's property, including that ranch. Red's sister-in-law had married into the Cullum family, whose members were very prominent business leaders in Dallas. Bob Cullum, for example, owned the Tom Thumb grocery store chain, and he was one of the most influential men in Dallas politics. The Cullums were big supporters of SMU, and, of course, Red had gone to school there. I got Red to call his brother-in-law, George Cullum, to find out who was in charge of SMU's land business at the bank. George agreed to make an appointment for us to meet with this person—he was a senior vice president—the next day in Dallas. Red and I flew to Dallas early the next morning for the meeting. The bank officer had full authority to make the deal, so within about forty-five minutes we had made a trade with him to buy the ranch.

I made the deal to buy the Gato Creek Ranch. My father had once owned part of it but lost it during Depression, which was one reason why I wanted to buy it. I had sentimental reasons for wanting to buy the Gato Creek, but it really was a very good ranch. I had to drag Red into that deal. He was afraid that it was too risky, but we bought it at the right time. It turned out to be an outstanding deal.

Working with Red

Talking Red into buying the Gato Creek Ranch was a quite an accomplishment. Red was a strong personality, and he could be the most stubborn individual you could ever imagine. I learned pretty fast that Red was the operator, and he was going to conduct our business his way. Some of the people who worked for him would say that there was a right way and a wrong way and then there was the Red Nunley way, and Red Nunley was going to do it his way. Early in our partnership, I tried to operate independently. I'd buy us some cattle without consulting Red, and he would sort of grind his teeth and not say much, but I could tell it didn't suit him. And then I'd sell something, and he'd also grind his teeth and not say anything, but I knew that didn't suit him either. I soon realized that if I acted on my own, the partnership wasn't going to work. If it was going to survive for a number of years, I needed to stay away and let him run the operation. In many ways, it's an unbelievable story that the only way that our partnership was going to survive was for me to stay out of his way, but it's true, and it worked.

Another reason our partnership worked was because Red Nunley was a man of absolute integrity. A lot of partners in the cattle business don't trust each other. If they are selling cattle, for example, each partner will insist on being at the sale because they want to make certain that they get their fair share. With Red, I never had to worry about getting my fair share. In fact, I really knew that if I didn't attend the sale, Red would make certain that I would get more than my fair share.

And, of course, the main reason our partnership was a success was that Red was one of the best ranch managers and cattle operators in the country. He just knew much more about the business than I did. I never had to worry about Red neglecting anything. And it didn't make any difference to him how long it took to get something done, he would get it done. He ran a ranch frugally. He didn't waste money, and even when we were making money, he didn't believe in spending it. Red knew where everything was on our ranches at all times. Like many ranchers of his generation, Red kept a little folding notebook in his shirt pocket where he would record the number of cattle we had at each ranch. I remember that my father kept up with his cattle the same way. Every few months, Red came to my office, pulled this little notebook out of his pocket, and told me how many cows we had at each ranch. I never got a very good look at his notebook. He always treated the information as his confidential material. After giving me the numbers, Red closed his little book and slipped it back in his pocket.

That was the extent that I knew of exactly how many cattle there were on each ranch, but I certainly wasn't the least bit concerned. Of course, I had a general idea where and what we had because we kept all the books in my office in Uvalde.

Although Red managed our business, he always insisted that I go with him to the ranches to see what he was doing and how he was doing it. I enjoyed going out with him. It was fascinating to watch him in action. When Red worked a bunch of cattle in the pen, he always said that he liked to operate with a high degree of flexibility. That was an understatement. Red would start working cattle one direction through the pen and about halfway through he might change his mind and bring them back the other direction. He knew how to work a bunch of cattle. And when he got through, they really had been worked. Red might run over a few people while he did it, and he might alienate a few others who might have come to watch him work, but he would get the job done.

With Red managing the day-to-day operation, I never worried about our business. Our ranches made money every year. Some years it wasn't very much, especially when we had a drought and the cattle prices were down, but Red's operating philosophy and his hard work ethic kept us going even in those hard times. Red never quit working. If there was something in the business that needed attention, he took take care of it.

The business absolutely came first; nothing else mattered. For example, one Christmas Eve morning during the first year of our Longfellow lease, Red called me on the telephone. He was absolutely torn up and upset. He said, "Dolph, we have to go to the Longfellow right now."

And I asked, "Red, what's the matter with you? This is Christmas Eve." He said that didn't make one bit of difference: "We have to go to the Longfellow and we have to go now."

I asked him what had happened. And he answered that our ranch hands were upset for some reason and that we had to go out there and straighten things out. Red was afraid they were going to quit.

I said, "Well, Red, I'll be glad to go with you after Christmas, but Janey is expecting me home pretty quick. We're going to celebrate Christmas Eve at our house. Janey's parents, her brother and his wife, and their three children are on their way to town. And my mother and our three children are going to be there. There is no way that I can go to the Longfellow Ranch tonight, it will have to wait until after Christmas."

That didn't impress Red. "Nope," he replied, "we have to go right now."

I immediately realized that I might be making a decision between my partnership and my marriage. I knew that if I left town after Janey had made all of these family plans for Christmas Eve and Christmas Day it would have been the end. Of course, it wasn't that hard of a decision, regardless of what the problem might have been on the Longfellow. The ranch could have burned up, and we still could have waited a few days. It didn't sound to me like it was very important, anyway. Aware that this might be the end of our partnership, I told Red that there was no way that I could go, and that there was no reason for him to go either. Red's wife, Dorothy, was back at their home in Sabinal. Whatever the problem at Longfellow, it could wait a couple of days. I wasn't surprised when Red got mad and hung up the telephone on me. I thought, well, there goes my partnership, but at least I've saved my marriage.

I did not hear from Red for several weeks after Christmas. He wouldn't speak to me. I thought that was the end. But finally he came by to see me, and everything was all right. He never mentioned the incident, and we continued our partnership. I never knew what the problem had been on the Longfellow. I just left it alone. Everything turned out all right, but it was a critical test for our relationship.

Airborne

Red was amazing in lots of ways and as smart as they come. He could learn anything he wanted to learn. He even learned to fly—both airplanes and helicopters—and he excelled at both. I didn't fly for a while after I left the university. Eventually, I bought a single-engine Cessna that was large enough to take Janey and the kids on trips. We bought an airplane that didn't have back doors, and we closed it up tightly. The kids could holler and fight all they wanted to, but they couldn't get out.

Red and I took that Cessna to a cattle sale on the Longfellow before we acquired the lease. We flew there, landed at their little airstrip, and attended the cattle sale. When it was time for us to leave, we got in our little airplane and I took off. Mountains surrounded the airstrip. They weren't big, but they were mountains. I had to circle and circle over and over again until I could get a high enough altitude to get over those mountains. It seemed to Red and me that we circled forever before I could get out of that valley. I decided then that I needed a more powerful airplane if Red and I were going to be flying

Airplanes and helicopters have replaced the horse as the primary means of transportation on a large ranch. *Courtesy of the Briscoe family.*

out that way often. I got a larger Cessna that I soon replaced with an even bigger Beechcraft.

But after that episode, Red decided that he would get his own airplane. He certainly wasn't going to be dependent on me for his transportation, and I didn't want him to be. He needed his own airplane to go from ranch to ranch. As usual, Red learned to fly his own way. He hired a pilot to teach him: no formal courses for Red and no messing with a license. Fortunately, Red was a natural flier, and he learned quickly. He never bothered to get a license, however, which meant that he couldn't land at any airport where he might have to show one. If he wanted to fly to San Antonio, he had to go with me or hire another pilot. That didn't matter much to him because all he wanted to do was to be able to fly from ranch to ranch.

Later, Red worked our cattle with helicopters. It wasn't any cheaper than by horseback because helicopters are expensive to hire, but it certainly was much faster. We hired a helicopter service to work pastures on a daily basis. We still work that way. At one point, Red and

I made some money, so Red decided he wanted to buy a helicopter. Whatever Red wanted to do was fine with me, because, after all, he'd made the money. So if he wanted to spend it on a helicopter that was okay. It might as well have been okay because he was going to do it anyway. Red bought a four-seat Bell Jet Ranger. Red also decided that the boys we were hiring to fly helicopters didn't know how to maneuver well enough to work the cattle as well as he wanted. So, Red decided that he was going to fly a helicopter and give directions.

Flying a helicopter is entirely different from flying an airplane. I never did learn how to fly a helicopter. Typically, Red never had a lesson, but he learned how to fly the helicopter anyway. Not having the benefit of professional training, he never had a helicopter license. Red didn't care because he only flew that helicopter on our ranches. He loved his helicopter. It was expensive to operate it, but it made it possible for him to see just about everything he needed to see on several ranches in one day. Red took that helicopter from waterhole to waterhole. He would discover if a fence was down, or if windmill wasn't working, or if the water was getting low in the concrete reservoir. He saw everything; he could really cover things in that helicopter.

And of course, he actually worked cattle with his Jet Ranger. Red would hire three or four other helicopters to work a pasture, and he'd fly above and connect with them by radio. He would tell the other pilots what to do as he hovered above them. He got on the radio and gave directions such as "Hey, you missed a cow; go back and get it," or, "Let that cow stay—she's got a baby calf—leave her alone." He directed the show from up in the air. And those boys who flew the other helicopters couldn't believe that he could do it, but he did. He could handle that thing like I don't think anybody else could.

I flew with Red a lot in that helicopter. Red was the best helicopter pilot I ever flew with, and I ended up flying with quite a few of them during the time I was in Austin. He was an outstanding helicopter pilot, but he refused to get a license. To Red, that was an invasion of his privacy and a restriction on his liberty, and he wasn't about to do it. He disliked government regulations of any kind, and he wasn't about to comply with that. Of course, it also meant we didn't have any insurance, but luck stayed with us, and we never had an accident.

The Nunley–Briscoe Partnership Continues

Red was an incredible character, but you could never have a more loyal friend. The only thing about Red that I would have changed if it had been within my power was his attitude about people in general. Red's view was that anybody he met was a sorry SOB until they proved differently. That attitude bothered Dorothy, his wife, who was one of the sweetest people I ever knew. She was a great lady who helped smooth over Red's rough spots, especially his suspicious view of people that he did not know well. She passed away about ten years before Red did, which was a sad thing. I tend to assume that most of the people I meet are going to be honest and trustworthy. I may be too trusting—at least that's what Red thought. But our different attitudes probably helped our partnership. I never had to worry about Red being gullible. Nobody was ever going to fool him. He was never going to take any wooden nickels.

As I said, Red was extremely frugal, but he did save his money for certain things that he wanted, such as his airplane and his helicopter, and then he paid cash for them. Another thing that he wanted was a big lodge on his ranch south of Sabinal. And he also wanted a large lake in front of the house. In the early 1970s, a gas field was discovered on the portion of Catarina that is near the Rio Grande. That field continues to produce gas. A gas field was also found on the Nicholson Ranch about the same time. The income from those fields made it possible for us both to do some things that we otherwise could not have done. With his royalty income from the gas fields, Red was able to pay cash to build the house of his dreams as well as the lake in front of it. And of course, he didn't get a permit to build the lake, which was consistent with his method of operation. That eventually became a problem, but there is a permit in place now.

Red had an intense interest in politics, but he didn't really have time to be politically active. Of course, he was very conservative. When I had an opportunity to get back into politics, Red was all in favor of it, and he encouraged me to do it. He was strongly supportive in every way, including being very generous with his own personal funds on my behalf.

Red died in December 1983. It is difficult for me to comprehend, but he has been gone now for nearly twenty-five years. Time has passed faster than I have realized. I was executor of Red's estate and the trustee of the trust that he set up. Red and his wife had one son who in turn had two sons. Their son has also passed away, but his sons—Red's and Dorothy's two grandsons—were my partners in our Nunley-Briscoe operations for several years after Red died. There are so many examples of these kinds of arrangements falling apart and everybody fighting, but Red's grandsons and I never had a problem. They're fine boys. They're very serious about their ranching business, and they are very hard workers. I've never known two finer young men. I feel about them as if they were my own sons.

Red also had his own cattle business, which the grandsons continue. They still own the home ranch south of Sabinal. They also operate the Junco Ranch east of Encinal, which had been part of the old Callahan Ranch, one of the most famous ranches in South Texas. My father had acquired that 30,000 acres and had never operated it but had leased it to Red. We later traded out on it. They bought the ranch in Cochran County, which was part of the Long-S, the old C. C. Slaughter Ranch.

Red Nunley was the greatest partner and friend anyone could have. His word was his bond and his integrity was beyond question. I will always be grateful for what he did for me after the death of my father, and I will never forget the wonderful times we had together building the Nunley–Briscoe operation. Besides my father, I never knew a more capable or successful rancher.

Chapter 8

BRISCOE RANCHES

Aﬆer my father's death in 1954, I assumed management of the various business operations that he had owned separate from his partnership with Red Nunley. Most of those operations were part of the entity that we later called Briscoe Ranches, which included the Margaritas Ranch in Mexico, the 45,000-acre Fowlerton Ranch in McMullen county, a 30,000-acre section of the old Callahan Land Company in Webb and LaSalle counties, and the 100,000-acre Catarina. The latter was my father's largest ranch in Texas. And, of course, I made our Rio Frio Ranch up in the hills north of Uvalde part of Briscoe Ranches.

When I took over Briscoe Ranches, it was my good fortune to have Les Brown, a top-notch ranch manager, already running the ranch at Catarina. My father had hired Les in 1939 to be the foreman of that ranch, a job that he would do extraordinarily well for more than five decades. Les came from a fine Catholic family residing in Batesville, Texas. He was a very young man when my father hired him to work as the ranch manager. Les eventually became much more to us than just an employee; he became a member of our family. Les was not only a talented cattleman, he also was a skilled engineer. His wife, Dorothy, was a medical doctor, and they raised their four children on the Catarina Ranch. She had her doctor's office on the ranch and treated our employees and people from the surrounding area. Their son, Charlie, is still at Catarina working with my son, Chip. Les took care of the ranch like it was his own. I was lucky indeed to have the benefit of his knowledge and skill. With men such as Les Brown and Red Nunley advising and guiding me, I was in great shape.

In December 1967, a long-standing dream of mine came true when I was able to purchase the Chupadera Ranch from Bill Lloyd of Houston. As I have detailed in an earlier chapter, the historic old Chupadera, which adjoins the Catarina, had been the ranch of my childhood. Ross Sterling lost the Chupadera during the Depression, and for many years it had been my goal to recover the ranch and make it part of my Briscoe Ranches holdings. The Chupadera acquisition included a paved and lighted airstrip and airplane hanger as well as the old ranch headquarters.

Managing a cattle operation like Briscoe Ranches may seem to be a straightforward proposition. You have land, either leased or owned, and then you put cattle on it that you hope you can feed as cheaply as possible. With a lot of luck, those cattle survive and grow, and then you sell them for the highest price possible. That is certainly the essence of the enterprise, but there is much more to it than that. Actually, the cattle business is complex, and there are any number of problems that can occur that one must overcome to survive. Confronting some of those problems can be a real challenge, and resolving them can be extremely satisfying. I've had a few successes over the years, but there are two that really stand out in my memory. One was my work with a land management approach called root plowing; the other was the eradication of the screwworm.

Root Plowing

One of the major challenges for all ranchers in the drier regions of Texas is drought. There is barely enough water in good years to grow the grass we need to feed our cattle, but in drought conditions the problem can be severe enough to break you. As a result, we had to work as hard as we could to get as much feed as possible to our cattle. Burning pear, which I mentioned in an earlier chapter, is an example of one traditional method of surviving a drought. Even if there is enough rainfall, it is important to have the land in such condition that our grass growth is as productive as possible. One of the grass-growing methods that I employed very intensely and with much success during the 1950s was root plowing.

Bob Kleberg of the King Ranch, who was one of the most influential innovators in the history of ranching, pioneered the use of root plowing. This technique is aimed at two of the worst enemies of good grass: hard soil and dense brush. Much of the clay soil in South Texas is so hard it does not absorb rainfall. You get little benefit from the rain because so much of it runs off into the creeks and causes flash floods. As a result, the underlying soil is denied the moisture needed to grow some of the most productive grasses, and grass seed sprouts can't penetrate the hard surface. And, of course, mesquite and other types of brush crowd out the grass and draw out much of the moisture that the soil does retain. Root plowing takes out the brush and opens the ground.

Actually, when you root plow you don't use a plow. A type of very sharp knife or cutter is attached to a tractor. Running parallel with the ground, the cutter digs about twelve inches into the dirt and cuts the roots of mesquite trees and other brush. It is an effective and efficient method of removing the brush while also breaking up the hard crust of the soil to allow the seeding and growth of grass. I had a great deal of success with the method at Catarina, so much that the *Saturday Evening Post*, which was a very popular national magazine in the 1950s, ran a major story about our efforts in its January 1959 issue. We began our program in 1954 during one of the worst droughts in recorded Texas history. We root plowed and seeded 80,000 acres of Catarina. After restoring the grass, we were able to produce more beef than before. We had beef yields of fifty pounds per acre with as little as eight inches of annual rainfall.

I tried several grasses during the root plowing program. The first was blue panic grass, which was excellent, but it played out. The cattle eat it out, and it doesn't come back. And then we used imported buffel grass, which worked well. Buffel grass is a fine seed and tonnage producer. Eventually, however, we had several days when the temperature remained below freezing, and that killed out the buffel. The buffel grass that was in clay soil didn't come back, but the grass in the

On his 100,000-acre Catarina Ranch, cattleman Dolph Briscoe, Jr. (center), inspects rootplowing operations. The specially designed plow blade at left is the key weapon in the attack on ravaged grazing land.

TEXAS GRASS IS COMING BACK

By JOHN BIRD

For more than fifty years cattlemen have fought a losing battle against a blight that threatened to destroy the range. Here's how they have turned the tide.

Photographs by Bill Shrout

When Texans talk about their "brush country" they are guilty—for once—of understatement. For the thickets of South Texas are no modest collection of shrubbery, but rather a vicious, invading jungle that has engulfed millions of acres of once-rich grasslands, described in early days as "the best wild pastures in the world," bringing calamity that could be equaled only if all the state's oil wells went dry. For more than half a century hard-pressed cattlemen have tried to beat back this creeping blight of spiny trees and cactus, only to see it spread, driving out the prairie grass, leaving the soil as bare and unproductive as an old

Rootplowing has doubled the per-acre beef yield for Briscoe (below, with his daughter, Cele, 2).

This is the story about our root plowing work that was published in the *Saturday Evening Post* in 1959. You can see the root cutter in the magazine picture. Cele was good at climbing fences, even at a tender age. Saturday Evening Post, *vol. 231, no. 32-33, p. 76.*

135

sandy soil did grow back eventually. The problem is that Catarina has much more clay than sandy soil. Now we use Kleberg grass, which was developed by the King Ranch and does not freeze out. It is an excellent grass.

We still root plow today, but not as much as we once did. The economic benefits are not what they were in the 1950s for a couple of reasons. One is that the cost per acre of root plowing, which includes much higher fuel prices, has increased tremendously. The other reason is that recreational use of the land has become much more profitable than it was in the 1950s. After World War II, none of our land was leased to hunters. There was no demand for hunting leases. There was plenty of hunting going on, but the hunters were the owners and their family and friends. It was not a business. The hunting lease business gradually developed in the 1950s. In the last twenty years, selling hunting leases has become such a big business that it may be the most important economic factor on Hill Country and South Texas ranch land today. Affluent urban business leaders and professionals, especially physicians and attorneys from Houston, Dallas, and San Antonio, have made hunting one of the most popular recreational activities in Texas. In the late 1990s, we were getting as much as twelve dollars an acre for hunting leases, but grazing leases were generating only about three dollars an acre. To foster the best conditions for hunting on your land, you have to preserve wildlife habitat, which requires plenty of brush to provide cover for game animals. Ironically, the brush that we previously eliminated by root plowing now generates more revenue than grass.

Eradicating the Screwworm

As I've pointed out in an earlier chapter, the screwworm was a terrible scourge that had plagued livestock growers since the beginning of the livestock industry in Texas. Janey and I spent many hundreds of hours combating this pest on our sheep and goat ranch in the late 1940s and throughout the 1950s. In 1960, when I was elected president of the Texas and Southwestern Cattle Raisers Association, I made the eradication of the screwworm my major project.

The screwworm eradication program actually began when I was vice president of the association, but I made it the association's primary project. The association played the leadership role in a coalition that included the Sheep and Goat Raisers Association and the Texas Farm Bureau. All of my life, I had witnessed the terrible destruction that this parasite had caused in the livestock industry, and I longed for the day when it could be eliminated. Few people thought the screwworm problem could be solved. A screwworm fly lays eggs on any wound or cut that an animal might have. The eggs develop into worms, which ranchers call screwworms. If left untreated, the worms usually kill their host. In the northern ranching areas, screwworms weren't a problem because freezing temperatures kill off infestations. The prevalence of screwworms in the much warmer southern regions of Texas increased our production costs and made it harder for us to compete with cattle production in colder climates. We had to work livestock every day, looking for sick animals. No matter how much time, labor, and money we put into the effort, the worms would kill our young calves, sheep, and goats.

In the late 1950s, my colleagues and I at the Cattle Raisers Association heard about a program that was being conducted in Florida to eradicate screwworms. We were interested in anything that might work, so I went with the association's president, Norman Moser, and the association's other vice president, Leo Welder, to Florida to meet with the researchers who were working on the program. We met with one of the USDA's entomologists, Dr. R. C. Bushland, and his team. They and another scientist, Dr. E. F. Knipling, had developed a method to stop the pests that they called the sterile male technique. The female fly mates only once in her life span. If that female fly mates with a sterile male fly, then her life cycle stops and she will never produce eggs. In the Florida program, they released millions of sterile male flies to mate with the females. This process, when supplemented with a strenuous effort to treat existing infections in animals, was a tremendous success. It quickly eliminated the screwworm population in Florida.

We ranchers in Texas were eager to start the eradication program in our state. A group of us asked Lyndon Johnson, who was in his last months as Senate majority leader, for a federal appropriation to start the program. Earlier, I had talked to Lyndon about the screwworm project in Florida during his visit to Uvalde for Mr. Garner's ninetieth birthday party, but he hadn't shown much interest, mainly because he didn't believe it would work. Later, however, when we asked for an appropriation to help us fight the screwworm, Lyndon agreed to get us the money. We had no problem with the request in the House, but in the Senate, Richard Russell, the powerful senior senator from Georgia, opposed the appropriation and nearly killed it. Lyndon, wily legislative manipulator that he was, just kept the Senate in session late enough one night until Russell gave up and went home to bed. In Russell's absence, the Senate passed an appropriation for $200,000 for screwworm research. Congress later increased its support to $6 million.

In 1961, we created the Southwest Animal Health Research Foundation to raise money to support research about how the program in Florida might work in Texas. Most of our contributors were ranchers, but we also received donations from hunters because screwworms were devastating our wildlife population. We often lost to screwworms as much as a third of the entire fawn population born every year. The foundation asked ranchers to contribute fifty cents for each cow and horse they owned and ten cents for each sheep, goat, and pig. That effort raised $3 million for the program. The Texas Legislature contributed another $2.8 million.

We had an ambitious program, but the U.S. Department of Agriculture refused to cooperate with us. Most of their scientists didn't think the program would work in Texas because of new flies coming in from south of our border. Florida is virtually surrounded by water, and it is relatively easy to prevent recontamination from the adjoining areas, especially with the adjoining areas located to the north, where freezing weather occurs often enough to offer protection. Arguing that reinfestation would be impossible to prevent in Texas, the USDA simply refused to cooperate with us. Fortunately, Dr. Bushland protested his agency's decision. He believed the program could work in Texas, and he voiced that opinion strongly enough to put his job in jeopardy.

Lyndon Johnson had just become president when our problems

We set up field labs on our ranches during the war on the screwworm. *Briscoe Papers.*

with the Department of Agriculture intensified. I decided to try and get Lyndon's help. I was especially concerned about Dr. Bushland because there were people at the department who wanted to fire him for saying that our project was workable. I knew that my old friend, Jack Brooks, who had become a key member of LBJ's legislative team in Congress, could get me access to the president. Jack didn't know anything about the screwworm, and he didn't care, but he agreed to arrange a meeting with the president.

Jack and I went to the White House and visited with Lyndon in his small work area next to the Oval Office, where we talked about a number of issues that Lyndon wanted to discuss, none of which had anything to do with screwworms. It was early in the evening, so Lyndon asked us to come upstairs to the private quarters and have dinner with him and Mrs. Johnson. Dinner wasn't the time to get into a conversation about screwworms, so I didn't mention it. After dinner, we watched a movie with the president and first lady. When the movie was over and we were leaving the White House, Jack whispered to me that I had not said a word about our screwworm project. So I got my courage up and finally asked Lyndon to do something about our problem in the agriculture department.

"All right," Lyndon replied, "I'll call [Agriculture Secretary] Orville [Freeman] in the morning." This was great news, because I knew that Lyndon still had doubts about the program. That next morning, the Department of Agriculture announced that it had changed its position. It would now cooperate with us. I don't know what Lyndon said to Secretary Freeman, but it worked. The president also prevented Dr. Bushland's dismissal. Equally important, he connected us with the officials in Mexico whose cooperation we needed to carry the program out on their side of the Rio Grande.

We also had significant help from Houston businessman Herman Brown, whose company, Brown and Root, built a facility at Mission in the lower Rio Grande Valley to produce sterile screwworm flies for the program. Brown and Root built the plant on an old abandoned air force base and charged only for their actual cost. We dropped the sterile flies from airplanes flying low over the region on both sides of the Rio Grande where the screwworms proliferated. The Mexican gov-

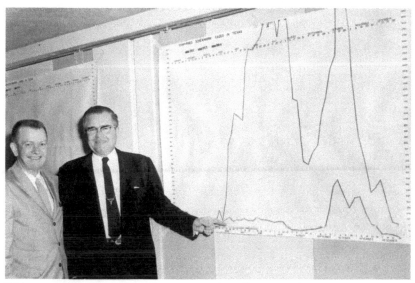

This graph chart indicates our success in the effort to eradicate the screwworm. *Briscoe Papers.*

ernment allowed the airplanes to fly over its territory to drop flies. That was critical, because the program could not succeed if we could- n't work both sides of the border. To my great delight, the program did succeed. By 1966 the United States was completely free of the screw- worm. We experienced a couple of outbreaks before the eradication program in Mexico was completed in 1991, but those episodes were manageable. The program has since been conducted all the way south to Panama, with the same wonderful success. One historian has declared that the eradication effort may have been of more benefit to the livestock industry in Texas than any other program in the twenti- eth century. I am very pleased that I had the opportunity to play a role in removing this terrible pest from our state.

THE TEXAS AND SOUTHWESTERN CATTLE RAISERS ASSOCIATION

I have been a member of the Texas and Southwestern Cattle Raisers Association for several decades now. Ever since it was organized in

As president of the Texas and Southwestern Cattle Raisers Association, I was called on to speak to a large number of civic and business organizations throughout the state. *Briscoe Papers.*

1877, the association has played a key and critical role in the development of the cattle industry in Texas. Of all the organizations in which I have been an active member, the Cattle Raisers Association ranks at the top when measured in terms of effectiveness and success in carrying out its important mission. The association was probably the first business organization I ever knew about as a child. My father was a very active member who served in several offices, including the presidency. I often heard him talk about how much the association and the friends he made among the other members meant to him. Naturally, with that background, I joined the association and became an active member soon after I returned home from the army.

The association was organized more than 125 years ago by cattlemen who met in the North Texas town of Graham to address the problem of cattle theft, which was rampant in the region at the time. Its founding members included legendary cattlemen such as James

Loving, Col. Kit Carter, Samuel Burk Burnett, and C. C. Slaughter. Apparently, the theft of livestock had gotten so bad that the cattle business in Texas was in danger of collapse. Not long after it was organized, the association started a program in which their inspectors monitored trails, shipping points, and terminal markets looking for cattle that had somehow become a part of herds to which they did not belong. I should emphasize that not all of the cattle they found in these inspections were stolen. As late as the 1880s and 1890s, much of the rangeland in west and northwest Texas was not fenced. Cattle often were picked up accidentally during a trail drive. The inspectors would check the brands on cattle in herds going north and remove those that had different brands from the brands they were supposed to have. Many cattle were stolen, however, and the association's inspection system helped to alleviate that problem. Eventually, the association hired its own attorneys and created a division to help prosecute cattle thieves.

The prevention of cattle theft was the primary purpose of the Cattle Raisers Association when it was founded, and that is still its first purpose. The association now has a force of some sixty or seventy inspectors who have a special ranger's commission that gives them the same legal authority as a Texas Ranger. Although they work for the association, the agents are trained and supervised by the Texas Department of Public Safety. The inspectors conduct brand inspections at every auction ring in Texas. The association keeps a computer record of the brand marks and other identifying characteristics of every animal that goes through those auction rings.

When they're shipped young, a lot of cattle are not branded. For example, we don't brand our cattle until after we wean them. If we ship them as calves, there's no brand on them, but they'll have an earmark, and that earmark will be recorded officially. That makes it possible to trace the animals if they are stolen. It's difficult for a thief to sell cattle because of that system. It is possible to sell cattle directly to a small butcher shop, but that would raise suspicions on the part of the butcher buying them. And most of these young cattle shipped that way aren't fat. They aren't butcher cattle.

Eventually, of course, the Cattle Raisers Association evolved into an advocate agency for the cattle industry, as well as continuing to serve its original purpose. That role really developed when the railroads spread throughout Texas and became the chief means of hauling cattle to market. Cattle raisers drove their herds to a railroad pen and then loaded them on the train for delivery to markets. The railroad companies were pretty ruthless in those days, and they colluded to fix high rates on cattle shipments. The railroads had a monopoly on routes, so the cattle raisers had no choice but to pay whatever rate the railroad demanded. That soon got the association active as an agency to represent the cattle raiser's cause in Washington and in Austin. It is now involved in many other issues, including those related to land use and water rights.

Sam Rayburn

I first became an officer in the Cattle Raisers Association in the late 1950s and eventually served as vice president and president. During that period, I traveled frequently to Washington, D.C., on association business. I would meet with various members of Congress and officials in the Department of Agriculture to make arguments in support of legislation or other federal decisions important to Texas cattle raisers, including the screwworm eradication program.

By this time, Jack Brooks, my old college and legislative friend, was serving as an influential member of the Texas delegation in the U.S. House of Representatives. Jack was always a big help to me when I was in Washington. I also was extremely fortunate to be on good terms with Sam Rayburn, who was at the height of his influence as Speaker of the House of Representatives. I had first met Mr. Rayburn in 1948 when he came to Uvalde with President Truman. My close relationship with D. B. Hardeman, who had become a trusted member of Mr. Rayburn's staff, as well as the fact that Jack Brooks was one of the Speaker's lieutenants in the House, facilitated my relationship with Mr. Rayburn. D. B. had joined Speaker Rayburn's staff in Washington in 1956. He and journalist Don Bacon eventually co-authored Rayburn's biography.

D. B. was especially helpful to me on my frequent trips to Washington. Through D. B., I got to know every one of Mr. Rayburn's assistants, as well as some of the key members of the staffs of other Texas congressmen. I was up there so frequently that I became sort of an unpaid member of the Speaker's staff. Mr. Rayburn was very generous; he gave me the run of his office. I had desk space and access to his telephones. Whenever I found it difficult to make an appointment with a federal official to discuss Cattle Raisers Association business, Mr. Rayburn would call the official and make the appointment for me. Naturally, Mr. Rayburn had no problem getting anyone on the telephone. For example, I couldn't get an appointment to see the Secretary of Agriculture during one of my visits. One telephone call from the Speaker, and I was in the secretary's office the first thing the next morning.

Mr. Rayburn even invited me to attend his legendary "board of education" sessions, which was a ritual of Mr. Garner's that Mr. Rayburn had continued. These meetings were held in a little private room on the ground floor of the Capitol that he reserved just for late afternoon get-togethers with close colleagues. There was nothing luxurious about the place. It had no windows and was furnished with an old couch, a few comfortable leather chairs, and some straight-backed wooden chairs that probably dated back to Mr. Garner's days or even earlier. Mr. Rayburn would usually sit in a swivel chair behind an old desk. Jack Brooks was a regular visitor to those sessions, so I often went with him. In that period, which was during Eisenhower's second term as president, Lyndon Johnson was running the Senate and Mr. Rayburn was running the House. Sometimes Lyndon would come over from the Senate, and he and Mr. Rayburn would talk legislative strategy. They might disagree a little bit on some matter, and finally Mr. Rayburn would just flat out say "Now, that's fine Lyndon, but *this* is what we are going to do." It was fascinating to watch those two operate together.

My role at those board of education meetings was to listen silently and to help keep the drinks flowing. Bottles of bourbon and scotch were always available. It was quite an honor for me to be invited to these little gatherings because it meant that Mr. Rayburn trusted me. It was absolutely forbidden to repeat what anyone said in these sessions to anyone who had not been there. "What is said in this room stays in this room" was Mr. Rayburn's warning to visitors. That was a rule that he enforced rigidly. Those who violated that code were never in that room again.

Mr. Rayburn told me that when John Garner was Speaker, he enjoyed bringing colleagues into the room and plying them with the cheap red whiskey that he served in beat-up old tin cups. He would not allow any visitor with whom he intended to do business to refuse the whiskey. Mr. Garner would stress that it was his personal rule never to have a serious talk with anyone who had not had a drink, if he had had one first. And, of course, he made sure that he had always had the first drink. Mr. Garner would pour himself just a little bit of whiskey, but he would fill the other cups to the top. And then he would lift his cup and say "down the hatch." His colleagues would be expected to gulp their drink in one quick shot—"Texas style," as Mr. Garner would say. If you sipped a drink, then he had no use for you. But Mr. Garner used those drinking sessions as a tool to get information out of his colleagues that they might not otherwise have shared with him. It was his version of the "loose lips sink ships" game. I never saw Mr. Rayburn use alcohol that way. In fact, it was always my understanding that if you drank too much at a board of education session it was likely that you wouldn't get invited back.

In the fall of 1959, when I was attending one of these board of education sessions with Jack Brooks, Mr. Rayburn made a comment about how much he enjoyed fishing. When we left the meeting, Jack said that he wanted me to invite Mr. Rayburn to Catarina. Rayburn's comment about fishing had given Jack an idea. This was when Jack was trying to get Congress to appropriate several million dollars to expand the size of an ongoing project for a dam on the Angelina River that would generate electric power and create a reservoir for flood control. The dam and reservoir, located eighty miles north of Beaumont, were in his congressional district. The Army Corps of Engineers, which didn't think the expanded project was necessary, opposed Jack's plan. Jack decided that if he could be alone with Mr. Rayburn during a fishing trip at Catarina, he might be able to persuade the Speaker to support his dam.

I loved the idea of Mr. Rayburn being a guest at Catarina and, of course, I wanted to help Jack out, so I invited the Speaker to come down and try his luck on some of the water tanks that we had stocked with bass. I was a little surprised but very pleased when Mr. Rayburn accepted the invitation. He and Jack Brooks came down that November during a congressional recess. Someone flew them to Uvalde in a private airplane, and then we flew in my airplane to Catarina, which is about eighty miles away. Before we departed from Uvalde, I asked Mr. Rayburn if he wanted to visit Mr. Garner. He said no—quickly and sharply—without further discussion. Mr. Rayburn didn't want to see Mr. Garner because he knew that he would lecture him like he was a freshman member of Congress and point out everything that he thought Mr. Rayburn was doing wrong. Once you were Mr. Garner's protégé, you remained a protégé. It didn't matter that Mr. Rayburn was Speaker of the House and Mr. Garner was in retirement.

I appreciated Mr. Rayburn's feelings about his relationship with Mr. Garner. A few years prior to this, when I was in the state legislature, Mr. Rayburn had passed through Uvalde, and he had stopped for dinner at Mr. Garner's. I wasn't invited to the dinner, but Mr. Garner was kind enough to invite me to come by after their meal. I was embarrassed by the insulting way Mr. Garner lectured to Mr. Rayburn that night. Mr. Rayburn had the good manners not to get up and leave, and he kept quiet and didn't argue, but I could see him smoldering quietly.

We flew straight to Catarina. I gave Mr. Rayburn one of the bedrooms in the wing of the ranch house that we used to lodge our hunting and fishing guests. After Mr. Rayburn went to Washington, we named the room after him with the intention of it serving as his quarters for future visits. Unfortunately, his last illness struck him down several months later, and he never returned.

Mr. Rayburn did love to fish, and he and Jack stayed three or four days. Janey and our kids were there, which pleased Mr. Rayburn because he enjoyed children, and he was very fond of Janey. Jack and I went out with Mr. Rayburn every morning to a nearby tank just north of the house. He had left his hat in Bonham, and he needed something to protect his bald head from the sunlight. As we were walking out of the ranch house, Mr. Rayburn spied an old straw hat hanging from a post in the hallway. "That's a great hat," he declared. "That will work fine for me." I told him that it had been my father's hat, implying that no one had used it since he had died. Mr. Rayburn smiled and said, "Dolph, your father and I were friends," which was true. "He wouldn't mind me wearing his hat." That pleased me very much, so Mr. Rayburn wore my father's straw hat on our fishing expeditions.

We fished all morning and then returned to the house for lunch, followed by a little siesta. Later, we went to a tank farther out on the south part of the ranch. It was great fun. Mr. Rayburn was easy to be around. He made everyone feel comfortable. He had a keen sense of humor, and he was good at small talk. It was a pleasure trip, but, naturally, Jack Brooks took the opportunity occasionally to bring up his dam project, and I wasn't shy about mentioning some legislation that the ranching community favored. Mr. Rayburn was interested in our ranch, and he was full of questions about how we operated it and what kind of problems we faced.

During his last day at Catarina, Mr. Rayburn caught a large bass at the south tank. Catching that beautiful fish pleased him deeply. On our way back to the ranch house, we had to travel in our pickup truck over some bad ruts in the dirt road, and Mr. Rayburn was tossed around a little. When we finally arrived, Mr. Rayburn said he wanted to weigh his fish. Exhausted, Jack and I assured him that it wasn't necessary. We were certain that it weighed at least twelve pounds. He replied, "Nope, we gotta weigh it." We weighed it, and it was ten and one-half pounds. Mr. Rayburn scowled in a way that only he could scowl and said, "Well, if you boys hadn't bounced that fish around so much in the pickup coming back here it would have weighed twelve pounds! It's your damn fault!" And that ended the conversation.

After we returned to Uvalde, I noticed that Mr. Rayburn had become very quiet and contemplative. Finally, he said, "Well, I guess I gotta go by there," which we knew was a reference to Mr. Garner's house. "Now look," he declared, "I do not want to stay very long; say as little as you can while we're there. I want to get in and get out and I want you two to shut up." We agreed, of course, and we paid a very quick visit. Thankfully, Mr. Garner was on his best behavior. We had

Here I am with Jack Brooks and Mr. Rayburn, who is wearing my father's hat and proudly showing the fish he caught on the Catarina Ranch. *Briscoe Papers; di_03993.*

I'm showing Mr. Garner the bass Mr. Rayburn caught on the Catarina Ranch. Mr. Rayburn was eager to make the visit with his congressional mentor as short as possible. *Rayburn Papers, CN 11088.*

a picture taken of Mr. Rayburn proudly showing his prized bass to Mr. Garner, himself a dedicated fisherman who could appreciate Mr. Rayburn's catch, even if he did have to tell us about a bigger one he had caught years before.

In November 1961, exactly two years after his visit to Catarina, Mr. Rayburn died. He was seventy-nine years old and he had lived long enough to see a Democrat, John F. Kennedy, back in the White House and his protégé, Lyndon Johnson, elected to the vice presidency. His passing was a major loss to this country. No member of Congress during my lifetime has exceeded Sam Rayburn's record of faithful and accomplished service to his country. And there have been few public servants in American history that could match his reputation for honesty and integrity. Sadly, they don't seem to be making them like Mr. Rayburn any more.

Chapter 9

A RETURN TO POLITICS

AFTER I LEFT THE TEXAS LEGISLATURE in 1956, I did not seek another elective office for almost twelve years. Nevertheless, my interest in Texas politics remained strong, and I stayed active in the affairs of the state Democratic Party. Janey and I attended nearly every Democratic Party state convention in those years when I was not a candidate. Although Dwight Eisenhower had carried Texas in the presidential elections of 1952 and 1956, the Republican Party had negligible influence in Texas at the state level in those days. Instead of a two-party political system, Texas had three factions within one party—the Democratic Party.

Gov. Allan Shivers led the most conservative faction, which was strongly anti-labor union. Its adherents usually voted Republican in the presidential elections. The liberal faction, which supported Ralph Yarborough in his races for governor and for the U.S. Senate, considered themselves the true party loyalists. The Yarborough faction was allied closely with the labor unions, and it always supported the Democratic candidate for president. A third faction, which was led by Sam Rayburn and Lyndon Johnson, was more moderate and tended to vote with the conservatives at the state level and the so-called loyalists at the national level. Although we had good friends in each group and it was difficult sometimes to stay with the loyalist side, Janey and I usually sided with the Rayburn/Johnson faction.

LBJ

I first became acquainted with Lyndon Johnson in 1948, when he ran against Coke Stevenson for the Democratic nomination for the U.S. Senate. I was too deeply involved in my own legislative race to pay much attention to Lyndon's race, but I did vote for him. Much has been written and said about Lyndon's controversial victory in that year. I have nothing to add to that famous story except to note that counting votes in my home state, especially in South Texas and East Texas, has frequently been a mystical process in close elections. Certainly the stories Mr. Garner told me about the old political bosses and his own elections, as well as the problem Mr. Sterling experienced when he was defeated for reelection, provided me with ample evidence of just how tricky our system of voting can get. The episode in Florida during the 2000 election indicated that Texas is not the only state where vote counting can be complicated.

I really did not get to know Lyndon Johnson very well until he came through Uvalde in 1952 during one of his periodic swings through the state to visit with voters. He was not up for reelection to the Senate until 1954, but that didn't matter because Lyndon was always campaigning. Part of his success, of course, was that he never stopped campaigning. I admired how disciplined he was in that way.

I got a first-hand view of Lyndon in action during that visit. I received a telephone call to pick him up at the Uvalde airport, where he arrived in a private plane in which he and the pilot were the only passengers. When Lyndon got into my car, I noticed that his hand was badly swollen from shaking hands during the previous days. Despite his objections, I took him to my physician, Dr. Ray Eads, who applied some ointment and bandaged his hand. We then drove to the Kincaid Hotel, which Lyndon remembered correctly as the gathering place in town for coffee breaks and lunch. You could always find a group of locals in the shop chatting and sharing news over cups of coffee. Lyndon went from table to table visiting with everyone and listening to their concerns.

When he had talked to everyone in the coffee shop, I took him to the *Uvalde Leader-News* office to be interviewed by the publisher,

This photograph of me with Mr. Garner and Sen. Lyndon Johnson was taken during LBJ's overnight visit to Uvalde in 1954. *Photograph courtesy of the* Uvalde Leader-News *Collection, El Progresso Memorial Library Archives.*

Harry Hornby. After the interview, we paid a visit to Mr. Garner, where he and Lyndon had a good political talk. We finished the day at the Uvalde High School auditorium, where Lyndon gave a rousing speech to a crowd of town folk and then answered questions. It was a masterful performance by a natural politician working in his native element.

Afterward, Janey and I took him to our Frio River Ranch for dinner and to spend the night. We had just added a little guestroom to our house, and we had put a folding bed in it. Unfortunately, the bed was too short for the senator, who was well over six feet in height. Apparently, his feet hung over the end of the bed all night. At some point in the middle of the night, Lyndon needed to visit the bathroom. It was a little difficult to find the bathroom from the guestroom, and Lyndon couldn't locate the lightswitch. Trying to make his way through the dark, he walked into a wall and bumped his face rather hard. It was a miserable night for him, and the next morning at breakfast he proceeded to tell Janey and me all about it.

After breakfast, Janey and I agreed to drive Lyndon to Kerrville, about eighty miles northeast of Uvalde, where he was to attend a noon civic club meeting with the prominent rancher Scott Schreiner. Before we went in that direction, however, I reminded Lyndon that Dr. Eads wanted him to come back to treat his hand and change the bandage. That did not fit into his scheme of things, but I insisted, and, since I was driving, we returned to Uvalde over his somewhat strenuous objections. Dr. Eads treated his hand despite Lyndon's protests. We drove him to Kerrville in time for his meeting, and then we took him to his ranch on the Pedernales River near Stonewall. His wonderful wife, Lady Bird, put us up for the night in one of their guesthouses. Lyndon never stopped. That night he went out to some local hall to make yet another speech.

Janey and I enjoyed those two days with Lyndon immensely. It was the first and only time we had an opportunity to be alone with him for an extended period of time. Lyndon was very easy to be with because he never quit talking. There was never any worrying about what to say. And I don't think Lyndon ever had a conversation with anybody without an intent and purpose. He was not one for small talk. Instead, he tested a number of his legislative ideas on us and soaked up all the information we had about how the people out in our part of Texas felt about a wide range of issues.

Later, I supported Lyndon's reelection to the U.S. Senate in 1954, his race for the vice presidency in 1960, and his election to the presidency in 1964. I thought Lyndon was an outstanding president. I was unhappy about his decision not to run for reelection in 1968, but I certainly understood it. I was never in Lyndon's inner circle like John Connally. I'm not sure if I was in the second circle or the third circle of LBJ's friends, but I was out there somewhere. He had lots of circles, of course. Lyndon was an interesting fellow in every way. He always liked to have people around, and he never wanted to be alone. There are individuals who need to be by themselves sometime, but Lyndon always struck me as someone who just couldn't stand to be alone. Maybe it's just that he liked to talk, and that's hard to do when you're by yourself.

PRICE DANIEL AND JOHN B. CONNALLY

With three active and vocal factions struggling for control of the Texas Democratic Party, state political conventions quite often were very tumultuous, exciting, and freewheeling affairs during the 1950s and 1960s. Despite the rambunctious nature of those gatherings, Janey and I always enjoyed them. They were never dull. No group of people could fight harder among themselves and generate more heated rhetoric than Texas Democrats in those days. I remember one especially fractious state convention when Price Daniel was governor. I was the parliamentarian, so I was up at the front table near the podium. I remember that we had to get the police out to protect the speakers on the podium from the delegates. When it came time to end the convention, we literally had to pull the plug on all the microphones. It was the only way we could stop the speech-making.

Janey and I supported Price Daniel in his three successful races for governor in 1956, 1958, and 1960. Price was a moderate Democrat and a decent man who operated independent of the three factions. He and his wife, Jean, had stayed with us at the Catarina Ranch, and we were good friends. Harry Hornby, the newspaper publisher in Uvalde, had been Daniel's classmate at Baylor University, and he was very close to him. In 1962 there was speculation that he might run for a fourth term. I was close enough to Price to ask him if he was going to run again. I needed to know, because if he wanted to run for a fourth term, I would support him. If not, I needed to decide on another candidate. But I couldn't get an answer out of Price. He just kept putting off the decision. Along with many others, I just concluded that he was not going to run again.

Assuming that Price wasn't going to be a candidate, I decided to support John B. Connally, who had resigned his post as Secretary of the Navy in the Kennedy administration to return to Texas to run for governor. I had met Connally during one of Lyndon Johnson's campaigns for the Senate. Connally had not yet announced his candidacy, but I knew that he had decided to run. In early December 1961, soon after I committed to Connally, I learned that he and his inner circle were looking for a private location to plan the campaign. I offered to host the meeting at our Catarina Ranch headquarters. Catarina is a perfect site for a private gathering because it is remote, and it has a lighted, paved landing strip, which makes it easy to get to by airplane. We had plenty of room for visitors, and we had a good cook. About fifteen people attended, including Austin attorney Frank Erwin, Dallas attorney Bob Strauss, Congressman Joe Kilgore, Dallas businessman Eugene Locke, state Rep. Ben Barnes, and John Connally's brother, Merrill. That was the first time most of us had met Barnes, who was a very young freshman legislator.

Connally's main objective at that meeting was to make certain that he had the absolute support of those individuals in attendance, which he did. I remember that most of the members of the group feared that a liberal attorney from Houston, Don Yarborough, who was closely aligned with labor, might be able to win the Democratic primary. We were aware that Yarborough would have the full support of the liberal-labor faction led by Mrs. Frankie Randolph, Maj. J. R. Parten, Bernard Rapoport, and Walter Hall. Yarborough would not lack money, and he would benefit from having the same last name as U.S. Sen. Ralph Yarborough, although they weren't related. He had labor's

John Connally, center, with Jack Valenti, right, during the 1962 campaign for governor. *Center for American History UT Texas Student Publications, Inc., Photographs; di_03940.*

active support, and labor was much stronger and effective politically then in Texas than it is today.

At that meeting in Catarina, we laid out a plan for the campaign. We decided how much money we needed to raise, who was going to raise the money, and generally what individual roles we each would play. The campaign really began as soon as everyone departed from Catarina. A few days after our meeting, on December 6, 1961, Connally announced his candidacy to the press.

Shortly thereafter, Price Daniel surprised us all by announcing that he would run again. That put many of us in an embarrassing and painful position. Price was very unhappy. I couldn't blame him for feeling that way, but he just waited too long to make his decision. I believe that one of the reasons why he ultimately lost the primary election to Connally was because he delayed his announcement until it was too late. Too many of his key supporters had already made commitments, thinking that he wasn't going to run. I believe that was a critical factor in his losing because he was a popular, highly regarded governor. John Connally was relatively unknown to most Texans. His initial polls indicated that he was supported by only 4 percent of the voters.

I worked almost full time in the Connally campaign. I flew Connally and his campaign staff all over Texas in my Beechcraft Bonanza airplane. Although it was exhausting physically, I had a lot of fun. The experience was so enjoyable that it made me realize that I might like to make my own statewide race as a candidate.

John Connally, of course, won the governor's race in 1962. John was a very effective governor. He had excellent political instincts. John was a charismatic person who loved having an audience. I think he was a greater actor as a political figure than Ronald Reagan. Actually, John would have been a tremendous success if he had gone into professional acting. He was that good. During his student days at the University of Texas, John had been head of the Curtain Club, the student drama group. He was quite an actor. He could take a subject that he didn't know a thing about and make people believe he was an expert. He had that kind of unique ability.

John believed that to be a successful political candidate, one has to pick enemies and then keep them. You have to have some political whipping posts that you can contrast yourself with in front of the voters. It's an effective method, and many people have used it and made it work. That's what John Connally did with Ralph Yarborough and his liberal followers. Ralph was a good and decent Christian gentleman, but John picked Ralph to be his enemy, and he demonized him to the greatest extent that he could. And he made it work for him. Although I never supported Ralph in his various campaigns, I always respected his integrity and tenacity.

John had a lot of ability and a tremendous personality. He also had the ego to go with it. Some people might even say that he was arrogant. I think even John would have admitted that there might have been a little bit of arrogance in him. Let's just say that he was not short of self-confidence. For whatever reasons, John never supported me when I ran for governor, but even in the later years when for some reason we weren't getting along very well, I always enjoyed being with him. He was really a fun kind of a fellow to be around. And I always thought it was because we understood each other.

I was governor when John announced in 1973 that he would leave the Democratic Party to become a Republican. There were a few people that I think he felt like he had to call before making his announcement. As governor of Texas, I was one of them. So, John called and told me he was going to break the news that morning. I tried to dissuade him, which was a waste of time because he'd already made up his mind. I could see his point of view, however, which was that he had a bright political future in the Republican Party. His relationship with President Nixon, which was close, really directed his decision. I was convinced at the time that Nixon, who was at the beginning of his second term, would back John as his successor. I don't think there's any doubt about that. At the time when John switched parties, Nixon was riding high. If it hadn't have been for Watergate and Nixon's resignation, Connally would have been the designated heir and the beneficiary of Nixon's influence, which was tremendous at the time. Nixon was riding about as high in the saddle as anyone ever rode when he caused his own downfall. Because of events beyond John's control, the party switch didn't work out for him.

THE FIRST CAMPAIGN FOR GOVERNOR

In November 1967 John Connally announced that he would not run for a fourth term as governor in 1968. With John out of the campaign, the governor's race suddenly seemed wide open. This proved to be too great a temptation for me to ignore. As I've said before, I had dreamed of serving as governor of Texas ever since that night I spent sleeping in the Sam Houston bed back when Ross Sterling was governor and I was a child.

I was forty-four years old, and my energy level was very high, so I decided that 1968, with no incumbent in the race, looked like my chance to make a successful bid for the governor's office. To be honest, I also missed being in an elected office, and I yearned to return.

The desire to run for elected office can be similar to having a fever, and it is a highly contagious condition. It's not very difficult to diagnose the condition, but it is hard, if not impossible, to cure. I should have stayed in the legislature back in 1956. I missed my life as a legislator terribly after I left. But in those first months after my father's death, I thought for certain that my political life was finished.

In 1968, however, my personal business affairs were in excellent order, and my highly successful partnership with Red Nunley meant that the ranches would be in good shape while I concentrated on the campaign. To be candid, I realized that the ranches probably would be in better shape with me out of the way. Red was going to run the business anyway, no matter what I did! And Red liked the idea of my running. He was very supportive.

Nine other individuals felt the same way that I did about the governor's race being wide-open, and they soon jumped into the Democratic primary campaign. The candidates included my former legislative colleague Preston Smith, labor union favorite Don Yarborough, former attorney general Waggoner Carr, Houston attorney John Hill, and a Connally associate, Eugene Locke. Despite the crowded field, I felt that my chances of winning the primary were excellent. I knew that I wasn't well-known throughout the state, but most of the other candidates weren't that well-known either. Although Preston Smith had served as lieutenant governor since 1962, it was no secret that he and John Connally had not gotten along well. Preston really was not one of the Connally crowd, so I doubted that Connally's supporters would swing over to him. Waggoner Carr was not a Connally ally either.

I made my announcement that I was a candidate for governor in the Democratic Party primary on January 25, 1968. We held the announcement event in front of the porch of John Nance Garner's house, the very porch that served as my roller skating rink when I was a child. Mr. Garner had died at the age of ninety-nine just two months earlier. Borrowing one of Mr. Garner's statements, I declared that "there are just two things to this government, as I see it. The first is to safeguard the lives and property of our people. The second is to insure that each of us has a chance to work out his destiny according to his talents." I stressed that my campaign would be for better law enforcement, improved schools, accelerated road construction, reduction of air and water pollution, and expansion of the tourist industry. I opened my state campaign headquarters in my father's old wool and mohair warehouse.

I informed the press that I had talked to John Connally about the campaign and that he had assured me of his neutrality. Naively, as it turned out, I also declared that I would have the support of John Connally's friends. Afterward, I flew in my airplane to Austin to hold another press conference and to pay my filing fee.

Soon after I announced my candidacy, Alfred Petsch from Fredericksburg came to Uvalde and told me that I shouldn't run. He feared that the same thing that had happened to Mr. Sterling when he was governor would happen to me. Alfred Petsch had been in the legislature when Mr. Sterling was governor. He said, "Dolph, you'll go broke. If you get elected you'll go broke just like Mr. Sterling did." He had been a strong supporter of Mr. Sterling's. I appreciated his concerns, but I knew that the real culprit behind Governor Sterling's bankruptcy was the Depression.

My main strategy in 1968 was to become better known to the voters. I thought that I could generate enough publicity by traveling around the state and by advertising. I believed that I could run my campaign the way campaigns had been conducted twenty years before, by making as many speeches as possible all over the state. I worked hard, but Texas had grown too much in population. It wasn't like a legislative race. I couldn't knock on every door. Times had changed, and I misjudged the situation very seriously.

Janey supported my decision to run, but I think she read the political situation more realistically than I did. She knew that it would be a very difficult uphill fight. I was much more optimistic. I thought I had a lot more support out in the state than I actually had. For example, I assumed that I would get the endorsement of the influential Harte-Hanks newspaper in San Angelo, but I didn't. Because of my business activities in San Antonio, I thought that I was strong there. My work in San Antonio, however, failed to generate as many votes as I thought it should have. The fact is that my campaign was not very good, and there was no one to blame for that but me.

Campaigning for the Democratic nomination for governor in 1968. *Briscoe Papers.*

I don't have a lot of memories about specific events during that campaign. That's the way campaigns tend to be, just a blur of towns, meetings, and people. I do remember, however, that Eugene Locke, who turned out to be John Connally's candidate, had this very catchy campaign jingle. It seemed like every time I turned on the radio, I heard that silly song. He certainly had more radio and television commercials than I or the other candidates did.

I wound up in fourth place on election day, which was deeply disappointing. Don Yarborough, who had the unified support of the liberal-labor union faction of the party, came in first place, but he failed to attract enough votes to win the nomination. The rest of us spilt the moderate and conservative vote, but Preston Smith received enough of those votes to finish in second place and make the runoff. Waggoner Carr finished in third place. I received about 226,000 votes. Supported by a united group of moderates and conservatives, Preston defeated Yarborough in the runoff.

After I lost the election, I realized that the business lobby had lined up behind Preston, and that had given him the edge. The business lobby had worked with him as lieutenant governor, and he was a known quantity. He'd been in the state government for a long time. They thought they could continue to work with him. The word they would have used to describe Preston was "dependable." And so they got behind him.

I also realized that I had started my campaign too late, and I had badly underestimated the importance of Preston's six years as lieutenant governor and the critical name recognition that gave him with the voters. Preston had spent years on the road building his organization, while I spent only a few months on my campaign. I was upset about losing, but I wasn't upset that Preston won. I got to know him well during my legislative years. Preston was a typically sound West Texan and a good man.

I learned a lot about conducting a state campaign in 1968, however, and I was able to use that knowledge effectively when I ran again in 1972. The number one lesson was that I had to be better known. As soon as I lost the primary in 1968, I immediately decided that I would try again. I just didn't know if it would be in 1970 or 1972. It just depended on how things looked in 1970 and whether or not Preston Smith would run again. But I knew that I needed to lay the groundwork immediately. I had a lot of work to do. I also knew that I had to attract to my side some of those who had played important roles in my opponents' campaigns in 1968.

I guess it was difficult to accept defeat. Any time you lose a political campaign, there is a period of depression afterward, regardless of how hard you try not to let it happen. And that was true in 1968 even though I probably should have known that I couldn't win when I got into it. But I didn't see it that way at the beginning and didn't see it during the campaign. Those bad feelings didn't last long. I realized that if I was ever going to make it to the Governor's Mansion I had to get over the defeat and start working right away. I would not wait until the very last moment to get rolling the next time. I learned that I had better put together an organization that I could depend on in every county. I didn't have much of a grassroots organization in 1968.

I began to travel the state as much as possible to become better known and to lay the local organizational groundwork to run again. Obviously, running a statewide effort is quite different from campaigning in four rural counties. And the magnitude of running for public office in a state as large as Texas is quite a challenge, to say the least. So I had to take advantage of every opportunity I had to go somewhere, make an appearance, make some friends, try to influence some people, and try to get going. I accepted every speaking engagement I received. By the fall of 1970, I was giving four or five speeches every week to local civic and business groups around the state. I had a steady stream of guests to spend the weekends at Catarina. I attended every kind of event that I was invited to and quite a few that I wasn't. I knew that I had to keep my name in front of people.

I considered running in 1970 against Preston Smith. I did not rule out entering the race until very close to filing time. I decided that it would not be smart to run against an incumbent governor who wanted a second term. Unless there is some scandal or other controversy affecting the governor's popularity, it had been the tradition in Texas when the terms were only two years in length to grant a governor at least two terms in office. I also felt that I needed more time to prepare for a campaign.

By the fall of 1970, I had made my decision to run for governor in the next Democratic primary in May 1972, no matter what anyone else decided to do. I told the *Dallas Morning News* in December 1970 that "what others may end up doing is really their business. I'm looking after my own affairs." Of course, that decision was made in tandem with Janey, who supported it absolutely. Janey was always that way. If I wanted to do it, she wanted to do it. There was never any argument about it. There might have been some discussion at first, but if after we discussed it and I still wanted to do it, then it was fine with her. I couldn't have had a more supportive wife.

I planned to enter a race for governor in the Democratic primary that I knew would include as major candidates my friend Preston Smith, the incumbent who was seeking reelection to a third term, and Ben Barnes, the very popular lieutenant governor. Eventually, Frances "Sissy" Farenthold, a liberal state representative from Corpus Christi, would become the fourth major candidate for governor.

In early 1971, some newspaper columnists reported that Lyndon Johnson had asked me not to run for governor in 1972 against Ben Barnes, a protégé of John Connally's who had been elected lieutenant governor in 1968. The truth is that Johnson never discussed the governor's race with me. I certainly did not get any encouragement to run for governor from any of Johnson's associates. But Lyndon never said anything to me about it. He did endorse Ben Barnes for governor in a widely reported speech, however, and it was obvious that his support for Barnes was strong.

There also was some speculation in the press that Johnson and Barnes were trying to persuade me to run for the U.S. Senate against the incumbent, Republican John Tower, instead of running for governor. But I had no interest in running for the U.S. Senate. I did not want to live in Washington, D.C. At that time, my children were still in school in Texas. Being a member of Congress is a more than full-time job, and you lose control of your time completely. It was not a practical thing for me to do.

Of course, I didn't discourage any of these rumors. I just let the rumors flow because it kept my name in circulation.

Several of Barnes's friends tried to persuade me not to run for governor. The *Houston Chronicle* even planted stories that I might run for lieutenant governor and that Barnes's supporters would help me if I did. It was clear to me that the *Chronicle*, which was managed by close friends of John Connally and Ben Barnes, was sending a message to me from the Barnes camp.

Finally, Ben Barnes personally tried to persuade me not to run. I met Ben in Austin for lunch while the legislature was still in session. Ben is a likable person, and he is easy to visit with. There is absolutely nothing abrasive about him or anything like that, so we had a nice visit. And as it has turned out, we have remained on good terms ever

Ben Barnes when he was lieutenant governor of Texas. *UT Texas Student Publications, Inc., Photographs; di_03939.*

since and never had any real bad feelings about it. There are always hard feelings after a campaign but most of the time they don't last too long. That was the only time that he and I actually talked about it, and that was really basically all we talked about that day. He was going to run, and it was only reasonable that he didn't want opposition.

He wanted to clear the field as much as he could. I told him he ought to run for the Senate instead. I was encouraging him. I thought that if a fellow his age, and he was pretty young at the time, could get elected to the U.S. Senate, he had the opportunity to accumulate a lot of seniority. The odds would have been that if he had won, he would have had a secure seat. Most incumbent U.S. Senators from Texas stay there for a long time. Then he would have had an opportunity in the United States Senate to become a vice presidential nominee. Even in those days, a Democrat from Texas would have an extremely difficult if not an impossible time getting the Democratic nomination for president. Unfortunately, Lloyd Bentsen Jr. found that out in 1976.

The more I was pressured to get out of the governor's race, the more confident I became about my chances for success. It was clear that my potential opposition believed that I had a decent chance to get elected, and that gave me some hope. Although I decided to wait until the early fall of 1971 to make a formal announcement of my candidacy for governor, I made it clear in several newspaper interviews during the summer of 1971 that I was in the race.

That summer of 1971, as I prepared for the coming campaign, my associates and I believed that there were large numbers of voters who could be attracted to a campaign that was moderately conservative as well as anti-Austin establishment. I also felt that the voters would respond favorably to my call for less government and no new taxes. I could see that ordinary Texans were fed up with the never-ending growth of government at all levels and the resulting increase in their tax burden. In fact, it was evident that a tax rebellion was spreading across the country. Although Preston Smith had been governor for four years, he was not part of the Connally-Barnes group that held the real power in state government. That group had expanded the size and power of state government, and I believed that Texans were no longer enamored with activist, big spending, big government—at the national or state levels. The Connally-Barnes crowd had raised state taxes, and it was clear that they would continue raising them. I felt that more and more voters wanted less, not more government. That was one of the reasons for Nixon's election in 1968.

Despite my belief that my no new taxes and limited government message would appeal to many Texans, I realized that it was going to be difficult to compete against Ben Barnes. I did not take Preston Smith for granted, but I realized fully that Barnes was my most formidable opponent. The odds were heavily in his favor because he had the LBJ–John Connally political establishment solidly behind him. That meant that he also had the support of most of the state's newspapers. And he would have all of the money that he would need. Barnes had everything going for him. He was the type of charismatic candidate whose personal attractiveness could easily divert the attention of many voters away from the substantive issues. Although I was betting that my message would be heard and that it would resonate with the voters, it was clear that I was facing an uphill fight just to get their attention. But I felt that if I could make it into a runoff against Barnes, I had a fighting chance to win. I also believed that the Connally-Barnes crowd had become arrogant and openly acted as though they were entitled to hold power. I thought that the voters might resent that arrogance and the potential it harbored for corruption. I had no inkling, of course, that corruption was, in fact, ready to bare its ugly head and turn the campaign upside down.

By the end of the summer, the political environment in Texas had changed in an unanticipated and dramatic way. A major scandal in state government suddenly threatened to turn the Austin establishment upside down. I was eager to get on the campaign trail.

Chapter 10

BECOMING GOVERNOR

The Campaign of 1972

ꙮ

IN JANUARY 1971, the Securities and Exchange Commission (SEC) filed a civil suit in the court of federal Judge Sarah T. Hughes claiming that Houston banker and land developer Frank Sharp and some of his associates had engaged in multiple incidents of stock fraud. Former Texas attorney general Waggoner Carr was the only well-known politician named in the suit.

A few days later, the SEC submitted papers to Judge Hughes revealing that Preston Smith, House Speaker Gus Mutscher, two other members of the legislature, and two legislative aides had enjoyed quick and large profits from unusual deals with Frank Sharp. Smith and Elmer Baum, chair of the state Democratic Executive Committee, had received a large unsecured loan from Frank Sharp's bank. They had used the loan to buy stock in Sharp's National Bankers Life Insurance Company of Dallas, which they subsequently sold to a Jesuit school in Houston for a quick $62,500 profit. Sharp persuaded the Jesuits to purchase Preston's stock at above market rates. Mutscher had borrowed even larger sums from Sharp, also without collateral, and he had reaped financial profits from selling stock to the Jesuits. Preston, Gus Mutscher, and the other officials had made these deals at the same time the legislature was considering banking bills that Sharp had requested. The legislature passed the bills with much haste and without benefit of committee hearings during a special session in September 1969.

The story continued to unfold slowly through the spring and summer, reaching a climax in September 1971, when a Travis County grand jury indicted House Speaker Gus Mutscher, state Sen. Tommy Shannon, and two of Mutscher's assistants. The grand jury indicted Mutscher for bribery, while all four were indicted for conspiracy to accept a bribe. The grand jury charged that they had conspired with Frank Sharp to pass two bills designed to establish a deposit insurance system for state banks that would allow Sharp's bank to cancel its Federal Deposit Insurance Corporation coverage and thus avoid regulation by federal bank examiners.

THE IMPACT OF SHARPSTOWN

News of those indictments received statewide attention. As I remember it, when the story broke I was in Houston making plans for my formal announcement as a candidate for governor in the Democratic primary. It was obvious that the stock fraud affair, which soon became known as the Sharpstown scandal, would have a significant impact on the primary. My advisors and I assumed that Preston's entanglement in the scandal would damage his chances for reelection. Preston had vetoed the banking bills after their passage during a special session of the legislature, but he had been hurt badly by the revelation that he had been involved with Sharp in a fast-buck stock deal. Neither Preston nor Ben Barnes was indicted, but it seemed at the very least that both had questionable relationships with Sharp and his legislation. Sharp's bills had passed with haste through the Senate, which Barnes presided over as the powerful lieutenant governor. Barnes explained later that he was not presiding on the day the legislation passed, but anyone who knows how the Senate works knows that no bill of any consequence makes it through that body without the lieutenant governor being fully aware of it.

The 1972 governor's race was a great example of how the direction of a political campaign can be completely turned around by unanticipated developments. For me, the Sharpstown issue was an extremely lucky event from a political strategy point of view. I was a major beneficiary of the scandal. It handed me a hot campaign issue that

The calm before the storm: Gus Mutscher, Preston Smith, LBJ, and Ben Barnes in Brenham, Texas, in 1970 before the Sharpstown scandal became news. *Texas State Library and Archives Commission Prints and Photographs Collection.*

attracted much more attention than the other points in my platform. As an outsider not connected to the Austin political establishment, the call to restore public confidence in state government was an especially good issue for me to pursue. My record was strong in this respect, because as a legislator during the 1950s I had pushed for the investigation that helped to expose the veterans land scandal.

It was a sad situation, of course, for our state. The Sharpstown scandal became the symbol of what people thought was wrong with state government. It encouraged the view that with enough money you could get anything you wanted from the legislature and that the state government was for sale.

I made my gubernatorial candidacy official at a press conference at the Capitol in Austin on September 29, 1971. In my announcement, I stressed my belief that there was no need for new taxes and that the state could operate within the income generated by the existing tax structure. That message, however, was not the part of my speech that

Frances "Sissy" Farenthold. *Farenthold (Frances "Sissy") Papers, Center for American History; di_03958.*

caught the attention of the press. What made the headlines was my demand that Ben Barnes explain to the people of Texas why the special legislation for Frank Sharp was given such VIP treatment in the Texas Senate. I had served public notice that the Sharpstown scandal would define the coming campaign. An interesting point about the Sharpstown scandal was that it was not as extensive or as significant as other scandals previously affecting state government in Texas. It's just that the timing was so crucial. The other scandals didn't occur during a heavily contested political primary.

As the campaign picked up momentum in the first weeks of 1972, it became obvious that the fallout from the Sharpstown scandal was taking its toll on Preston Smith and Ben Barnes. I made certain to mention the scandal in every speech that I made. Of course, Frances "Sissy" Farenthold, who also was running against the Austin establishment, did the same thing. She was benefiting from the scandal as much as I was. Sissy Farenthold was a member of the state legislature from Corpus Christi. I did not know Mrs. Farenthold, but I knew some of her kinfolk, including Judge Dudley Daugherty, who was a leading citizen of the South Texas town of Beeville. I served in the legislature with his son, Dudley Daugherty Jr.

I really didn't pay much attention to Sissy Farenthold during the first primary campaign. Ben Barnes and Preston Smith were the people to beat. Mrs. Farenthold wasn't a factor in my strategy. As the campaign went along, however, it was obvious from the polls that she was getting stronger. For one thing, she quickly became the preferred candidate of the liberal wing of the Democratic Party. Although that was a minority faction, it was not inconsequential because the moderate/conservative side of the party usually attracted several candidates as it did in 1972. That made the liberal side, if they had only one candidate, a much more significant factor in the primary.

Before the Sharpstown scandal broke, I had not received any major newspaper editorial endorsements. Sharpstown changed that situation. My first significant endorsements came from the *Austin American-Statesman* and the *Waco News-Tribune*, both owned by the Fentress newspaper company. The editors, Harry Provence in Waco and Sam Wood in Austin, wrote editorials endorsing me for governor.

They stressed that I offered "fresh, untarnished leadership" that the state needed to restore the confidence of the people. Those endorsements were a tremendous help. Fortunately, both of those editors knew me well, and they believed in me.

Harry Provence and Sam Wood were highly respected in the newspaper industry in Texas. Both had spent their lives dedicated to using their newspapers to build a better Texas. And they put out good newspapers that reported events as they saw them, and their editorial pages were vocal about how things should be. There is no way that I could have had a more important boost in the campaign than that. At that time, Harry Provence was chairman of the Texas Coordinating Board for Higher Education, and he knew what was going on in state government. I think he and Sam Wood were ready for an end to the high-flying days that had existed since John Connally's administration.

The Fentress endorsement caused other newspapers to take another look at my campaign. It was especially important to have the endorsement of the Austin newspaper because all of the political reporters for the other major newspapers in the state read the capital city newspaper. That endorsement sent a shock wave through the establishment in Austin and throughout the state. Actually, it took some courage for the Fentress newspapers to go against the political establishment. John Connally had done a great job of getting the establishment, including Lyndon Johnson, behind Ben Barnes. In those days, that was a very powerful group, and it would have been easy for the Fentress newspapers just to go along.

I remember meeting with the editorial boards of all of the major newspapers in Texas. In those meetings, I tried to make it clear that I was not a one-issue candidate with a single-minded focus on the Sharpstown scandal. The members of those editorial boards also wanted to know my views on the state's fiscal policies. I stressed that I was running on a pledge of no new taxes. With one exception, every newspaper editorial board argued that it would be impossible for me to hold the line on taxes. Every administration since Coke Stevenson's in the 1940s had increased taxes. Many of the editors simply assumed the attitude that I didn't know what I was talking about.

I knew, however, that Texas had a robust economy and that all signs pointed to continued growth. Our oil and gas production was expanding tax revenue rapidly, and other sources of state income were increasing. I could see no reason for additional taxes. We were in great fiscal shape, and I felt that the increasing revenues from our existing tax system could easily accommodate whatever growth in spending that we might need to take care of state needs. That was my point, but I really wasn't getting it across. The news media didn't believe me. They thought my no new taxes pledge was an idle campaign promise. I can't blame the press too much for dismissing my pledge. After all, other candidates had made the same pledge in the past and had broken it once they were in office. I believe the doubt was based less on questions about my truthfulness and more on the general view that I simply did not know what I was talking about.

THE CAMPAIGN

As my campaign built momentum, I had some talented people on my side to help it along. Calvin Guest, who later became chairman of the Democratic Party, played a key role in building my team. Calvin's strengths included his capacity for hard work, his dedication to the job, and his loyalty to the cause. Calvin also had a tremendously high degree of good old common sense. That is a rarer commodity in politics than you might think. Howard Richards, a young and enterprising attorney practicing law with Chilton O'Brien in Beaumont, organized the campaign in Southeast Texas and later joined my personal staff. To help with my speechwriting and overall public relations and advertising, I hired the Deloss Walker firm in Tennessee. Walker was highly skilled and his firm did a great job.

Of course, my beloved Janey was the most important member of my team. She made a major contribution to all of my speeches. Janey was an excellent judge of people. Whenever I went against her judgment, I always regretted it later. Not just every now and then, but every single time. She was a much better judge of people than I am. She just had a natural skill when it came to sizing people up. Janey could see through the phonies and crass opportunists. It was impossible to fool her. That kind of perception is perhaps the most valuable asset you can have when you're running for political office. I always tested my ideas with her first. I considered her opinions to be better than mine in every case.

Just as I never would have been elected to the legislature without Janey, I never would have been elected governor of Texas without her. She campaigned for me on her own, and then we campaigned a lot together. Janey campaigned as hard as I did. She never gave out or got tired, and she never quit working.

Our three children, however, did not like my decision to run for

Janey, the tireless campaigner, in 1972. *Briscoe Papers, Box 255; di_04105.*

The official 1972 campaign portrait of our family at the Frio Ranch. *Briscoe Papers; di_03949.*

governor. Our son and daughters are very private people who have no desire for public acclaim or recognition. Our oldest daughter, Janey, was born in 1950, and Dolph III, who goes by "Chip," was born in 1953. Our youngest daughter, Cele, was born in 1956, and she was still in high school in Uvalde in 1972. Janey and Chip were students at the University of Texas at Austin. Even today, they probably still wish I hadn't run for governor. But once I jumped in, they couldn't have been more supportive. They campaigned out on their own. We had campaign bus trips out of Uvalde that our kids went on. I admit that they were reluctant campaigners at first, but I think they enjoyed it to some extent once they started. It just wasn't easy for them to start. It really wasn't their thing.

The campaign was tough on the kids because they had to bear the personal attacks on their father that political campaigns generate too often. Before we began the campaign, Janey and I expected a certain amount of personal criticism, although we didn't expect some of the dirty tactics that our opponents employed. We had been through it all before, but the 1968 campaign was relatively free of dirt. It's hard enough when you are the candidate and the target of personal attacks, but it is especially difficult if you're a kid and your parents are being attacked. I well remember how much it hurt when I was a kid and I thought that somebody had criticized my mother or my father.

But I never really went through anything like my kids did. So it's difficult for me to realize just how tough it is when a person puts his family in that kind of position. And that's what a person does when he or she becomes a candidate for a statewide office or, certainly, a national office. I didn't realize fully what a strain I was putting on my family. My father never ran for office, so I did not go through it as a kid. I know what it is like to be criticized in public, and there's nothing easy about that. I was in politics for a good while, so you might think that after all the years, personal criticism would not bother me, but it did. I've known people who were in politics a lot longer than I have been, and it never stopped bothering them. I know it bothered Lyndon Johnson all his life. You think you might get iron-hard skin or something, but you don't. What you have to do, however, is learn how to act as though personal criticism doesn't bother you. I think I succeeded at that eventually. At least I hope that I did.

In our case, the children also had to endure personal attacks aimed at their mother, and that is especially tough. When they start criticizing your wife, that really gets under your skin. That is something that Ronald Reagan and Bill Clinton and their children had to endure. That really hurts. Janey was the target of the same kind of personal criticism that Nancy Reagan and Hillary Clinton attracted. It was terribly unfair and unwarranted. I'm not talking about criticism of their views about public policy, because that certainly is part of the game. If you can't take that kind of heat, you really have no business in public life. What I'm talking about is *ad hominem* attacks.

There are some things you can control in a campaign, but you can't keep your opponents from engaging in personal attacks. You can do a lot to shield your family, but the fact is that your family reads the paper, and they watch television and listen to the radio. Naturally, they want to know what's happening to their father and mother. And it's not always a pretty picture.

THE ROAD TO "NOWHERE"

A month before the primary election, the polls were indicating that none of the candidates would be able to win the nomination without a runoff election. They also indicated that I had a slight lead. It seemed likely that I would make the runoff. That was when the Barnes campaign panicked and resorted to mudslinging.

The first attack claimed that I had improperly influenced the construction of a thirteen-mile farm-to-market road in Dimmit County that went by my Catarina Ranch. The allegation claimed that it was my personal road to "nowhere." Two Barnes supporters in the state Senate made the allegation and they admitted that one of Barnes's campaign aides had given them the information. The allegation evaporated immediately, however, when the state highway commission issued the facts about the road's construction. The state highway department built the road in the early 1960s, several years after I had left the legislature. The Dimmit County Commissioners Court made the formal request to the state to have the road built. It was the subject of three separate public hearings, and all three members of the highway commission voted to approve it. Traffic on the road averaged one hundred cars a day, while the state average for farm-to-market roads was thirty to forty cars a day. It was hardly a "road to nowhere."

As soon as the "road to nowhere" allegation died at birth, the Barnes campaign stooped even lower. They spread the false rumor that I had been treated for a mental illness. Frank Erwin, the politically powerful Austin attorney and University of Texas Board of Regents chairman, was the person behind the rumor. Erwin certainly never admitted that to me, but he did admit it to others. I had known Frank for a number of years. He had attended the meeting at Catarina in 1962 when we started the John Connally campaign. I never could say that I knew Frank well enough to be close to him or anything like that. But I knew him through the years, and I had thought that we were on good terms. I didn't realize we were on the kind of terms that we were.

Erwin attempted to get my private airplane flight logs as evidence that I had gone to the University of Texas Medical Branch in Galveston for psychiatric help. I had never gone anywhere for psychiatric help, so that was easy to disprove. The allegation was so far-fetched that I never did think it had any great deal of effect. I've been fortunate in that I have enjoyed good health, both mental and physical, my entire life. I certainly never needed or sought psychiatric help of any type.

It's not hard to determine their motivation for spreading the rumor. The Barnes camp decided that it was time to gut me. It's that simple. That was about as low as you can get. At that time, I couldn't be certain whether I had Barnes on the run or not. Nevertheless, I thought it was an act of desperation on their part, and I pointed that out in the campaign. Actually, I saw the incident as the first sign that I was causing the Barnes campaign major concern. There was no other reason for them to resort to such a loathsome tactic. But I had to answer the charge and I did. I gave permission to my personal physicians to talk to the press about my private medical history. They certified that I had never had any need for psychiatric care and that I had never been treated for psychiatric problems of any kind.

Erwin's rumormongering about the state of my mental health didn't die easily, despite the complete falseness of the claim. Two years later, when I had a severe kidney infection that forced me to spend a few days in the hospital in San Antonio, the old rumors resurfaced. I had spent nearly a month at my mother's bedside. The day after her funeral in December 1974, I was hit with this terrible infection, which was life-threatening, and I entered the hospital. The combination of the lengthy absence to be with my dying mother and this hospitalization was enough to set the rumors flying. They were widespread enough that I felt it necessary, against the advice of my associates, to hold a press conference as soon as I left the hospital to demonstrate to the press that my problems had been physical, not mental. When I held the press conference, I still felt awful physically. I meant it when I told the reporters that I felt like I had been run over by a truck. Some members of the press ridiculed me for making a public statement

Frank Erwin, chairman of the University of Texas Board of Regents. *Center for American History Prints and Photographs Collection; di_01352.*

denying a rumor that had not been reported in the newspapers, therefore giving publicity to the very charges I was denying. That did not bother me one bit. I believed then, and I believe now that it was important for me to confront the rumors publicly. The rumors were there, I wanted to deal with them directly, and I did. I don't regret having done that.

THE RUNOFF AGAINST FARENTHOLD

On election day, May 6, 1972, I felt that I had an excellent chance to make the runoff. I had always taken it for granted that Ben Barnes would be my opponent. To everyone's shock, including mine, Barnes suffered a decisive defeat. He was eliminated along with Preston Smith. I came in first, with Mrs. Farenthold a distant second, more than 340,000 votes behind me. I don't think anyone had properly gauged how strongly the voters had linked Barnes to the Sharpstown scandal. Sharpstown inspired a lot of Texans to vote for reform. Sissy Farenthold received many of those reform votes, and she made it into the runoff with me. The voters wanted a change, so they swept Preston Smith and Ben Barnes out of office.

I was now facing an opponent in the runoff that I had not anticipated. A runoff campaign is very different from the general primary campaign when you have several opponents. You only have a month to campaign, and the campaign dynamic changes. And in this runoff, even the issues changed. The Sharpstown scandal, which had dominated the first primary, was no longer a factor because neither Sissy Farenthold nor I had been tainted by it. The campaign evolved into the more traditional liberal-versus-conservative confrontation, which focused more on philosophical issues. I believe it would have been easier for me to run against Ben Barnes or Preston Smith than Sissy Farenthold. I had geared my campaign to make maximum use of the Sharpstown scandal. I had planned to hang Sharpstown around Ben Barnes's neck. When he lost, Sharpstown was no longer an issue, and we had an entirely new campaign. I found myself on the defense instead of the offense. That's not where I had planned to be.

Sissy Farenthold's campaign now described me as the establishment candidate. But I had never been in the establishment. The establishment now had to come to me, not the other way around. But the real point here is that she labeled me as the establishment candidate. That allowed her to continue the political strategy she had used in the general primary, because her entire campaign had been anti-establishment. She just substituted Dolph Briscoe for Ben Barnes in her speeches. That's pretty much the way the rest of the runoff campaign went.

I would have preferred not to have a woman to run against. Ask anyone who has ever run against a female. It is tough. It was especially difficult in those days and in this state. Our culture, which is a mix of the old South and the rugged West, demands that you be a gentleman around women. That is certainly the way I was raised. There was a rigid line that you did not cross in your formal relationship with other women. I knew that if I was not careful in my criticisms of Sissy Farenthold, I could be perceived as a bully. You can be a lot more aggressive when you are running against another man.

Sissy Farenthold is also an extremely well educated and intelligent person. She knew what she was doing every step of the way. She knew how to take advantage of everything there was to take advantage of. She was a tough opponent. This was the first election in Texas held after the voting age had been lowered to eighteen years of age. Sissy Farenthold really went after that youth vote. And she was able to take advantage of the environment of reform that dominated the election. As a member of the legislature, Sissy Farenthold had been one of the leaders of the reform coalition known as the "Dirty Thirty" that had rebelled against the power of the Speaker of the House, Gus Mutscher. That gave her a lot of credibility and momentum in the campaign.

Sissy Farenthold did give me a very big break, however. In one widely reported speech, she took the position that the state's elite and legendary police force, the Texas Rangers, should be abolished. When I heard that, I realized that I had been handed a wonderful campaign issue. I am a traditionalist, and I have always viewed the Texas Rangers as a heroic part of our Texas history. To me, they were heroes that brought law and order to many parts of the state during the nineteenth century. In modern Texas, they have become a highly professional police enforcement and investigative agency. As far as I was concerned, there was much truth in the old saying, "One riot; one Ranger." I have always had the greatest admiration for the Texas Rangers.

My respect for the Texas Rangers goes back to the time when I was a kid. Governor Sterling's Chief of Texas Rangers was named Bill Sterling. I got to meet him when I was a child, and I remember him well. He and my father became very good friends. Bill Sterling was an extremely impressive man for whom I had deep respect. Coincidentally, his family in Austin was close to Janey's family, and they also admired Sterling and the Texas Rangers. I was most appreciative of Mrs. Farenthold's remark about abolishing the Texas Rangers, because I knew that most Texans admire them and cherish their legacy as much as I do. She handed me a wonderful issue to use against her.

Sissy Farenthold also challenged me to a series of public debates, but I refused. My campaign staff, especially Deloss Walker, opposed the idea because we were so far ahead in the polls. Walker was insistent about my need to stay away from meetings and presentations that he and his staff had not tightly scripted and controlled. In hindsight, I think that strategy hurt more than it helped. The thinking was that Sissy Farenthold had to debate because she was losing. We did not need to take the risks that are always there when you debate. And we did not want to give her any free publicity. In other words, she had nothing to lose, but we would be taking an unnecessary risk. I agreed with that advice then, but in retrospect, I think it was a mistake. It gave Mrs. Farenthold another issue to use against me: "Why won't Dolph Briscoe debate me?" I didn't like that. I think a lot of people hear a challenge like that and, naturally, they think, "what is that boy afraid of?"

I remember being in Dallas during that runoff campaign. We were going from building to building and walking the streets in Dallas, handing out literature and talking to voters. Some women came up to me and asked, "Why don't you debate Sissy? What's wrong with you? Are you scared or something?" That bothered me a great deal. I really didn't have what I thought was an acceptable answer or at least not one I could be proud of. What do you say to the voters? I'm too far ahead to debate? I wish now that I had accepted her challenge. I regret not doing it.

But you have to remember that at the time debating was not a standard part of campaigning. The damage that Richard Nixon suffered from his debate with John F. Kennedy had a chilling effect on political debates for a number of years. It wasn't until the 1976 campaign that the presidential candidates once again held debates. Johnson refused to debate Barry Goldwater in 1964. Nixon refused to debate in 1968 and 1972. It was not the standard procedure then that it is today.

That race in 1972 against Sissy Farenthold was a mean campaign. I think that was to be expected, given the turmoil of the times, with the war in Vietnam being fought and all of the other social tumult the nation was experiencing. A few days before the runoff election, U.S. Sen. Adlai Stevenson III of Illinois came to Texas to campaign on Farenthold's behalf. Stevenson was chair of the migratory labor subcommittee at the time. He claimed that I was employing so-called "wetback" labor on my ranches, which was not true. Our main ranch, Catarina, is down on the Rio Grande, where the border patrol had a camp and patrolled twenty-four hours a day, seven days a week. And that was with our approval. We needed them there, and we wanted them there. I was able to prove that we were not working illegal immigrants. The border patrol's official records documented that. The federal authorities verified that we had cooperated fully with them in this matter. They even had a key to our ranch gates, and they could come and go at will. We obviously had nothing to hide from them. It would be pretty stupid to have the border patrol camped out on your ranch if you were employing illegal immigrants from Mexico.

At the time, I was so irritated by the Farenthold campaign's tactics that I didn't appreciate how interesting a campaign it must have been to the public. But it was a campaign in which one day I was an anti-establishment candidate and the next day I was an establishment candidate running against a very talented charismatic woman who was appealing to a large block of new baby-boom voters. And all of this occurred after the incumbent governor had been defeated rather decisively, along with the boy wonder of Texas politics, Ben Barnes. These developments had been completely unforeseen by the political pundits.

Despite everything Sissy Farenthold threw at me, however, I did prevail. I received 1,099,993 votes and Sissy Farenthold received 887,665. It was not as close as I had feared it might be, and that gave me a good feeling. The election of 1972 marked the end of the power of the old political guard in Texas that John Connally had created. It was a political earthquake. I was lucky to be a part of it.

THE POLITICAL STRUGGLES OF 1972 CONTINUE

I had won the Democratic nomination for governor, but the struggle was far from finished. As soon as I won the primary, I had to contend with a Texas Democratic Party that was deeply divided among the Sissy Farenthold liberals on the left, the establishment regulars in the center and on the right, and a vocal group of activists on the far right. These factions, of course, supported different candidates for the Democratic presidential nomination. The liberal wing supported U.S. Sen. George McGovern of South Dakota, and the far-right group supported Alabama Gov. George Wallace, who had won forty-five electoral votes in 1968. The center of the party was dominated by a diverse group of moderates and conservatives. Many of the members of this group had been associated with the John Connally–Ben Barnes party establishment. Some of them supported Sen. Henry "Scoop" Jackson of Washington for the presidential nomination, while others were uncommitted.

The leadership of the liberal faction of the party did nothing to try to bring the party together for the general election campaign. They wanted to keep the party as divided as possible. That led to a nasty fight and a bitter time at the state and national conventions. Whatever efforts I made to try to unify our state party were mostly rejected. It really was a tough year.

Roy Orr, the chairman of the state Democratic Executive Committee, volunteered to step aside for a chairman of my selection. Roy and I got along well, but he was a controversial figure in the party, and I wanted to bring in someone who could unite us. There really wasn't any fight over the chair; Roy offered to step aside. At that time it was traditional for the governor to get whoever he wanted for the chair. As the party's nominee for governor, I appointed Calvin Guest, who had served as my campaign manager, to serve as the new chairman. Roy Orr, who was a Dallas County Commissioner, became a good friend and strong supporter of mine.

The George Wallace forces were a very strong presence at the Democratic Party's state convention in San Antonio. Wallace had increased his following in Texas largely on his vocal opposition to the court-mandated busing of children to accelerate racial integration of the public schools. Busing as a means to achieve racial balance was an extremely unpopular concept in Texas. I also thought it was a terrible idea and said as much during my campaign. Wallace had fifty-two delegates, McGovern had forty-one, and Henry Jackson had thirty-two. The Texas delegation that went to the National Democratic Convention in Miami was pretty much divided among all three of the factions.

Unfortunately, I misjudged the situation. I thought we could follow the tradition of the Roosevelt-Garner days, when the delegates to the 1932 Democratic national convention put the interests of Texas over their personal agendas. I believed we could unite when we got to Miami. I was really naive about that. Exactly the opposite happened. I was unprepared for the "what's in it for me" attitude that ran rampant in the delegation. I learned my lesson in Miami, perhaps the hard way, but I certainly learned it. There were those who were only interested in "what position do I get now in the party?" and "if I don't get that position I'm going to do this, that, and the other," all of which further divided and fractionalized the state party.

We had divisiveness and self-interest in spades in Miami. Even before the state convention, I thought that we could bring it together. I hoped that everyone could accept that we can disagree, but we're not going to be disagreeable. It didn't work out that way. The tradition in Texas had been for the state Democratic Party delegation to unite by the time they went to a national convention. We usually had our factional fight at the state convention, and then we pulled together.

Before 1972, of course, members of the state delegation really had to come together because the party convention operated under the unit rule. When we lost the unit rule, we lost that unity. The unit rule was good from the point of view of the state being effective at the national convention. Without the unit rule, the Texas delegation was fractionalized, resulting in a significant loss of influence.

I went to the national convention in Miami as an uncommitted delegate, but I also was a vigorous opponent of Senator McGovern's candidacy. I opposed McGovern for several reasons. I was upset by his harsh and unfair criticism of former President Johnson, who I admired greatly even though he didn't support my bid for the gubernatorial nomination. I believed at the time, and I still believe, that Lyndon was one of the greatest presidents this country has ever had. I felt that as a senator, McGovern had tried to undermine Lyndon in every way that he could. I thought he had behaved in a very cowardly and low manner. McGovern continued to attack Lyndon's handling of the war even after he left the White House.

I deeply resented McGovern's attacks. In my opinion, Lyndon took the blame for a war that he didn't start. He inherited it. I believe the record will show that President Dwight Eisenhower is the person who got us involved by sending the first military advisors. John F. Kennedy increased and expanded an effort that essentially began with Eisenhower. After Kennedy's assassination, Lyndon faced a no-win situation. If he had pulled out, the Republicans would have called him either a coward or a communist. The Republicans would have killed him on that issue. In my opinion, the military leadership just flat-out lied to him about the war. There is no doubt that Secretary of Defense Robert McNamara misled and deceived him. McNamara has even admitted it. Lyndon's military advisors kept telling him, "Just send another hundred thousand troops and another thousand airplanes and we'll win." He kept sending them, but it didn't end the war. Lyndon trusted the military, but he found out too late that he couldn't trust the Pentagon. In retrospect, anybody can look back and say, "that was a war that shouldn't have been fought." I can't disagree with that judgment. We should have stayed out of that war, but it wasn't Lyndon who put us there. Eisenhower made the first mistake. The presidents who preceded LBJ created an impossible situation for him, made worse by horrible and wrong-headed advice from the Pentagon.

I further thought that McGovern's work as chairman of the commission to reform the Democratic Party's structure and procedures did much to destroy the effectiveness of the Democratic Party as a campaign organization. I thought as well that there was absolutely no way that George McGovern could win Texas as a presidential candidate. He was much too far to the left to carry this state. And being that far to the left, I believed his election would have been nothing less than a national calamity. Obviously, I did not want him to be president. After all these years, I haven't changed my mind a bit about his candidacy. George McGovern's economic and foreign policies would have been a disaster for the country.

Most of McGovern's support among Democrats resulted from his pledge to withdraw the U.S. military from Vietnam. I understood why so many of our citizens wanted to pull out of Vietnam. It was an awful war. But I was opposed to a unilateral withdrawal. Of course, the governor of Texas obviously couldn't do anything about the Vietnam War. But it was such a hot issue that it surfaced a lot during the state primary and during the general election campaign. Even though I believed that we should never have been in Vietnam in the first place, I felt like we needed to win the war. I felt that once we were in, we needed to do whatever was necessary to win it, or at least get it to a point where we could withdraw without losing. Do it, get it done, and get it over with. But we were just too far in. We ended up, of course, with a disgraceful pull-out. It was one of the saddest chapters in the history of the United States.

But that war should never have happened. One serious problem with our decision to get involved in Vietnam was that the decision-makers, Republican and Democratic, knew next to nothing about the history of the place. We didn't appreciate or understand that the Vietnamese were fighting a civil war, and we had no business getting into the middle of it.

There is something else that we didn't think enough about at the time: Generals in the army can't make their reputation in history without a war. And the army's officers in the lower ranks find it much more difficult to get promotions in peacetime than in a war. The promotions come pretty fast during a war. That's a cold way to look at it, but it's the truth. I think the military likes to fight a war every now and then for reasons of individual self-promotion. That is also true of the president. To improve popularity ratings, a president sometimes needs a war. It's a pretty cold, hard, cruel way to look at it, but I think it is reality.

So, 1972 was a difficult time to be a candidate for governor or for any prominent public office. It did not matter if the office you were running for had nothing to do with Vietnam. That war just stirred people up so much that it affected just about everything. Of course, George Wallace's candidacy for the Democratic Party's presidential nomination just shook up an already agitated situation even more. Governor Wallace was a formidable force in Texas politics in 1972. Because of his strength in my state, I decided to vote for him for the presidential nomination during the first ballot. To say my vote was controversial would be an understatement. I voted for Wallace for this reason: I thought that if the Democrats were going to have a chance of beating Richard Nixon, we needed a ticket that would challenge him in the South. My hope was that the convention would be dead-locked, and the delegates would turn to someone like Henry Jackson, who might have selected Wallace for his running mate as part of the deal to get the nomination. Wallace would have cut deeply into Nixon's strength in the South. That would have been a balanced ticket similar to the Franklin D. Roosevelt and John Nance Garner ticket in 1932 and 1936. It wouldn't have been that dissimilar to the Kennedy–LBJ ticket in 1960.

I thought Wallace deserved a chance. There was no question that he had made his mistakes as governor, and I certainly did not approve of the stand he took against racial integration, but I believe he would have been a real populist in national office in Washington. I believed then, and I believe now, that he would have dropped his racial stance once he got away from the voters in Alabama. You know, when Lyndon Johnson was the senator from Texas, he had to talk and vote a certain way to get elected. But once he had a national constituency, his behavior changed. George Wallace eventually won the support of the African American people in Alabama because he admitted his mistakes and he changed his ways. I think he was ready to do that in 1972.

I certainly didn't think a McGovern–Wallace ticket was possible. But I voted for Wallace because I thought it was a way to come out of that convention with a constructive ticket rather than the disaster we got. I also wanted to send a message to the Wallace supporters back in Texas that I would listen to their concerns and that they should remain in the Democratic Party.

I also voted against the crazy platform that the McGovern supporters passed at the convention. The document was full of radical and harebrained proposals. I knew it would never be accepted in Texas, and I was not going to have it hung around my neck by Hank Grover, my Republican opponent.

Janey and I did vote for McGovern when it became obvious that he would receive the nomination. Eleven other delegates who had voted against McGovern earlier also changed their votes in his favor. We made the switch because of our belief in traditional party unity. My switch to McGovern, which was purely symbolic, outraged a number of Wallace delegates. So in the end, my attempts to unify this badly split delegation for the upcoming campaign in Texas really blew up in my face. By voting for Wallace on the first ballot, I unintentionally alienated some African American and Mexican American voters. By voting for McGovern at the end, I offended the Wallace vote.

Later, when Wallace's followers threatened to split from the Texas Democratic Party during the state convention in September, Wallace sent a telegram to his Texas leaders, declaring "Dolph Briscoe is a friend of mine." His telegram was read to the convention, and it prevented a split. During the period when I was governor, I got to know Wallace much better because of our participation in the annual meetings of the Southern Governor's Conference. I developed an admiration for his courage in dealing with the terrible physical pain that he continued to suffer for the rest of his life and for the way that he continued to lead his life in the face of such overwhelming disability. You can't help but wonder how history was changed by the attempt on Wallace's life. He had won the Florida primary, and he was flying high at the time.

I would have been better off politically if I hadn't been a delegate to the national convention in Miami. I should have just told them, "Y'all go on and have all the planks and arguments that you want and I'm going to run my own campaign. I'll run as a Democrat but I'm going to run my own campaign." The fact is that there were some people who didn't want unity in the Democratic Party. And I couldn't make them unify. It's like the old saying, "You can lead a horse to water but you can't make him drink." Well, that applied to the situation in Texas. I could lead them to the convention, but I couldn't make them unify.

After the national convention, I announced that I would vote the straight Democratic Party ticket in the general election, as I always had in the past. I also announced that I would not actively campaign in Texas for the McGovern ticket because I knew that I had an active opponent on the Republican side and that I had to concentrate on my own race.

Janey and me with Gov. George Wallace of Alabama and his second wife, Cornelia, at the Southern Governors Conference in Lakeway, Texas, in September 1974. *Briscoe Papers; di_03950.*

Miami was a disastrous convention, and the McGovern campaign was even more of a disaster. It was a complete catastrophe here in Texas. It was really the beginning of the downfall of our Democratic Party in Texas. After 1972, Jimmy Carter was the only Democratic candidate for president to carry Texas, and he barely won the state. It was easy to see in 1972 that the Texas Democratic Party was going downhill because of what was happening with the national party. Texas was then, and is today, very conservative, and the national party moved too far to the left for most Texans. I had to be sure that whenever George McGovern was in Texas, I was at the opposite end of the state, because it was obvious that any association with him would be harmful, if not disastrous.

HANK GROVER AND RAMSEY MUNIZ

I came back to Texas and launched my general election campaign against a serious Republican opponent, Hank Grover, a state senator from Houston. I could not afford to take Grover lightly because he had plenty of money behind him, and the Republicans were beginning to demonstrate increasing political clout. Paul Eggars, the Republican candidate for governor in 1970, had shown surprising strength against Preston Smith. In addition, the state Democratic Party was falling apart around me; they were squabbling like a bunch of little kids. And I had a very weak presidential candidate at the top of the national Democratic ticket. I also had the distraction of being opposed by Ramsey Muniz, the candidate of the La Raza Unida Party. His candidacy was guaranteed to siphon away some votes that would normally have gone to the Democratic candidate. It was not a promising situation.

Ramsey Muniz's candidacy meant that I had to work much harder for the Mexican American vote than Democratic candidates had worked previously. Accordingly, we beefed up our organization in the Mexican American community. We had excellent leadership, especially in South Texas. Rudy Flores, a brilliant attorney from Uvalde, played a major role in my effort with Mexican American voters. After the election, Rudy joined my gubernatorial staff in Austin. Later, he served as city attorney for Uvalde. Dr. Hector Garcia, a physician in Corpus Christi who was the national leader of LULAC, gave me his active support. And we had strong organizations throughout the Rio Grande Valley, in Webb County, and throughout South Texas. It succeeded in minimizing the vote for Ramsey Muniz. I think Zavala County, which was the hotbed for the La Raza party, was the only county in which I did not win a majority of the Mexican American vote. La Raza was in control of the city government, the county government, the school district, and just about everything else in Zavala County.

Some political reporters thought Muniz would hurt me much worse than he did, but I don't think they understood how basically conservative the Mexican American vote is. It is a pro-family, law-abiding vote, much to their credit. And of course, it's a very strong Catholic vote. The radicalism of La Raza did not suit the majority of Mexican Americans. I carried the Mexican American vote despite the efforts of La Raza Unida. But Muniz was a distraction because he was an appealing fellow. He was articulate, handsome, and well educated. And that attracted some of the Farenthold group, which provided a large percentage of his vote. Muniz received more than 100,000 votes. It was only 5 percent, but when you're talking about a close race, that's a lot. Muniz played a role in making that race much closer than it would have been otherwise. But a more important reason for the close election was Richard Nixon's coattails and McGovern's drag on the rest of the state's Democratic candidates.

It was a strange campaign year. According to the Farenthold campaign during the primary runoff, I was an ultra-conservative whose politics were to the right of Attila the Hun. During the fall campaign, Hank Grover claimed that I was a "big government" liberal. I really didn't know Grover before the campaign. I got to know him later, and he was a decent, nice fellow. He was a former schoolteacher who had taught history at a high school in Houston.

On election night, the early returns seemed to indicate that Hank Grover might win. Some news organizations projected a Grover victory, and those projections were reported on the ten o'clock television news programs around the state. Media commentators on some of the

Ramsey Muniz, the La Raza Unida candidate for governor of Texas, 1972. The *Cactus (1973), p. 63; di_03938.*

radio stations predicted my defeat. Naturally, I was concerned as I listened to these reports, but I also knew that the first votes to be reported were from urban precincts where Republicans had done very well in the recent past. The rural boxes, especially in East and South Texas, were always the last boxes to be reported because the votes were on paper ballots instead of on machines. I knew that my strongest support was in those areas. When those votes were finally reported sometime in the early morning of the next day, I emerged with a very narrow victory. The vote was so close, however, that Grover did not concede defeat for a few days afterward.

The final count gave me 48 percent of the vote to Hank Grover's 47 percent. Ramsey Muniz's 5 percent almost gave the election to Grover. It was the smallest margin for any Democrat who had become Texas governor in at least fifty years. This move toward Texas becoming a two-party state had been brewing for a long time, really as far back as 1944 with the Texas Regulars who opposed FDR's fourth term. It was now obvious that the Republicans were going to start fielding much stronger candidates.

Officially, I had campaigned for governor for a period of twelve months on a nonstop basis. Unofficially, I had been campaigning ever since my defeat in 1968. To be the governor of Texas had been my great dream ever since that night I spent in Sam Houston's bed in the Governor's Mansion four decades earlier. My childhood dream had come true.

Chapter 11

THE FIRST TERM

Legislative Success and a Chicken Ranch

W HEN JANEY AND I WENT TO AUSTIN in January 1973
for my inauguration as the fortieth governor of Texas, we
were filled with excitement and eager to take on the responsibilities
that the voters of Texas had bestowed on us. Being governor of Texas
was, of course, the fulfillment of my longtime personal dream. My
excitement and satisfaction did not blind me to the seriousness of the
task ahead, but I can say quite honestly that I was not intimidated by
the job as the state's chief executive.

Austin was like a second home to Janey and me, so the environment was familiar, and we had plenty of good friends and family
nearby. A more significant reason for my self-confidence, however,
was my previous service as a state legislator. The eight years I was in
the legislature gave me a very useful background to draw on when I
assumed the duties of governor. I knew from firsthand experience
exactly how the legislature operated and how its members viewed the
governor's role in the process. In addition, as a representative I had
observed closely the performance of two governors: Beauford Jester
and Allan Shivers. And as a kid, I had the privilege of knowing and
watching Gov. Ross Sterling. As a result, the job was not a mystery to
me, and I had a clear view of what I wanted to do with it.

FIRST TERM GOALS

Because of the Sharpstown scandal, my most important goal as I moved into the Governor's Mansion was to do everything possible to restore public confidence in our state government. As governor, I was determined to set the highest ethical standards and to establish a strictly moral tone in office. I tried at all times to bring to the governor's office the same principles of integrity and honesty that I have lived by in my personal life. In my opinion, the governor is the one elected official in Texas who can serve most effectively as an example to our citizens, especially for our youth. The person who serves as governor has a responsibility to conduct his or her public and personal life in a manner that can make every Texan proud.

In my lifetime, Texans have taken a great interest in their governor as a person. Texans might not know who their United States senators are, but they know the name of their governor. As a result, the governor lives in a bright spotlight at all times. And he or she will be on the front page of the newspaper quite frequently, sometimes for reasons that aren't especially flattering, often on a matter that the governor had nothing to do with. Whoever serves as governor of Texas must be prepared for microscopic scrutiny by the media. But the media exposure also provides a useful forum for a governor to serve as a positive example to his or her fellow citizens. Teddy Roosevelt called the White House a "bully pulpit." I certainly never saw the Governor's Mansion as a pulpit, but I was keenly aware of the need for its occupant to serve as a model citizen.

My other major goal was to do all that I could to ensure that the financial needs of state government were met without increasing existing taxes or creating entirely new taxes. I had made the "no new taxes" pledge a cornerstone of my campaign, and fulfilling that pledge was a major part of what I wanted to accomplish. Coke Stevenson in 1946 had been the last Texas governor to hold the line on taxation. In the twenty-six years since Stevenson's departure, state government had been allowed to grow rapidly, sometimes to meet essential needs, but too often simply to pay for pork-barrel legislation or to throw money at problems that can't or shouldn't be solved at the state level.

This rapid growth in government had to be paid for with new taxes and increases in already established taxes.

I entered office with the firm belief that our taxpayers were eager for less government, not more. It was clear to me that our people were tired of the biennial increases in their tax bills. I thought I could see that the rapid expansion of the Texas economy in the early 1970s would increase state revenues sufficiently to pay for the basic needs of the state without resorting to another tax increase. The pattern in the recent past had been to increase services beyond the ability of the expanding economy to support them. I was determined to end that practice.

Another of my major goals was to increase the number of Mexican Americans and African Americans working in state government and to appoint more from both groups to various state agencies, boards, and commissions. At the beginning of my term I appointed two distinguished Mexican Americans, Rodolfo Flores and Lauro Cruz, to serve on my staff. I asked Cruz, who was a former member of the legislature, to work on minority recruitment.

I am proud that I appointed a far greater number of Mexican Americans and African Americans to influential positions in state government than any of my predecessors. The initial appointments included Corpus Christi attorney and La Raza Unida leader Tony Bonilla, who I placed on the Coordinating Board for Higher Education, and Dr. Robert Bacon, an African American from Houston, who I appointed to the Texas Board of Corrections. Early in my first term, I also appointed the first African American district judge and the first African American members of the state Pharmaceutical Board and the Board of Medical Examiners.

I also wanted qualified individuals from the labor unions to have state appointments. Previous governors had been openly hostile to the labor movement in Texas. The labor leaders that I knew, however, were pro-capitalist, patriotic Americans who simply wanted fair wages and a safe working environment for their members. I couldn't see anything that was unpatriotic or that was "liberal" or "conservative" about those goals. I've never been comfortable with extreme political labels such as ultra-conservative or ultra-liberal. I was called a liberal during my years in the legislature, and I was called a conservative governor. I tried to ignore those labels when I made gubernatorial appointments. I am especially proud of my work to make certain that labor had a strong voice in my administration.

INAUGURATION DAY

Inauguration day in Austin on January 16, 1973, was cold, windy, and cloudy, but for Janey and me, the weather was irrelevant; in our minds it was a beautiful and glorious day. It began with a prayer breakfast featuring Tom Landry, the head coach of the Dallas Cowboys, who delivered an inspirational talk that set the moral tone for the remainder of the inauguration. William P. "Bill" Hobby Jr., the newly elected lieutenant governor, and his wife, Diana, also attended the breakfast.

At noon, Bill Hobby and I, accompanied by our families, went to the grounds on the south side of the Capitol to take our separate oaths of office from Robert Calvert, the chief justice of the Texas Supreme Court. As we walked up to the platform under the archway of drawn swords formed by the Sul Ross Volunteer honor guard of cadets from Texas A&M University, a nineteen-gun salute echoed across the Capitol grounds. Surrounding us on the platform were the members of the Texas House and Senate, the majority of whom were serving their first term. Special guests included former Texas governors Alan Shivers, Price Daniel, and Preston Smith; and Bill Hobby's mother, newspaper publisher and former Eisenhower cabinet member Oveta Culp Hobby. Former President Lyndon Johnson and his wife, Lady Bird, braved the cold and windy weather to attend the inaugural. The Johnsons were there at the invitation of Bill Hobby. Lyndon had made few public appearances since leaving office four years earlier, so Janey and I were honored by his and Lady Bird's presence. After the inauguration ceremonies, Janey and I invited the Johnsons to join us for the official luncheon in the Governor's Mansion. At first, Lyndon declined, saying that he really didn't want to impose on our special event, but he eventually accepted the invitation. He and Lady Bird got to the mansion before Janey and I. When we entered the dining room,

Former President Lyndon Johnson holding court at the luncheon in the Governor's Mansion the day of my inauguration in January 1973. *Briscoe Papers; di_03951.*

we were surprised (but not shocked), to find Lyndon sitting at the head of the governor's table, holding court.

That luncheon would be the last time we would ever see Lyndon. He died of a heart attack on January 22 at his ranch in the Hill Country. Janey and I attended his funeral in Washington, D.C., and then went to his ranch for the burial. The Rev. Billy Graham rode in our car with us as we drove to the ranch.

The inauguration was broadcast live over a statewide television network. One of my fondest memories of the event was looking into the crowd of several thousand people and seeing about two thousand of my neighbors and friends from Uvalde, including the Uvalde High School band, which later marched in the inaugural parade. I have been honored with the solid support and steadfast friendship of the citizens of Uvalde throughout my political career. Their presence in such large numbers at the inauguration meant a great deal to me and to Janey. After lunch that day, we hosted a special reception at the Governor's Mansion just for the citizens of Uvalde.

Inauguration day in 1973 on the steps of the Capitol. Lyndon Johnson can be seen to the left of Janey as he walked through the honor guard from Texas A&M. *Texas State Library and Archives Commission, 1974/29-5, photograph by Bill Malone.*

Janey and I enjoying the inaugural parade. It was a wonderful day. *Texas State Library and Archives Commission, 1974/33-35.*

I've never favored lengthy speeches, even for an inaugural, so I kept mine to a relatively short ten minutes. I stressed the themes on which I had campaigned: restoration of public confidence in state government, no new taxes, effective and efficient government services, enhanced educational opportunities for all Texans, and a fight against crime. I duly noted that the audience of five thousand gave me its longest and loudest applause when I promised "no new taxes in 1973."

After Bill Hobby took his oath of office, he delivered a speech in which he made generous and gracious comments about me, pledging that in performing the duties of lieutenant governor, he would remain "at the right hand of Dolph Briscoe, whom we principally honor here today." Bill Hobby would be true to his word. In the six years that we served together, even when we disagreed on specific issues such as the proposed new Texas Constitution, Bill was always a steadfast friend. We collaborated whenever we could, and in those few cases when we couldn't, our disagreements never became angry or disrespectful.

After the inaugural parade down Congress Avenue, Bill Hobby and I hosted a public reception in the great rotunda of the Capitol. There were no special or invited guests for this event. Bill and I felt strongly that we should be available to greet and shake the hand of any member of the general public who wanted to attend. The Sharpstown scandal had badly eroded the public's trust in its state officials, so we wanted to throw open the doors of the Capitol for an event to symbolize our determination to conduct a state government that would be open to the scrutiny of the people.

That night, after the various inaugural balls, Janey and I hosted a slumber party at the mansion for forty of our daughter Cele's classmates at Uvalde High School. It made a very long day and night, and the next morning I was as exhausted as I have ever been in my life, but I have never been happier. I was tired, but eager to get to work.

The Governor's Powers

Texans perceive the governor to be the head of state government. They look to the governor for leadership, and they hold that person to be responsible for the condition of the state. These are understandable expectations. The reality is, however, that the Texas Constitution did not establish a form of government in which the governor controls the executive branch.

In Texas, the executive branch is divided among several separately elected officials and the members of the various independent commissions and boards that have executive authority. Unlike the president of the United States, the governor does not have a cabinet. The authors of the Texas Constitution, which was written at the end of the era of Reconstruction in 1876, purposely created a state government in which power is distributed among a multiplicity of office holders, commissioners, and board members. The governor appoints the members of those boards and commissions, with confirmation by the Senate. These board and commission members are completely independent of the governor, often to the governor's chagrin. And their terms of office are structured in such a way as to insure that any newly elected governor will serve most of his or her first term in office with a large number of holdovers appointed by the previous governor. The reality is that the independent departments such as the Office of Attorney General, the Agriculture Department, the General Land Office, and the independent boards and commissions administer our state government, not the governor. This has created a very contradictory situation. People want some person—the governor—to be responsible for resolving problems in state government, but they don't want to give that person enough power to do much about those problems.

I often heard comments from my fellow Texans about strong actions that I, as governor, should be taking to remedy various problems over which the governor has absolutely no authority. I must admit, however, that campaign rhetoric is a major source for this widespread misunderstanding about the governor's power. Every election, the candidates for governor issue statements and make pledges that if they are elected they will crack down on some problem, such as violent crime or illegal immigration, or take an action to improve some situation, such as traffic jams or teachers salaries. My own campaign speeches included such promises. The reality is, of course, that the powers of the governor of Texas are severely limited by the state constitution. For example, the governor has no meaningful law enforcement power, and he or she has no authority over the public schools. The candidates for governor that I have known understood that when they promised to "crack down on crime," or to "raise teacher salaries," they really meant that they would appoint officials to the relevant boards who would carry out these pledges and they would veto bills that violated them. The message doesn't come across to the public that way, however.

The fact that Texas has independently elected officials running the key state departments greatly complicates the administration of state government. There is no question about that. The governor doesn't even have his or her own attorney general, whose office has the authority over the state's legal matters. Often the governor has an attorney general who is looking enviously at the governor's job. The governor can't fire the state's lawyer. The governor has a lawyer the people elected, and there's nothing the governor can do about it except hire a lawyer for his or her staff. A governor has counsel on his staff, which is really the counsel he or she depends on. But that counsel has no legal authority.

Although the administration of state government is complicated somewhat by the present constitutional structure, I actually favor our system over one in which the governor has extensive powers. One of the strengths of Texas state government is the fact that we have these independent agencies and boards. I believe this system makes it more likely that the individual board and commission members will do what they believe is best for the citizens served by the agencies they govern. They are able to make decisions free of the political pressure that comes with a system in which they serve at the governor's pleasure.

THE GOVERNOR AND THE LEGISLATURE

In my opinion, the governor of Texas does have adequate power and influence. The governor's authority to veto any law passed by the legislature is an extremely strong tool for influencing the direction of a bill while it is being legislated. The governor's veto power is enhanced by the constitutional provision allowing line-item vetoes. Of course, the veto is a negative power, but the threat of a veto can be a positive power if the governor uses it to create an opportunity to negotiate with the sponsors of a bill to iron out problems before that bill ever reaches the governor's desk. The members of the legislature know that if the governor vetoes legislation it is usually very difficult to override that veto; it requires the vote of two-thirds of the members. Overriding a veto is nearly impossible if the governor has worked closely with the legislature during the session and he or she has developed a good relationship with the leadership. The members, therefore, have a good deal of inducement to work with the governor to solve the problems in a bill before it passes.

In addition, many members of the legislature will want some item of personal privilege from the governor at some point, such as an appointment to a state board for one of their constituents. The governor also might decide not to sign some special local bill that applies only to the member's district. Whenever a governor kills a local bill, it is a terrible embarrassment to the representative or senator whose district is affected. So, the governor does have some tools to influence legislation. Of course, a very popular governor also can appeal directly to the people through the media to pressure the legislature to pass or not to pass certain bills. That tactic, however, is just as likely to backfire as it is to work because it can cause resentments that can result in uniting the legislature against the governor. Naturally, most of the members prefer quiet negotiations away from the media. Public grandstanding by a governor can itself become more of an issue than the original legislative problem. The governor should be solving problems, not be the problem.

SPECIAL SESSIONS OF THE LEGISLATURE

The governor also has the exclusive power to call a special session of the legislature. The legislature knows that it can be called back into a special session if the governor feels strongly that a specific problem failed to be solved during the regular session. The threat of the members being called back to Austin and having their family lives and careers disrupted is another tool that a governor can use to influence legislation. Thankfully, Texas does not have a full-time legislature. The vast majority of the members have other jobs back home. I believe strongly in a citizen legislature because it's important that members of the legislature spend a major part of their time back home among the people that they are representing. The more time they spend back home, the better they will represent their constituents.

In my case, however, the threat of calling a special session was not an effective weapon. I don't believe in special sessions, and I made that clear to the legislature at the beginning of my first term. The legislature had been having too many special sessions in the years prior to my being governor, and I wanted to put a stop to it. Special sessions are an unnecessary expense to the taxpayer, and the knowledge that a particular governor doesn't mind calling them can actually impede progress during the regular session. The members assume the attitude that they can always come back in special session and take care of important business that they failed to deal with at the proper time. My policy was to call a special session only if there was an emergency or some critical problem that could not wait until the next regular session.

Actually, I used the governor's exclusive authority to call special sessions in a different way. My threat was that if the legislature didn't get its business done during the regular session, then they could just go home looking like a failure. I wasn't going to call them back to Austin.

I called three special sessions during the six years I was governor. I called one in December 1973 to lower the state highway speed limit to fifty-five miles per hour. That session lasted only three days, and it was an emergency necessitated by the Arab oil boycott. Texas would have lost $240 million in federal highway support if we had not lowered the speed limit. I called a special session in July 1977 to deal with public school finance issues, and that session lasted only ten days. The final special session I called was in July 1978 to enact tax relief measures.

WORKING WITH THE BIG THREE

As governor, I knew that it was essential that I work closely with the three office holders who were the most important players in the overall legislative process: the lieutenant governor, the attorney general, and the Speaker of the House. Fortunately, the three individuals who held those posts while I was governor were Democrats, so partisan rivalry was not a problem. Nonetheless, close coordination between the governor and the holders of those offices is not easy to accomplish, even when everyone is from the same party. As I stated before, the fact that each is independently elected, with a separate power base and political organization, creates problems even in the best of situations. Strong personal ambitions and egos also affect relationships. Each office holder is a unique personality with his or her own personal traits and opinions that may or may not match well with the governor's. So, there are a lot of variables that affect the governor's relationship with those three key officials.

The lieutenant governor has a special constitutional relationship with the governor because the state constitution provides for the lieutenant governor to become the state's chief executive in the event of the governor's resignation, death, or impeachment (all three situations have occurred in Texas history). The constitution also gives him or her the duty of presiding over the state Senate. In case of a tie vote in the Senate, the lieutenant governor can cast the deciding ballot. Although the vice president of the United States has the same constitutional role at the federal level, those are the only two provisions that the two offices have in common. The rules of the Texas Senate give the lieutenant governor a number of important legislative powers that the federal vice president does not have. For example, the lieutenant governor appoints the chairs of Senate committees and serves as the chairman of the Legislative Budget Board, which has great influence over the writing of the state budget.

Houston businessman Bill Hobby was lieutenant governor for both of my terms as governor. I did not know Bill well before the election in 1972, but during the inauguration we became better acquainted, and we quickly developed an excellent working relationship. Because his father had been governor, Bill had tremendous respect for the office of governor, which was very helpful to our relationship. Bill was extremely easy to work with. At the start of our relationship, he made it clear that he wanted a close and harmonious relationship with me. We agreed that Bill would be the person to work directly with the members of the Senate in all legislative matters, but

Lt. Gov. William P. Hobby Jr. *Bentsen (Lloyd M.) Papers, Center for American History [cropped from original print]; di_03936.*

only after he and I conferred and reached an agreement on general legislative direction. I thought that was a good deal because he and I had very similar goals, and the lieutenant governor has the overwhelming power in the Senate. To put it another way, I understood that as governor I shouldn't try to go around him unless we had a serious disagreement over some very critical issue. As it turned out, we had a few disagreements, but I don't remember ever having one that was so serious that I had to appeal directly to the members of the Senate. We made a good team.

The Speaker is the key individual in the House of Representatives and it is equally important that the governor also have a good working relationship with him. The first two years that I was in office the Speaker was Price Daniel Jr., from the southeast Texas town of Liberty, who, like Bill Hobby, was the son of a former governor. Price Jr. initially was elected to the state legislature in 1968. At the age of thirty-one, after only two terms as representative, Price's House colleagues elected him their Speaker. Handsome and energetic, Price was widely viewed as the new boy wonder of Texas politics, replacing the recently vanquished Ben Barnes. *Time* magazine recognized him as one of the nation's top one hundred leaders. Before I became governor, I didn't know Price Junior, but I knew his father well.

Unfortunately, my relationship with Price Daniel Jr. didn't work out that well. When I became governor, I reached out to Price in the same way that I reached out to Bill Hobby. We had pleasant meetings during which we would work out some agreement on legislation, but too often Price would agree to do one thing and then do the opposite after he left my office. That kind of behavior makes it difficult to work with a fellow. Where I come from a person is as good as their word. I regret to say that I could never count on Price's word. In addition, I felt that Price played too much to the press. I often thought that he was more interested in getting his name in the media than he was with doing the best job possible for the people of Texas. He had a tendency to flop around on important issues and to try to be all things to all people. That trait eventually caught up with him during the Texas Constitutional Convention in 1974, but more about that later.

The truth is that I never could understand Price Jr., and we did not

Speaker of the House Price Daniel Jr., right, with state representative Hawkins Menefee of Houston. Texas Observer *Records; di_03937*.

end up with a good working relationship. There were many bills that he supported and wanted that I was strongly in favor of also, so we worked fine on those. But overall, we didn't enjoy a good relationship, certainly nothing like I had with Bill Hobby or that I had with Price's successor, Billy Clayton. When Billy Clayton became speaker in 1975, whatever he agreed to do he did. We worked well together. I never had to watch my back with either Bill Hobby or Bill Clayton. But that was not the case with Price Daniel Jr.

Another state official who is vitally important to the governor is the attorney general. The attorney general of Texas is the state's lawyer, but the office has broad authority that can impact every entity of state government. This authority can also be used to influence the legislative process because the attorney general provides opinions concerning the constitutionality of acts passed by the legislature. Although this opinion function is advisory, the state courts rarely overturn the attorney general's rulings.

John Hill was the newly elected attorney general when I assumed my duties as governor. I first met Hill when he and I were students at the University of Texas. After his graduation from the university's School of Law, Hill made quite a reputation as a trial lawyer in Houston. He served as John Connally's secretary of state during Connally's last term as governor. As secretary of state, Hill worked overtime to increase his visibility to enhance his opportunities for election to a higher public office. When John Connally decided against running for another term in 1968, Hill quickly announced his candidacy for governor. He and I both hoped for Connally's endorsement in that race, but Connally's support went to another candidate, Eugene Locke. Preston Smith won the election, I wound up in fourth place, and Hill finished sixth.

After 1968, it was clear that Hill and I would continue to be rivals for the governor's chair. Apparently, Hill decided in 1972 that Ben Barnes could not be beaten in the governor's race, so he entered the campaign for attorney general. According to the *Houston Chronicle*, he filed his candidacy ten minutes before the deadline. He defeated the incumbent, Crawford Martin, without a runoff. I'm sure that Hill was shocked when I won the governor's race. I always felt that he had deep regrets about his last-minute decision to run for attorney general instead of governor. Throughout my tenure as governor, Hill acted as though I had usurped his rightful place as the state's chief executive. I never had any doubts that he was eager to run against me when he felt the time was right. It didn't take long during my first term for me to realize that the attorney general's office was not going to be especially helpful whenever my office had a controversy to confront or a sensitive issue to resolve.

The Secretary of State

The secretary of state is the one executive officer appointed by the governor with the consent of the Senate. The office has a variety of important but routine bureaucratic functions, such as affixing the state seal to official documents, compiling and publishing state laws, and appointing the notaries public. The secretary of state also serves as the

Mark White, second from right, and his wife, Linda Gale, soon after his appointment as secretary of state. *Briscoe Papers; di_03945.*

state's chief election officer, responsible for overseeing the primaries and the general election. All of the functions of the office are managed and carried out by a professional and experienced bureaucracy, under the general oversight by the secretary. In practice the position functions as an arm of the governor's office, with the secretary often serving as an unofficial executive assistant, advisor, and legislative aide. For example, it was a tradition at the time that during legislative sessions the secretary of state would serve as the governor's liaison with the members of the Senate. For all of those reasons, the position can play a key role in the success or failure of the governor's general program.

When I began to consider candidates for secretary of state, I realized that it was crucial to appoint someone with legal training who shared my political views and who was loyal, energetic, and personable. It didn't take long for me to realize that a young attorney in Houston by the name of Mark White, who had worked in my election campaign, would be my best choice. Mark was with the Joe Reynolds law firm in Houston. Joe Reynolds was one of my best friends and one of my strongest supporters in the Houston area. Mark White had helped me tremendously in the campaign. He wrote some outstanding position papers for me, and he had worked tirelessly and effectively for my election. Mark was a brilliant and ambitious young lawyer as well as an extremely personable young man. I felt that he would make an excellent secretary of state. I called Mark and told him that I wanted him to come to Austin and talk to me about the secretary of state's office. He thought I meant working in that office, not being secretary of state. He was shocked when I told him I wanted him to be the secretary of state. That possibility had not occurred to him.

In my opinion, Mark White made as fine a secretary of state as any governor has ever had. He was always ready to work. He did an outstanding job administering the various functions of his office. During the legislative sessions, he served as my liaison with Bill Hobby. Whenever things weren't going well with one of our bills in the Senate, Mark was always ready to go to work on the senators who were having problems supporting the bill. He was a persuasive advocate for our program. Of course, Bill Hobby and I would talk about Mark's assignment beforehand. Some problem would surface with a vote and Mark, Bill, and I would split the senators up between us. Mark might be more effective with one senator, while another might respond better after a visit to my office. Who we each would work with depended on how effective we were with that particular individual. Then we would go back and have another vote. Mark did a great job. He enjoyed doing it, and he had excellent relations with the members of the Senate. Mark White's talent and ambition would eventually lead to his election as attorney general in 1978 and as governor in 1982. I'm proud to have played a small part in bringing his talents to state government.

The 1973 Legislative Session

In the election of 1972, fallout from the Sharpstown scandal resulted in a nearly 50 percent turnover in the membership of the legislature. It was the most extensive change in the composition of that body since 1946. The 1973 legislature featured seventy-six new state representatives and fifteen new senators. Most of these new members had campaigned—as had I—on the theme of cleaning up the mess in Austin,

Addressing the legislature during my first term as governor. *Texas State Library and Archives Commission, 1973/100-7, photograph by Bill Malone.*

so we shared a strong interest in reform legislation to help eliminate and prevent corruption in state government.

I urged such legislation in my address to a joint session of the legislature on January 18, 1973. Noting that "we will never have a better climate for great achievements," I called for a new ethics law to "return to morality in state government." And I asked the legislature to pass a stronger lobby registration act that would require lobbyists to identify their clients and to fully disclose the amount of money they were spending to defeat or to pass a bill. In addition to a call for the reform of drug laws and a major revision of the penal code, I reiterated my pledge to oppose any new taxes or tax hikes. I was deeply gratified by the legislature's enthusiastic reaction to my speech, which they demonstrated by giving me a lengthy standing ovation at the conclusion.

I worked hard to get my recommendations enacted into law. My style, however, was not to pressure or threaten individual members to do it my way or else. I had resented that type of tactic when I had served in the legislature. My style is much more deliberate and patient. In addition, as I have said, I agreed to let Bill Hobby lead the way in the Senate. I kept a low profile with the Senate, but I was happy to meet with individual senators who needed to see me, and I occasionally worked directly with some of the senators when Bill Hobby asked me to do that. In the Senate, I had excellent relationships with John Traeger from Seguin, Frank Lombardino from San Antonio, Bill Moore from Bryan, and A. M. Aikin from Paris. I had great respect for Senator Aikin, who had been in the Senate when I was in the House. Senator Aikin always played by the rules. He was a man of honor whose word was his bond.

Because of my excellent relationship with Bill Hobby, I usually focused more of my attention on the House. As I have said before, being a former member of the legislature, I was quite familiar with the various ways a governor could affect legislation. That experience was extremely helpful, particularly at the beginning of my first term. For example, I think personal relationships are important. Janey and I had many members of the legislature over to the mansion for breakfast and lunch so that we could get to know each other better. Some of the members who had been in the legislature for quite a few terms told me that it was the first time they had ever been in the Governor's Mansion. Those meals were as enjoyable as they could be. Everything was off the record. No members of the press were invited. We could talk, visit, and just have a good time. I might lobby a little with some of them, of course. It was a real good way for me to get some idea about what the legislative atmosphere was like.

I also found it more effective to call members of the legislature into the governor's office for discussions than going out on the floor of the House chamber to talk to them. In other words, you have somebody on your territory, not theirs. When you are on the floor of the House, you're on their territory. There's something about meeting in the office of the governor of Texas that I found to be more effective than meeting anywhere else. The governor's office is a symbol or whatever you want to call it of the power of the executive branch of state government. The person who happens to be governor is there only temporarily, but the office is there permanently, so there is a timelessness about the place that is impressive. Every time I've been in the Oval Office in the White House I have been deeply impressed. And every time I've been in the governor's office, even when I was the governor, I was very aware of all the history that has been made there and what the office represents. The grandeur of the place is greatly enhanced by it being in the Capitol, which is one of the most impressive buildings I have ever seen. I've been in awe of that building every time I've ever walked into it in my life: as a member of the legislature, as a visitor, or as governor.

I found the vast majority of the members of the legislature very easy to work with. I don't mean that they would always say yes; I mean that most of them would give you a decent chance to make your case, and then they would give your argument thoughtful consideration. I must admit that there were a few individuals that I couldn't work with at all. There were a couple of members that I gave up on completely, and I just ignored them the entire time I was in office. When I wanted the legislature to pass a bill or change some legislation, I knew that talking to them would be futile. There was just no point in even trying to talk to them. Thankfully, they were an extreme minority.

The legislator that I worked with in the House more effectively than just about anyone else was the representative from my home district, Jim Nugent from Kerrville. Jim was a longtime member of the House. He knew the rules well, and he knew how to get things done. Jim was very well respected. I worked him extremely hard, and he nearly always came through for me. Other members in the House with whom I worked closely included Jon Newton from Beeville and Benny Bock from New Braunfels.

For most of the session, I was pleased with the progress the legislature was making on moving important legislation through to conclusion. In May, however, about three weeks before the adjournment date required by law, I became alarmed by a stalemate that developed between the House and Senate over their different versions of several critical bills, including the lobby and ethics bills and drug law reform. Some of the differences were trivial, but legislators can become quite stubborn near the end of a long session.

Speaker Daniel made the problem worse when he denounced the entire Texas Senate during a press conference, claiming that the House bills had been "raped, pillaged, and ridiculed" by the senators. At that point, I threw my entire effort into breaking the stalemate by seeking compromises acceptable to both sides. I called Daniel, Hobby, and the members of the conference committee to my office and told them that I would not, under any circumstances, call a special session to finish business that should be settled in the regular session. I asked them to find a middle ground and get their work finished on time. I also sent Mark White to meet with the leadership of both houses to work out their differences in way that would also satisfy my office. He did a magnificent job, and, in doing so, he earned the trust of the legislative leaders. When you get near the end of a session and it looks as though important business is not going to be finished, that's usually when everybody starts getting together. It happens during those last two or three days. Sometimes it's the last day, sometimes it's the last few hours. But everybody knows the pressure is on to get something accomplished.

There were a few disappointments at the end, including the failure to pass a school finance reform bill, but by the time of adjournment much of our program had passed in acceptable form. Those achievements included new ethics and financial disclosure laws for public officials and governing election campaigns, revision of the open-meetings law, a new open records act, and stronger laws regulating lobbyists. And, of course, we had held the line on taxes.

It had been a productive session, and I was pleased with the results. I had to veto only twenty-two bills, some of which duplicated or contradicted other bills, and I used the line-item veto on six items in the budget. To find only $1.5 million to cut out of a $9.7 billion budget was strong evidence that the legislature and I had worked well together. The legislature passes hundreds of bills during a typical session, sometimes too quickly, and mistakes are always made. The veto process is the time to correct those mistakes. I vetoed only eight bills of any substance, including bills that would have raised mortgage rates unnecessarily, changed the dates for the state's fiscal year, and prohibited the police in small towns from using radar devices to detect speeders. I looked at the latter bill as a special interest law for the members of the legislature, who drove a little too fast on the trips back home. As I declared when I vetoed the bill, "we need all the help we can get in enforcing" our traffic laws.

The Chicken Ranch Affair

Satisfied with our accomplishments in the legislative session, I was looking forward to a relatively quiet summer in 1973. I suppose that is evidence of my naiveté about how much the news media was changing. With twenty-four-hours-a-day cable news, we are very aware today that the news media has a constant need to find sensational news to report, and, when they can't find any, they don't mind generating it themselves. This process was in its early stage when I became governor.

By the summer of 1973, the media, especially television, no longer accepted that there could be something called a slow news month. Carefully packaged news formats such as "Eyewitness News" were beginning to take over local television news. The formats typically featured a sensational daily report from the station's "investigative reporter" who breathlessly reported the discovery of cockroaches in the kitchen of a local restaurant or that the local police were getting free coffee and doughnuts at a local cafe. The *60 Minutes* program on CBS had become one of the most popular shows on television, and every local television reporter wanted to be Mike Wallace. They occasionally uncovered a legitimately serious problem or scandal, but those were few and far between. Anyway, truly serious problems have a way of uncovering themselves eventually.

By the summer of 1973, Marvin Zindler had become a very popular investigative reporter for KTRK television in Houston. I first met Marvin in Houston during my campaign in 1972. He was working in the consumer fraud division of the Harris County Sheriff's Department at that time. Marvin was an unforgettable fellow—flamboyant in style with a dapper moustache, a distinctively tailored wardrobe, and a memorable hairpiece that was similar to one worn by former ABC television network announcer Howard Cosell. His television delivery, which was rapid-fire and loud, was similar also to Cosell's. The truth is that I always liked Marvin. He had a tremendous following in Houston in the 1970s, and he did for years. Marvin was still on the air, as flamboyant as ever, until shortly before his death in July 2007.

In July 1973 Marvin called me and said that he wanted to come to my office at the Capitol and conduct an interview. He didn't say why he wanted to interview me, but I replied, "fine, come on up." So a couple of days later, he and a crew arrived and they set up the camera in the governor's inner office. I didn't expect that the interview would be anything unusual, just the normal questions and answers about issues of state government. We had a pleasant chat, I got comfortable, and then the camera came on. All of a sudden, Marvin asked me—in his highly dramatic style—"Did you know there is a *house of prostitution* called the 'Chicken Ranch' operating in clear violation of the law over in La Grange?"

La Grange is a lovely small town on the Colorado River in Fayette County about halfway between Houston and Austin. That question startled me, to say the least. Marvin definitely blindsided me on camera, which he had every right to do. Staring into the glare of his camera lights, all I could say was "no," because I had never heard of this place. Then I managed to blurt out: "How do you know that?" Marvin answered, "You see this young man who is operating our television

Houston television personality Marvin Zindler. *Center for American History Vertical File; di_03944.*

camera? He's unmarried. Last night we stayed in La Grange, and I paid his fee at the Chicken Ranch. He can tell you the truth." So, this young man spoke up and said, "Governor, I can assure you from personal experience that a brothel is in operation there." I didn't know how you could get any better proof than that. Marvin then asked me what the governor of Texas was going to do about it. Without hesitation, I said, "Marvin, we are going to close it up."

Thankfully, Marvin didn't ask me how I was going to close it up, because I had absolutely no idea. The stark fact is that the governor of Texas has no power to order a local police official such as a county sheriff or a chief of police to do anything. Many Texans, maybe even most, don't realize this. Sheriffs are independently elected, and the local police are under the authority of the town or city government. The governor is not the commander-in-chief of the police in the state. And that's the way it should be. We don't want a police state. No elected state officer has local police power, including the attorney general.

After Marvin left my office, I felt as though a bolt of lightning had hit me. I knew right away that I had a problem, because I had just stated on television that I would shut this place down, and I had absolutely no authority to do that. I knew I had to do something, of course, because prostitution is against the law, and I had taken an oath to uphold the laws of the state of Texas, even if I had no power to do so. I immediately called Col. Wilson Speir, who was head of the Texas Department of Public Safety (DPS), a couple of my staff lawyers, and John Hill, the attorney general. They came over the next morning, and we discussed our options. Colonel Speir confirmed that the state police had no jurisdiction in this matter. We silently contemplated this fact for a while.

Finally, Colonel Speir proposed to station an unmarked DPS car near the Chicken Ranch parking lot so that the officers could record the license plates of the car of every person who visited the establishment. The DPS would use the license plate numbers to learn the names of the patrons of the Chicken Ranch and then give them to the Austin newspaper for publication. He believed that action would stop all patronage and force the place out of business. We discussed this for some time, but we realized that we might be opening a political Pandora's box if we tried that tactic. Undoubtedly, some members of the legislature might find their names on that newspaper list. I asked Colonel Speir if he knew of an organized crime or Mafia connection with the brothel. If there was, the FBI might have jurisdiction, and we could pass the matter on to the federal government. He said there was no evidence of a Mafia connection, and that the operation, which had been in business for many years, was strictly local. That meant, obviously, that the Chicken Ranch had long enjoyed the protection of local politicians and law enforcement officers.

Then Colonel Speir got another idea. He said that he knew the Fayette County sheriff, Jim Flournoy. Speir said Flournoy had worked for many years as the foreman of the McGill Brothers Ranch in South

Texas before he became sheriff. I realized then that I also had known Flournoy when he was foreman of that ranch. Colonel Speir offered to call Flournoy to see if he would do his duty and close the place down. That was the obvious solution, but Colonel Speir suggested that many of the local citizens might not be pleased if the sheriff closed it down. In other words, the locally elected sheriff probably had an extremely sensitive political issue on his hands. Nevertheless, I agreed that Colonel Speir should make that call to Flournoy. About this time, my receptionist informed me that a crowd of news reporters was in the outer office wanting to ask me questions about the story Marvin had broadcast the evening before. As I moved toward the front door to meet with the press, I noticed the attorney general of Texas scurrying out the back door. He left me to fend for myself. I would have appreciated some support from the official who is supposed to be the state's attorney, but that was okay. I answered a few questions and made it through the press conference without too much of a problem.

When Colonel Speir asked Sheriff Flournoy what he intended to do, the sheriff replied that he would not close the brothel because it had the support of many local residents. Flournoy said that he had seen Zindler's television report and that he had anticipated Colonel Speir's call. He claimed that he had on his desk petitions signed by hundreds of residents of his county demanding that the brothel remain open. Flournoy was eager to deliver the petitions to the governor's office. Colonel Speir told him that we weren't interested in seeing the petitions. He also said that he was sorry to hear that Flournoy was refusing to enforce the law. Speir warned Flournoy that he was forcing the Department of Public Safety to publicize the license plates of the brothel's customers.

Speir's threat apparently made a strong impression on the sheriff. He soon called Speir back to say that if I would call him personally and order him to close down the Chicken Ranch, he would do it. An "order" from the governor of Texas would give him the local political cover he needed. We agreed to follow the sheriff's recommendation, so I called him and said, "Sheriff, I am ordering you to close what is known as the Chicken Ranch." To my relief, he answered that

The soon-to-be world-famous "Chicken Ranch" near La Grange, Texas. *Hobby (William P., Sr.) Family Papers, Center for American History; di_03935.*

although he disagreed with my decision, he would obey my order. On August 2, 1973, Flournoy closed the Chicken Ranch. He and I both knew that I had no authority to order him to close the place, but it was a practical way for us to get the law enforced in that county. For several days afterward I kept waiting for someone to point out that I had no legal authority to close the place down, but no one did. It would not have made any difference legally, of course, because the sheriff certainly had the power to do what he did.

I was delighted that we had solved the problem so rapidly and easily. I was not eager to try the option of publishing the names of customers. There was no telling where that would have led us, but I was ready to take that step if necessary.

I thought I had heard the end of the Chicken Ranch. Then Larry L. King, a Texas writer with a real talent for political humor, published a story about the Chicken Ranch episode in a popular magazine. That article attracted enough national attention to inspire King to use the story as the basis for a wildly successful Broadway musical, *The Best*

Little Whorehouse in Texas. Janey and I didn't go to see the musical in
New York, mainly because we didn't want to attract publicity. When
we made a trip to London, however, we decided to see the show there
because we thought no one would know us. Janey and I really enjoyed
the show. It was easy to see why it was so popular. It was very enter-
taining. I especially enjoyed it when the actor who was playing "the
governor" performed a wonderful Texas two-step. If only I could
dance that well. During the intermission, Janey and I went out to the
lobby for some coffee. We were surprised to find the lobby crowded
with Texans, some we knew personally—so much for anonymity.

It's funny, but I realize that it is quite possible that the main thing
for which I will be remembered in Texas history is that I was the governor who closed the Chicken Ranch!

Chapter 12

THE SECOND TERM

*Holding the Line on Taxes and a Tragedy
in Huntsville*

THERE WAS NEVER ANY QUESTION in my mind that I would
run for reelection in 1974, this time for a four-year term. An
amendment to the state constitution had increased the terms of
statewide office holders from two to four years beginning with the
1974 election. I felt that my first term had done much to restore confidence among voters in the integrity of state government. I had supported and worked actively for the successful passage of a new code of
ethics for public office holders. As a result, the legislature had passed
the most far-reaching ethics bill in Texas history.

I also had worked hard for insurance reform during my first term. I
appointed former state senator Joe Christie to serve as chairman of the
Insurance Board, and I had given him a directive to develop a competitive insurance rate system in Texas. Joe did an outstanding job. He
was a real friend of consumers. Under his leadership, the board took
actions that resulted in lower insurance rates. In addition, I pushed the
legislature to strengthen the Insurance Board's regulatory authority.

We also cracked down on the dope dealers by passing stiffer penal-
ties for selling hard drugs. At the same time, however, I also worked
successfully for a more rational law on possession of marijuana. It
made no sense to me to send young people who had no prior criminal
record to prison for making the mistake of having a small amount of

marijuana in their possession. Accordingly, the legislature reduced the crime of possessing a small amount of marijuana from a felony to a misdemeanor.

Janey had her own achievements during that first term, but the most significant was the establishment of "Operation Peace of Mind." Janey was deeply affected by a horrific serial murder case in Houston and Galveston in 1973 in which a number of the victims were teenage runaways. As a result, she became the leading advocate for the establishment of the nation's first toll-free telephone hotline system for runaway children. The system we established served as a model for a nationwide program.

I was proud that during my first term I appointed more than twenty women to state boards and commissions. That was a far larger number of appointments than any of my predecessors had made. We still had a long way to go in the effort to bring more women into the government, but it was a good start. As I mentioned in the previous chapter, I had worked equally hard to recruit minorities to serve in positions of authority in state government. In addition, I had an open-door policy for all members of the legislature, and I made a special effort to work with the African American and Mexican American legislative caucuses. Shortly after my inauguration, I became the first governor to host lunches at the Governor's Mansion for the leaders of the League of United Latin American Citizens (LULAC) and the American GI Forum, two important national organizations representing the interests of Hispanic Americans. And throughout the legislative session I had been a strong advocate for bilingual education in our public schools.

The polls indicated that seven out of ten voters were satisfied with my performance as governor and that I was viewed favorably in the minority communities. I knew that after coming so close to winning in 1972, the Republicans would mount a stiff challenge to my reelection. To strengthen my chances in the general election, it was important that I have minimal opposition in the Democratic Party primary in May 1974. I was aware that John Hill was making telephone calls to his friends to see if there was enthusiasm for his going against me in the primary. Recalling Price Daniel's mistake, I decided that it would

Janey and me with Jess and Betty Jo Hay. *Briscoe Papers.*

be wise to make an early official announcement of my reelection bid to help deter Hill and any other potential opponents from within the Democratic Party.

Accordingly, on October 30, 1973, my good friend and stalwart supporter Jess Hay of Dallas held a fundraising dinner in Austin at which I made my official announcement. I was delighted that U.S. Sen. Lloyd Bentsen gave the main dinner speech endorsing my reelection. I was especially honored when Lloyd declared that I was "an inherently decent man, with decent motives" and that I had established myself as a fiscally responsible governor who did not have his hands in the "people's pockets." I'm sure that Bentsen's endorsement went a long way to scare Hill from challenging me. Former congressman Joe Kilgore, another influential party leader, agreed to serve as my campaign manager. Joe and I had served together in the legislature.

In early January 1974 Hill announced that he would run for a second term as attorney general. It looked as though I might not attract

a major opponent in the primary. As late as January 1974, Sissy Farenthold, who we knew had been considering another campaign against
me, was reported to be interested in running for the Texas Railroad
Commission. In early February, however, she filed as a candidate for
governor.

THE CAMPAIGN LAWSUIT

A couple of days after Mrs. Farenthold announced her candidacy for
governor, she filed a $2.5 million lawsuit against me, Jess Hay, and Joe
Kilgore, alleging that we had violated a state campaign law by accept-
ing financial contributions prior to the appointment of a campaign
manager. Her suit claimed that my fundraising dinner in Austin in
October 1973 had violated the law. I had appointed Joe Kilgore as my
campaign manager the day of the dinner. The truth is that the purpose
of the dinner was to raise money to pay off the $825,000 in campaign
debt that remained from the previous campaign. Every cent raised at
the dinner was to pay the expense of the event and to retire my 1972
campaign debt. Farenthold's lawyers tried to have the trial initiated a
few weeks prior to the May 4 primary, but the judge agreed to post-
pone it until after the general election in November. The judge
announced that he did not want the trial to have any impact on the
elections. Nevertheless, the plaintiffs conducted depositions, issued
press releases, and generally kept the story in the newspapers throughout the remainder of 1974.

We eventually settled the Farenthold suit out of court in April 1975
because it was the easiest route to take. We knew we would prevail
ultimately, but the legal expenses that we would have incurred by
going forward with the suit would have been much greater than the
amount that we paid in the settlement. I had done nothing illegal or
unethical. The district attorney of Travis County examined our
fundraising reports closely and announced that he saw no evidence of
illegal activity. Nevertheless, the entire episode hurt me deeply. My
reputation for personal integrity means everything to me, and to have
it questioned so seriously was one of the most unpleasant experiences
I have ever had in public life.

1974 Campaign and Election

Despite the harassment and distraction of the Farenthold lawsuit, I felt very good about the primary campaign. You can never assume anything in politics, but I was confident of winning the Democratic nomination. Enthusiastic crowds greeted Janey and me at every campaign stop. I was much more comfortable and confident in my public appearances in 1974 than I had been two years earlier. My campaign motto was "He Kept the Promise," which referred to my 1972 campaign pledge of no new taxes. I stressed that I had kept my promise and that I would continue to do so. I knew that a majority of the voters appreciated a politician who, after getting elected, did exactly what he had promised. Sissy Farenthold generated much less enthusiasm than she had two years earlier. Her main attraction to voters in 1972 had been as a reform candidate running against corruption in state government. My administration had restored popular confidence in state government, and that left Sissy Farenthold without a substantive cause. In addition, I believe it was clear to the voters that her approach to government would lead inevitably to new taxes and that she was philosophically far to the left of most of the citizens of Texas.

On May 4 I received 68 percent of the vote in the primary and once again became the Democratic Party nominee for governor of Texas. And this time I would not have to wage a runoff campaign. I was especially pleased to win a solid majority of the Mexican American as well as the labor vote. It was a rousing vote of confidence, and it was a great way to begin my campaign for the general election in November.

What a difference two years had made in the internal affairs of the Democratic Party. In 1972 the national party had committed suicide with the McGovern candidacy, and the state party had been divided by bitter factionalism. Although you can never be confident that Democrats aren't going to squabble and fight among themselves, I felt very good about the unity we were enjoying in 1974. President Nixon and the Republican Party were neck-deep in the ongoing Watergate scandal, which helped our efforts to unify the Democratic Party. I was also in much better shape with the state's labor unions, and my relations with African Americans and Mexican Americans had improved

This photograph was taken soon after my reelection in November 1974 to a second term as governor of Texas. It was a happy and satisfying time. *Briscoe Papers.*

considerably during my first term in office. My appointments of African Americans and Mexican Americans to state boards and commissions were noted and appreciated.

THE CONSTITUTIONAL CONVENTION

During the primary campaign and after, the members of the legislature were in Austin to serve as delegates to a convention to write a new Texas constitution. The constitution they sought to rewrite was adopted in 1876 to replace the radical Reconstruction constitution of 1869. The 1869 document, which had been passed under pressure from the authorities in charge of Reconstruction in Texas, created a powerful and centralized state government featuring a strong governor and a number of state programs maintained by much higher taxes than Texans were used to paying. The constitution of 1869 accomplished some good things. For example, it created a common school system and strengthened civil rights. But a significant number of Texans opposed the document because it was a product of the hated Reconstruction government and enforced by the U.S. Army. Historically, Texans have been an extremely independent people, and they have never tolerated a powerful government or what they felt were high taxes, so it's not surprising that they were eager to toss the constitution out as soon as they could.

The constitution of 1876 was written in outraged reaction to the previous constitution. It severely restricted the powers of the legislature and the governor, returned control of public schools to local authorities, and basically established a commission form of executive administration. The legislature, which under the previous constitution held annual sessions, could meet no more than 140 days during odd-numbered years. It allowed for special sessions of no more than thirty days, but only if the governor called them. The governor was granted a veto over legislation, which can be overridden by a two-thirds majority of both houses of the legislature. The governor was given no authority over other elected state officials or over local officials. The document's authors carefully wrote it to keep state government out of their lives as much as possible. It had provisions that are unacceptable today, such as the requirement of racial segregation in the public schools and the levy of a poll tax, which are no longer operative, but it also established the University of Texas and enacted homestead protection. Although the constitution of 1876 was created to serve a Texas dominated by an agricultural economy with a vast majority of its citizens living in rural areas, it also provided a fairly easy method for passing amendments that made it possible to accommodate change. Accordingly, Texans have amended the constitution more than 230 times.

Although the 1876 constitution has served us relatively well, it is a lengthy document with a number of passages subject to a wide range of interpretations. There have been demands over the years to replace it with a "modern" charter. Those demands increased substantially in the late 1960s, ultimately influencing the legislature in 1971 to create a constitutional revision commission to draft a new charter to be considered by a convention that was scheduled to convene in January 1974. The constitutional convention was to be composed of the members of the Sixty-third Legislature. The convention's final document would not go into effect unless it was approved by a two-thirds majority of its members. A large majority of the voters approved this plan in the general election of 1972.

After receiving a draft document from the constitutional commission, which had been chaired by Robert Calvert, former chief justice of the Texas Supreme Court, the constitutional convention opened in Austin in January 1974. Price Daniel Jr., entering the last year of his service as the Speaker of the Texas House of Representatives, was elected presiding officer. Price Jr. aspired to higher political office and it was clear that he had hopes that a successful constitutional convention would catapult him into the governor's office eventually.

The convention, however, soon turned into a three-ring circus featuring heated disputes over a number of issues, some significant, many trivial. Every special interest in Texas had lobbyists pressuring the convention to write provisions securing their agendas in the constitution. One day the convention members would fight over provisions to overhaul the judiciary, while the next day they would battle over a provision to legalize bingo gambling for the purpose of charitable fundraising. One of the biggest battles centered on the issue of a right-to-work provision. Texas has long had a so-called right-to-work law, which makes it illegal to require an employee to join a labor union as a test for employment or job advancement. Several anti-labor delegates wanted to write that prohibition into the new constitution. They were fiercely opposed, of course, by the pro-labor delegates.

Because the decision to rewrite the constitution had been made by the legislature and the voters prior to my election as governor, it was clear to me that the governor would not have an official role to play in the deliberations, and I made no attempt to influence the process. Prior to the convention, I did state that I recognized that our current constitution had some problems and that I welcomed a thorough consideration of possible corrections. I added, however, that I had serious doubts about the need for an entirely new constitution. This statement was later misinterpreted by advocates of the new constitution as my endorsement of the final document.

When I had been an idealistic freshman member of the state legislature in 1949, I went to Austin convinced that the constitution needed to be rewritten completely. At the time, it seemed to me that the document was an out-of-date relic from the past. I could see that Texas faced a dynamic and exciting future that demanded a more active state government. When I left the legislature eight years later, however, I had a different view. My experience as a state representative gave me a deeper appreciation for the work done by the authors of the 1876 constitution. I understood how wise they had been to create a state government with strong limitations on its power.

My doubts about the need for a new constitution deepened as the convention continued into the summer of 1974. Among my chief concerns was the inclusion of a provision allowing annual sessions of the legislature. I was opposed to that provision. As a veteran of four legislative sessions, I came to appreciate the concept of the citizen legislator who returns home after the end of the session, who resides and works in his district, and is not a full-time politician. I believe that the closer the level of decision-making is to the people, the more capable government is of responding to the needs and wishes of the people. I believe our state system of biennial sessions keeps state government closer to the citizens that it is supposed to serve.

There are states where the legislature can call itself into session, and there are many states that have annual legislative sessions during which they are in session almost year round. Thank goodness we don't have annual sessions in Texas. I hope that we never have them. I feel very strongly that one problem with the federal government is that Congress is in session for so long. When John Garner was vice president, I can remember how he would return to Uvalde after Congress adjourned, and he would stay home for a few months. In those days, Congress was not in session nearly as long as it is today. As a practical matter, members of Congress now have to move their families to Washington if they are ever going to see them. And their constituency is not really their home anymore, so they don't spend much time there. They can't because they're in session most of the time. The good thing that we have in Texas is that we limit our legislative session to a specific number of days. And when midnight comes that day the session is over. One of the wisest sayings I ever heard when I was growing up in Uvalde was that the people's lives and property were in danger as long as the legislature was in session. I heard Governor Sterling make that observation, and my father often repeated it. They always laughed when they said it, but they really believed it—and so do I. As long as the legislature is in session, you never know what's going to happen. You never know what kind of bad legislative action might get out of there.

During the constitutional convention, the press asked frequently for my opinion about the various proposals, but I refused on the grounds that I had no role in the process. It should have been obvious, however, that I had no enthusiasm for it. I was relieved when the constitutional convention eventually adjourned without approving the new charter. It failed by only three votes, mainly due to the controversy over the right-to-work provision. The issue did not die, however. It would surface again in the next legislative session.

Fred Carrasco Prison Shoot-out

After my primary victory, I looked forward to a relatively peaceful summer as far as affairs of state are concerned. The constitutional convention continued until the end of July, but I was never invited to participate for the reasons I have already discussed. The legislature was not in session, so that front was quiet with one small exception. In August I had a brief flare-up with some legislators who were upset when I refused to call a special session to consider new pay raises for state employees and teachers. I argued that the regular legislative session in January 1975 was the proper time and forum to work on this issue. Everyone was exhausted by the constitutional convention, which had lasted for seven months. I did not see any compelling reason to bring the legislators back to Austin at a huge cost to taxpayers, especially with the regular session not that far away.

My wish for a peaceful summer wasn't granted, however. At 1 p.m. on July 24, Fred Gomez Carrasco, a thirty-four-year-old international drug smuggler who was serving a life sentence for murder, joined with two other prisoners in an attempt to escape from the Walls Unit of the state prison in Huntsville. Carrasco was a desperate criminal who was reputed to have murdered more than forty men during the time his gang was dealing heroin in San Antonio during the 1960s and early 1970s. The San Antonio police had captured him in a gunfight at a motel in July 1973.

A prison trusty had smuggled guns to Carrasco and his partners, twenty-seven-year-old Rudolfo Dominguez and forty-two-year-old Ignacio Cuevas. Dominguez was serving a fifteen-year sentence for assault to murder. Cuevas was a Mexican citizen serving a forty-five-year sentence for murder. Those three extremely dangerous convicts took twelve hostages in the escape attempt and held them in the prison library. Except for one prison guard and a Catholic priest, the hostages were librarians and teachers at the prison. One of the hostages suffered a heart attack soon after being taken hostage, and Carrasco released him. Carrasco demanded fifteen handcuffs and a television, which prison officials quickly gave him. He followed with another demand for six bulletproof vests, three bulletproof helmets, three walkie-talkie radios, three M-16 rifles, a large amount of ammunition, and some clothing. Carrasco declared that he had no intention of remaining in prison and that he would kill his hostages without remorse if his demands weren't met.

An hour or so after the hostages were taken, W. J. "Jim" Estelle, director of the Texas Department of Corrections, the independent state agency in charge of the prisons, called to brief me on the situation and to ask for my advice. I told Jim that I would defer to his expertise in this matter and that he would have my complete backing for his decisions. I did not want to interfere with the director and the professionals whose job it is to handle such situations. I also offered to go to Huntsville, but Jim counseled me to remain in Austin and monitor the situation with him over the telephone. He and the warden, H. H. Husbands, would manage the negotiations. Nevertheless, I told Jim that I would make certain that he had everything he needed and that I would be available to talk to the prisoners and the hostages if necessary. I cancelled several public appearances and other meetings, and I ordered the Texas Department of Public Safety to provide whatever help Jim Estelle requested. I remained in close contact with Jim throughout the siege. Except for the late night and early morning hours of the day, I would guess that we talked on the telephone every thirty minutes or so during the siege.

The day after Carrasco, Dominguez, and Cuevas took their hostages, Carrasco demanded that he be able to make his demands to me over the telephone. After getting advice from Jim Estelle, I decided to make the telephone call. We agreed that I would not make any commitments to Carrasco. We hoped the telephone call would buy additional time for us to find a way to end the siege without loss of life. I can't recall ever being more anxiety ridden. The lives of several innocent hostages were at stake. I spoke to Carrasco in a conference call that included his attorney, Ruben Montemayor. Carrasco spoke Spanish, and Montemayor translated. I understand spoken Spanish, so I could follow everything Carrasco said as he said it. He demanded armored vests, guns, and helmets that would provide them protection as they left the prison. Carrasco repeatedly asked when his demands were going to be met. "I've got to know," he said in Spanish. "I'll look into it," I responded. "I'll see." I also talked to several of the hostages. It was a heartrending situation. I could hear the fear in their voices as they pleaded with me to meet Carrasco's demands. They were extremely brave and heroic people. I talked one other time with

Carrasco, but it was essentially the same conversation that we had the first time. It had no effect on him whatsoever.

The siege lasted eleven days and ended at 9:30 p.m. on August 3. Jim Estelle arranged for the convicts, who used their hostages as human shields, to go to an armored car that they planned to use as an escape vehicle. As they left the library, prison security guards sprayed them with fire hoses, knocking them down. The convicts opened fire, and the police fired back. Carrasco and Dominquez were shot to death. A Department of Public Safety ballistics test indicated that Carrasco shot himself. Dominquez shot and killed hostage Julia Standley during the melee. Another hostage, Elizabeth Beseda, was also killed in the shoot-out. Jim had informed me of his plan two hours before it went forward, and I remained in my office monitoring the situation.

There is no way to express properly what a tragic situation that was. The needless and cruel death of those two innocent women was a horrible event. They were just doing their jobs in that library. They weren't guards. They were in the prison trying to help these prisoners. The next day Janey and I visited the victims' families. What could we say that could be meaningful to those families? After all of these years, I still don't know what else could have been done. It was a sad chapter in Texas history.

ELECTION TO A SECOND TERM

Jim Granberry, a forty-one-year-old orthodontist and former mayor of Lubbock, was my Republican opponent in the general election. Jim, of course, made the standard Republican charge that I was a liberal who was out of step with the conservative philosophy of most Texans. Ramsey Muniz was once again the candidate of the Raza Unida Party, but we were fairly confident of our standing with Mexican American voters. As the campaign neared its end, our polls indicated that Muniz would not be much of a factor in the election. In addition, it was clear that Granberry was finding it extremely difficult to find an effective issue to use against me. On election day, I received more than 61 percent of the votes to become the first Texas governor

Inauguration Day, 1975. *Texas State Library and Archives Commission, 1976/19, photograph by Bill Malone.*

to serve a four-year term. Granberry won only five of the 254 counties in Texas. I even carried Dallas County, which had become a Republican bastion. Muniz won less than half the votes he had attracted in 1972. To win reelection by that wide of a margin was the greatest honor I have ever received.

1975 Legislative Session

In 1975, Texas's economy was continuing to outpace the national economy, mainly due to increased revenue generated by rising energy prices. It was estimated that we would have a budget surplus of $1 billion without any increase in taxes. Accordingly, I proposed to the Sixty-fourth Legislature a program that included a 10 percent salary raise for state employees and public school teachers, as well as substantial increases in the budget for public health programs, medical and vocational education, and highway construction and maintenance. I also urged the legislature to make public school finance reform its most important priority. The state was under intense legal pressure from the courts to create a financial system that would make the quality of education in every independent school district as equal as possible.

In addition, I asked for increased authority for the Texas College Coordinating Board to control all new state college construction projects. I was alarmed at the rash of ill-considered and extravagant building projects that were being launched, primarily by the University of Texas System, the University of Houston, and Texas A&M University. Our state colleges, concerned more about prestige than accountability, were creating a host of new academic programs with no serious consideration of need or if they duplicated already existing programs. I told the legislature that the "squandering of the taxpayers' money without coordination, guidance, or direction has to stop." To be candid, my comments were aimed directly at Frank Erwin, who at that time was the chairman of the University of Texas Board of Regents. Erwin and his fellow regents openly ignored the coordinating board when making decisions about new construction on the university campus.

My other requests included tighter licensing and regulation of most child care facilities, tougher construction standards for the mobile home industry, stricter energy conservation measures for state office buildings, and a requirement that all insurance policies be written in a clear and readable style so that consumers could understand them more easily. Accompanying these proposals was my firm warning that I would veto any tax increases. Howard Richards, who served as my chief legislative liaison, worked tirelessly and effectively to persuade individual members to support our plan. Mark White, who remained as my secretary of state, continued his outstanding work with the members of the Senate.

Howard, Mark, and my other staff did a good job. Having a new Speaker of the House also helped our efforts. It was much easier for us to work with Billy Clayton than Price Daniel Jr. Clayton and I shared a rural, agricultural background, and we agreed on practically every issue. He was never unfair in his dealings with me, and he always kept his promises. The legislature eventually passed more than 60 percent of the programs I advocated during my "State of the State" address at the beginning of the session, including all of the requests that I discussed above. The bills that passed included one on public school finance in which few of us had any confidence. Someone called it a "band-aid" plan, and that is what it turned out to be. The problem would resurface in 1977, and it has continued to be a serious problem.

House Speaker Billy Clayton, with whom I enjoyed much better relations than I had with his predecessor. *Texas State Library and Archives Commission, 1978/99-2; di_02944.*

The defeats included my requests for a repeal of the state sales tax on utility bills, improvements in certain law enforcement procedures, stronger privacy laws, and a new antitrust act. In addition, the legislature passed a much bigger budget than I had requested, effectively wiping out our projected budget surplus and making tax reduction impossible. Nevertheless, we had completed the second legislative session in a row that did not pass or raise any taxes.

The budget that landed on my desk for signing was much larger than I believed was necessary, especially the appropriation for higher education, which included special riders authorizing 130 construction projects at sixteen state colleges. The projects included a new downtown campus for the University of Houston and an extensive expansion of the University of Texas Law School. The total cost of these projects was estimated to be in excess of $1 billion. The cost had to be estimated because the riders authorized these institutions to spend as much as necessary to complete the projects. This huge expense was in addition to the legislature's 62 percent increase in spending for higher education over the previous biennial budget. The legislative sponsors of these riders had inserted them at the end of the session, without public notice or hearings. I thought this was an outrageous and irresponsible use of public money. This legislative slight of hand also was similar to the maneuvering that had resulted in the Sharpstown scandal. I was not alone in my concern about these appropriations; eighty-one legislators petitioned me to veto them. I vetoed the riders, as well as other unnecessary higher education projects costing an additional $27 million.

I also was not pleased when the legislature resurrected the proposed new constitution that had been killed at the constitutional convention the previous summer. The legislature divided the failed constitution into eight sections and offered each for approval by the voters as amendments to the 1876 constitution. The voters could pick and chose which, if any, of the amendments they wanted to replace corresponding provisions in the current constitution.

It was at this point, in October 1975, that I decided it would be appropriate for me to announce my views about the proposed new constitution. Lieutenant Governor Hobby, Attorney General Hill, and Speaker Clayton were traveling across Texas, urging the voters to approve all of the amendments. Not every state official favored the entire document. Bob Bullock, who had been elected state comptroller in 1974, was critical of several of the amendments, and many of the state's judges opposed the amendment to reorganize the judiciary. While I was studying the matter, Justice Calvert came to my office and made an eloquent plea on behalf of the new constitution. A careful study of the document, however, confirmed my worst suspicions. I could not, in good conscience, come out in favor of the amendments. Although I had problems with numerous items, especially in the section on the judiciary, my opposition was based chiefly on the provision for annual legislative sessions.

At a press conference on October 14, 1975, I declared that it would be in the best interests of the state for all eight amendments to be defeated. I admitted that some of the proposed changes were good, but the bad changes far outweighed the good. I sincerely believed that the new amendments would result ultimately in a vast increase in state expenditures, which would require higher taxes, maybe even an income tax. I felt that reasonable means were available to the people of Texas to amend the existing constitution, which they have done more than 230 times since 1876.

I was attacked immediately by a number of state officials for being "out of step" with the citizens of Texas. My reaction was that the people of Texas were free to disagree with me by voting for the new constitution. If it turned out that I was out of step—and I didn't believe that I was—so be it. On November 4 the voters overwhelmingly defeated all eight of the amendments. When reporters asked Bill Hobby for an explanation for the defeat, he replied that "there's not enough of the body left for an autopsy." Price Daniel Jr. and John Hill told the press that I had killed the new constitution.

As I told the press, the election was not about personalities or what any politician had to say about the issue, it was about the fact that the voters had faith in their present constitution and saw no need to change. Because Price Jr. had tried to appease every faction at the convention, he ended up alienating just about everyone. His political career actually suffered as a result of his performance during the con-

This is the office I used whenever I returned to Uvalde during my terms as governor. It remains my office to this day. *Briscoe Papers*.

vention. In 1978 Price Jr. was a candidate for attorney general, but Mark White defeated him in the Democratic primary. Tragically, Price Jr. was killed in a gunshot incident in his home in Liberty in 1981.

I did not fully realize it at the time, but my opposition to the proposed constitution and my battle to bring the higher education budget under control had made me some powerful enemies. A few weeks after the voters killed the proposed constitution, reporters for the Associated Press in Austin released a series of articles, which were printed in most of the state's major newspapers, charging that I had been an "absentee governor" who had spent too much time away from my office in Austin. I was criticized particularly for the time I had spent back home in Uvalde and at my Catarina Ranch. A couple of popular newspaper columnists who had been fiercely critical of my opposition to the constitution repeated the allegations.

The criticisms grew so loud that Cactus Pryor, a very popular Austin radio and television personality, came to my defense. "Show me a man who can think more clearly in a smoke-filled room than on a clear-skied ranch in South Texas," Cactus declared, "and I'll show you a machine politician." Cactus added that lobbyists were the main source of complaints about my alleged inaccessibility. That was an accurate statement.

I always took the position that Austin is a poor place to learn what the voters want from their government. I told members of the capitol press corps that they would do themselves a world of good to get out of town more often. The truth is that it was important to me to maintain close contact with people who would tell me what they really thought, rather than what they believed I wanted to hear. I liked the kind of feedback that J. Frank Dobie used to describe as the truth "with the bark off." I did not feel that I could get candid and objective advice in Austin. There was a degree of isolation in the Governor's Mansion that, as our state has grown, has only increased with time. I found that if I stayed in Austin all the time, my contact was limited to those who are working in government and to those who are lobbying for some special interest. It is an artificial atmosphere. I tried to travel around the state as much as I could to escape that confining environment in Austin. Back home is also where I could receive feedback from long-time friends who weren't concerned about hurting my feelings.

I remember one instance when I thought I had really accomplished something wonderful by working hard to reduce the size of some state expenditure. I returned to Uvalde and went over to the Kincaid Hotel coffee shop to visit with some of the local folks who liked to gather there for conversation. The first thing they hit me with was why did I spend so much money! I got no credit for significantly reducing the expenditure. I had expected to be told about what a good job I had done, but I didn't hear that. Instead, I heard about how we were spending too much money. Well, that's simply not the kind of opinion I would have heard in Austin.

I never neglected my duties, and I made certain that the leaders of state government could find me no matter where I happened to be. Speaker Clayton told the press that "whenever I needed [Governor Briscoe], I always found him." These allegations bothered me, of course, but I understood that they were unfair accusations that had been encouraged by some of the special interests I had angered during the battle over the new constitution. I refused to let the episode change my routine.

In December 1975 the Texas Supreme Court ruled that I did not have constitutional authority to veto the special higher education riders in the budget. Supporters of the law school at the University of Texas at Austin had been among those requesting a ruling by the court, which declared that the only way I could have killed the riders would have been to veto the entire appropriations bill. If I had understood this at the end of the legislative session, I would have vetoed the entire bill, and I would have immediately called a special session for the legislature to pass a new appropriations bill without the riders. At any rate, I was now very aware of the power of the higher education lobby. I resolved nevertheless to continue my efforts to bring higher education spending, as well as overall state spending, under control.

THE JIMMY CARTER CAMPAIGN FOR PRESIDENT

Richard Nixon's resignation as president in August 1974 presented the Democratic Party with an excellent opportunity to recapture the White House in the 1976 presidential election. By the beginning of 1976, various candidates were lining up to make a run for the presidential nomination in the Democratic primaries. I decided very early in the process to support the bid of Texas Sen. Lloyd Bentsen Jr. It was an easy decision, but it was based on more than simple loyalty to a fellow Texas Democrat. I had known Lloyd Bentsen and his father favorably for many years. He and I shared a basic conservative Democratic political philosophy. Lloyd was an articulate and effective political leader who had made an impressive record as a freshman in the U.S. Senate. His campaign for president, however, never really got off the ground.

When Lloyd's presidential campaign failed, my support went to a fellow southerner, Gov. Jimmy Carter of Georgia. I first met Carter at a meeting of the Southern Governors Conference in 1974, and we soon became good friends. I felt that as the standard-bearer, he would return the national Democratic Party to its traditionally southern conservative roots. I also was attracted to the fact that he was a deeply moral man guided by sincerely held Christian beliefs, who would restore badly needed moral values to the White House. In addition,

I welcomed Egyptian President Anwar Sadat to Texas when he arrived at Ellington Air Force Base near Houston in 1975. *Briscoe Papers, Box 255.*

Carter assured Oklahoma Gov. David Boren, Louisiana Gov. Edwin Edwards, and me that, if elected president, he would remove price controls on natural gas. That was a critical issue for Texas, Oklahoma, and Louisiana because our states were the nation's leading producers of natural gas. Federal price controls had discouraged exploration for new sources and the artificially low prices had cut deeply into our tax revenue. After Lloyd Bentsen withdrew from the primaries, I was pleased to switch my support to Jimmy Carter. I campaigned vigorously for his nomination.

In July 1976 Janey and I attended the national Democratic Party convention in New York City during which Carter received the nomination. I served as chairman of the Texas delegation. I was not happy with his choice of Minnesota Sen. Walter Mondale for the vice presidency; my preference was Ohio Sen. John Glenn, but the decision did not lessen my enthusiasm for Carter's candidacy. After the convention, we returned to Texas to spearhead Carter's campaign. Janey and I traveled throughout the state to wage as vigorous a campaign as possible on Carter's behalf. We were on the road almost constantly, stressing Carter's moral values and his conservative fiscal views, including his pledge to deregulate natural gas prices. By election day, Janey had shaken so many hands that she developed a serious infection in her right hand. We were both exhausted at the end, but we were deeply satisfied when Texas was among the states that Carter carried. Jimmy Carter was my friend, and it was a great feeling to see a friend become president of the United States.

Unfortunately, our friendship didn't survive his presidency. It turned out that Carter made a lot of promises that he seemed to have no problem breaking. He promised me that if he became president, he would deregulate the natural gas industry, but once he was in the White House he forgot his promise. I traveled throughout Texas, as did governors Boren and Edwards in their respective states, telling the voters that they could trust Jimmy Carter to keep his promise to deregulate natural gas production. I walked out on a limb only to have him cut it off. I had made the argument to Carter that price controls never work the way they were intended. The federal government had imposed price controls as part of its program to blunt the effects of the energy crisis. The intention was to keep the price low. But most of the experts believed that with deregulation, exploration would open new fields that would increase the supply, and the price of gas would actually decrease. Time proved us right on this issue. When controls on natural gas were removed, prices did go up initially, but new drilling eventually caused the price of natural gas to fall below the previously regulated level. This was proof to me that price controls do not work. Natural gas prices now fluctuate according to the economic law of supply and demand, as they should.

I think Carter made a poor president for many reasons, not just because of his stand on natural gas. I completely disagreed with his administration's general economic policy of fighting inflation with high interest rates and unemployment. It was a bad policy that didn't work. Carter had the poorest, most inaccurate, sorriest economic advice a president ever had. He was one of the greatest disappointments of my political life. Although I voted the straight Democratic Party ticket, as I always do, I did not campaign for Carter when he ran for reelection in 1980. I was not surprised by Ronald Reagan's victory, and I did not mourn Carter's defeat.

THE LEGISLATIVE SESSION OF 1977

When the legislature convened for its session in 1977, Texas continued to enjoy unprecedented economic growth and prosperity, which resulted in greatly increased revenues from the existing tax structure. We opened the new session with a $1 billion surplus, and projections indicated an additional $2 billion would be added to that surplus during the next two years. Obviously, this significant increase in revenue made it much easier for me to maintain my position against new taxes. Increased revenue made it possible for us to enhance essential state services, especially our highway system, and to raise the average teacher's salary more than 50 percent without increasing the state tax burden. And by keeping a lid on taxes and by improving our state's infrastructure, we were able to attract new business to Texas, which created new jobs and added to the increase in our tax revenue.

Of course, many members of the state legislature were strongly tempted to use our surplus to enlarge the state bureaucracy and to send more pork barrel projects back to their districts. As a result, I spent much of my time during the legislative session attempting to restrain this impulse for bigger government. The most important fiscal reform that I fostered and worked for during the 1977 session was the Tax Relief Amendment to the constitution. The amendment created restrictions on taxing agricultural land as property according to market value, which frequently was far greater than the land's actual productive value. The amendment also allowed certain exemptions from taxes on homesteads and prohibited taxes on personal property. After a struggle, we were able to get the amendment out of the legislature and submitted to the voters as a constitutional amendment. The amendment was approved by 84 percent of the voters.

Public school financing was the one problem that continued to defy every well-intentioned attempt to solve it. As expected, the band-aid plan passed in 1975 had proven unworkable, and local school districts were facing financial disaster. The session ended with the various factions unable to compromise. Although I disliked special sessions, and, with one exception in 1973, had successfully avoided them, I knew that we had an emergency situation. I agreed to call a special session to convene in July 1977 to address school finance. The legislature produced a new plan within the allotted time for the session, but that plan also proved to be inadequate. Public school finance was the most vexing issue I faced during my six years as governor. The problem of how to equalize funding in all school districts and at the same time retain a high degree of local control would continue to plague the state. In my view, the complex problem of how to finance public education fairly and effectively will continue to be the most important issue Texas state government will have to confront in the coming years.

The 1977 regular session and the special session would be the last time the legislature would meet before the 1978 primary election. My term as governor would be up in 1978. I had an important decision to make.

Chapter 13

THIRD TERM DENIED

The Election of 1978

THE TRUTH IS that I never gave a thought to not running for a third term as governor. I was proud of my record, and I believed that a large majority of Texans were pleased with my conservative management of the executive office and my ability to hold the line on new taxes. Janey supported my decision to run again.

It was no surprise to me, of course, when John Hill announced in September 1977 his candidacy to be the 1978 Democratic Party nominee for governor. Hill had been running for governor ever since his defeat in the governor's race in 1968. I was confident, however, that I could beat him. In my view, Hill was too liberal for most Texas Democrats. I was confident of victory in the general election as well. Although it was obvious that the Republican Party was continuing to gain strength, I felt that my conservative record and the advantage of being an incumbent would carry me to success in the November election.

George Christian, a highly regarded political strategist who had served as President Johnson's press spokesman, agreed to run my campaign. George did an outstanding job, as he always did with any job he ever took on. The problem, however, is that I didn't really let George do his job. The overwhelming victories I had enjoyed in the primary and general elections in 1974 spoiled me. In retrospect, I can see that I was overconfident and complacent about my campaign. I took my reelection so much for granted that I ignored most of the advice of my campaign staff. Basically, I was my own campaign manager, despite having George Christian's talented services. The result was a poorly managed campaign—the worst I have ever run, even worse than the effort in 1968. I blame no one else but myself for that.

My campaign went backward in the sense that I operated in an outdated manner. I never did get the campaign organized properly. I depended too much on personal contact through travel and personal appearances at rallies and other events. I made extremely poor use of the media. My television campaign advertisements were awful; there is no other way to describe them. Money was not an issue. I had enough money to support the campaign adequately. I don't think I underestimated John Hill as an opponent; I knew he was articulate and energetic, but that didn't worry me.

The problem was that I failed to convey any sense of urgency, which made my leaders at the grassroots level complacent. I should have fired up the troops and made wake-up calls, but I didn't. As a result, I didn't get my voters to the polls. There were a few counties where my local campaign people did a good job, and the results indicated that. But I did not pay attention enough to the grassroots operation in each one of my strong counties and that hurt me badly. My strongholds had been in the rural areas of South, East, and West Texas; where I could depend on 60 to 80 percent of the vote. My reelection depended on a high voter turnout in those areas. I usually split the urban metropolitan areas with my opponents, so the rural vote was crucial to my campaign. In 1978, however, we failed to activate my base, particularly in South Texas. That was my fault entirely. I simply took it for granted that my supporters would vote in large numbers, but I never gave them a reason to be concerned enough to vote, so the turnout was light in the areas of my greatest strength.

In hindsight, I believe the issue of my serving a third term probably hurt my campaign more than any other issue. I was asking the voters to make me their governor for another four years, which would give me a total of ten years as the state's chief executive. Ten years is a long time. It would have been the longest period anyone had served as governor of Texas. There was a real need to explain to my fellow citizens why they should make me their governor for that length of time.

George Christian greeting us during the 1978 campaign. *Briscoe Papers.*

I did a poor job of answering that question because I failed to under-stand its importance.

I also mishandled the difficult issue of public education. I had sup-ported and worked for the passage of the highest percentage increase in teacher salaries in state history, but I received no credit for it. The Texas State Teachers Association did not support me, and that obvi-ously hurt.

Hill promised to spend $1 billion to raise the salaries of public school teachers, in addition to immense spending increases in a num-ber of other state programs. He promised everything to everybody, and he proposed to fulfill those promises without an increase in taxes. Quite frankly, Hill could not have carried out all of those promises without a tax increase, despite the increased revenue that the energy boom was providing Texas.

If I had done a better job of getting my voters to the polls, however, I don't believe Hill's issues would have defeated me.

I convinced myself that I was going to win, even when I saw the polls showing Hill had edged ahead. Near the end of the campaign, when the polls indicated that Hill might win, George Christian and Joe Kilgore met with me during a trip to Houston to urge me to call for a major tax cut. We knew that state revenues were increasing rapidly as a result of the spike in energy prices and that the legislature could be persuaded to cut taxes. In hindsight, I should have followed their advice, but I was afraid that it was too late in the campaign to announce suddenly that I was for a major tax cut. I feared that it would look like desperation. After the primary, I called a special session of the legislature, which did reduce taxes by approximately $1 billion, so it would not have been demagoguery for me to call for a tax cut during the election. Instead, I missed a golden opportunity to regain momentum for my campaign.

On May 7, 1978, I lost my reelection bid to John Hill by 179,000 votes. I have to admit that it was a bitterly disappointing defeat. I was angry, but my anger was more at myself for not working harder and wiser in the campaign. Don't let anyone who has been denied reelection to an important public office try to tell you that it doesn't hurt. And the hurt is deep when you feel that you had carried out the duties of that office very well. It is also a bitter feeling to see your opponent rewarded despite his mean-spirited personal attacks as well as his engaging in rhetoric that twisted and wholly misrepresented my actual record.

John Hill eventually lost the general election to the Republican candidate, Dallas oilman William P. Clements. If I had won the primary, I sincerely believe that I could have defeated Clements. Obviously, that is a big "if" that never happened. There is no question that a race against Bill Clements, who had access to a sizeable personal fortune, would have been costly and difficult. But it was still the case in 1978 that a conservative, business-oriented Democrat could have defeated a Republican in a statewide election in Texas. Jimmy Carter had carried our state only two years earlier. In 1978 Democrats won the races for lieutenant governor, attorney general, land commissioner, and comptroller. Lloyd Bentsen easily won reelecton to the U.S. Senate in 1982 and in 1988. Clements beat Hill by a tiny margin.

The main problem for Hill was that he had been a trial lawyer, and trial lawyers don't have a pro-business public image. I think election analysts have shown that Hill lost the votes of a lot of conservative Democrats who voted for me in the primary. Hill also ran a complacent campaign. He and his followers assumed his election was automatic because Texas had not elected a Republican governor since the days of Reconstruction. I know that I would have taken Bill Clements much more seriously than did Hill.

I should add here that I have always had a good relationship with Bill Clements. I first got to know Bill before I became governor, when we worked together in support of the Boy Scouts. I did not take his surprise decision to run for governor in 1978 as a personal attack on me. Bill felt that it was time for Texas to elect a Republican governor, and he wanted to be in office in 1980 to help in the effort to elect a Republican president. He had the personal resources, the ability, and the energy to be a formidable candidate. I was not shocked when he beat John Hill. He treated Janey and me with respect and friendship after I left office, even though I always rejected his frequent invitations for me to switch to the Republican Party. Bill honored Janey in January 1981 by appointing her to a six-year term on the University of Texas Board of Regents. She loved the time she served as a regent for her beloved alma mater.

In the months after my defeat, there was much speculation in the press that I would abandon the Democratic Party to become a Republican. I never gave one second of thought to changing parties. I have always been a Democrat, and I always will be a Democrat. I'm proud of being a Democrat and of what our party has done for Texas and for the nation.

Larger Achievements as Governor

I ran in 1968 and again in 1972 deeply committed to the goal of stopping the biennial increase in state taxes that had occurred since the administration of Coke Stevenson in the 1940s. I believed that some of those tax increases had been unwarranted and that state government had gone on a path of automatically increasing taxes every two years, whether or not those increases were really necessary. The state had developed a tax habit that needed breaking. I am proud that I achieved that goal. It was obvious in 1972 that the state's energy-based economy would continue to increase our tax revenues for years to come. I realized that state services would have to expand to meet the challenge of a larger population, but the increase in revenue from existing taxes would be sufficient to do the job well. My opponents claimed that state government stagnated during the six years that I was governor. The record will show that charge is false. Essential state services expanded, in some areas dramatically, while I was governor.

My agenda as I assumed the duties of governor in 1973 centered on my philosophy that Texans wanted less government, not more. I believed then, and I retain that belief today, that Texans are an independent people who basically want the government to leave them alone. That's not just a Texas trait; the truth is that most Americans feel that way. I think those who claim that Texans and their fellow Americans are anti-government are wrong. Our citizens certainly expect government to provide essential services, but they prefer to have as many of those services as possible to be controlled and administered by local government. I tried always to conduct the governor's office with that view in mind.

In the 1978 primary campaign, John Hill called me a "do-nothing" governor, which is a serious corruption of my "less government is best government" philosophy. I feel certain that Hill did not defeat me with that charge. As I have discussed earlier, other factors beat me. When Clements, who shares my view on the subject, defeated Hill in the general election, I believe Hill discovered that most Texans prefer the more conservative approach to government.

I think my management of the governor's office also played a significant role in restoring public confidence in the integrity of state government after the Sharpstown scandal. There were no special favors or jobs for sale from the governor's office while I was in charge. And I believe that the people of Texas knew that. I feel that my reputation for honesty and integrity was one of my major strengths as governor.

THINGS UNDONE AND A COUPLE OF REGRETS

Of course, I'm not entirely satisfied with my record. I do wish that I could have done more to improve our state educational system at every level, from kindergarten to graduate school. We took several steps forward, including increasing teacher salaries, but I wish we had done more to address the issue of accountability in the classroom and at the administrative levels of our educational system.

In retrospect, I realize that as governor I should have developed a closer relationship with the news media than I did. I made a mistake by not using the news media to reach the people. I should have had more one-on-one interviews, both with individual members of the print press and on radio and television. The resulting article or news report may not have been what I would have liked, but that's a risk I should have taken. I failed to take advantage of the opportunities that were available for me to use the media. I took the attitude that if I did a good job of keeping the state running well without new taxes it would be readily apparent to the citizens of Texas without my having to work the press. That was a mistake. I also should have conducted more press conferences. I should have given so many press conferences that they became routine and maybe even boring. At any rate, as I look back, there is no question that I should have given the press more access.

It may seem surprising reading this today, but it took me quite a while to realize that by the time I became governor in January 1973, the behavior of the capitol press had changed radically from the way it had operated when I was last in government in the early 1950s. I was surprised by how adversarial many of the reporters covering state government had become. I had not expected that. My experience as a member of the state legislature had been completely different. I had a good relationship with the local newspapers in my district. I also had gotten along well with the *Dallas Morning News*'s capitol correspondent Richard "Dick" Morehead, who was still at his post when I became governor. I guess I could best describe my relationship with the press during my legislative years as one of cooperation and friendship. It was naiveté in the extreme for me to think that I could enjoy that same type of relationship with the press after I became governor.

The capitol press corps had grown tremendously since my service in the legislature. In those days, the major urban newspapers would have only one capitol correspondent. When I became governor I discovered that some of those same newspapers had several reporters covering state government. We essentially had no television coverage in the early 1950s. When I was governor it seemed like every television station in Texas had a reporter and camera crew. As recently as the 1940s, the capitol press corps was so small that Gov. Coke Stevenson could take the entire group on hunting trips. In addition, what was supposed to be off the record during those hunting trips stayed off the record. It doesn't work that way now.

I can't blame my staff for the mistakes I made in my relations with the news media. My difficulties were strictly my own making. Bob Hardesty, who had worked as a speechwriter for President Johnson, did an outstanding job handling my relations with the press. Bob urged me to have more press conferences, but I basically ignored his good advice. I simply did not anticipate how much press interest there would be in my private and business life. I didn't realize that we had entered a new era in which the details of the private life of a public official were no longer considered off limits. When I was questioned about how much land I owned, for example, I refused to answer the question. Where I come from in the ranching world you never talk about how much land you own, and you never ask others that question. It is like going around telling people how much money you have in the bank. It's in bad taste and rude. So, I was extremely hesitant to talk about my land holdings. And that was a mistake. My refusal looked as though I had something to hide, which I did not. I should have answered immediately, and that would have ended that.

The initial problem I had with the press was that I had defeated Sissy Farenthold, who had become the darling of some reporters because she was colorful and made good news copy. In that respect, I did not compare well with Farenthold. I was the opposite of colorful, and I was not inclined to make outrageous comments, which meant that I was a bore to reporters who were eager for sensational stories.

If I ran for public office today, I would enter the race with the full knowledge and expectation that I would no longer have a private life that was off limits to the press. That is now the rule, for good or bad, and I would have to accept it. I regret my poor handling of the news media as governor. I would handle it differently if I had a chance to do it again.

THE FIRST LADY

Texas Monthly magazine once noted that the state legislative leadership and the lobbyists in Austin were amazed that as governor I seemed to have no close advisors other than Janey. In its articles about me, *Texas Monthly* rarely got anything right, but the magazine was correct on that point. I never had a kitchen cabinet or inner circle of advisors. As I look back, it seems very odd to me that anyone would have been surprised that she was my closest advisor. I always treated Janey as my full partner in everything in which I was involved, and that included my work as governor. Janey was highly intelligent, extremely well informed about public issues and current affairs, and full of plain old common sense. She had two degrees from the University of Texas, and she had been a keen observer of state politics as far back as her college days. She also happened to be my loving wife as well as my trusted best friend.

Some members of the press, as well as a few lobbyists and my critics within state government, resented the key role that Janey played in my administration. After I was inaugurated, some of the state's newspapers published articles that questioned the propriety of letting my wife have so much "influence." One joke that circulated around the Capitol referred to us as "the Governor and Mr. Briscoe." *Newsweek* ran an article about Janey that was titled "Boss Lady." The article included a picture of Janey talking with me. The caption read: "Janey and Dolph: Who's in charge here?"

It's sad to have to say this, but there is no doubt in my mind that many of Janey's detractors were inspired by an old-fashioned brand of male Texan *machismo*. Times have changed, thankfully, but in the early 1970s too many Texans believed that a woman had absolutely no place in state government. It's true that Texas elected Miriam Fergu-

Janey and me during our tough campaign for reelection in 1978. *Briscoe Papers; di_03968.*

son governor back in the 1920s and 1930s, but everyone knew that the decisions in the governor's office would be made by her husband, James Ferguson, who was banned from public office because of his impeachment as governor in 1917. With a few exceptions, such as those rare occasions when a woman was elected to the legislature, Texas government had been strictly a male enterprise. Janey was a strong woman, and that threatened some people who were still living in the past. Texas, of course, does not have a monopoly on that sort of outlook. There are many important examples of strong first ladies at the national level, and each one was attacked for being strong.

During my run for governor, Janey and I campaigned together. She worked the crowds and gave speeches. She was always the best worker in every campaign I ever ran. We were a team, and we never hid that fact. After the election, Janey said publicly that she would be an active participant in my administration, sort of a minister without portfolio. There were serious issues that Janey felt strongly about, and she was eager to make a contribution in those areas of her concern.

Janey worked with the Texas Department of Mental Health and Mental Retardation to provide work for people with disabilities. One of her achievements was the establishment of a state sheltered workshop program for the handicapped. She was the driving force behind the creation of the state's runaway hotline during an era when there had been no system available to help keep parents in touch with their kids who had left home and cut off contact with their families. She worked as a volunteer in an influenza vaccination program during the swine flu epidemic. Janey loved history, and she had a deep interest in historic preservation. One of her projects resulted in having the federal government designate the Governor's Mansion a national historical landmark.

Janey was an activist, she had her own opinions that she expressed openly, and she had a high profile throughout my years as governor, but she never, ever, interfered with or tried to intervene in any official matter. The younger generation may be surprised today that anyone would criticize Janey's activism as a first lady. The wonderful women who were first ladies after Janey, such as Rita Clements, Linda Gale White, and Laura Bush, were just as engaged in their own projects. And, of course, with Ann Richards, Texas finally elected a woman as governor on her own right.

I'm very proud of the fact that Janey made her own distinct contribution to the effort to educate our fellow citizens that women are as capable as men when it comes to serving the public good.

Chapter 14

LIFE AFTER THE GOVERNOR'S MANSION

INAUGURATION DAY ARRIVED in January 1979. All of our things had been packed and sent back to the ranch. Janey and I said good-bye to the mansion staff and the DPS guard detail. Trooper Bill Williamson drove us over to the Capitol, right up to the governor's office, where all our personal things had been sent back. It was about 9:30 or 10:00 a.m. We said goodbye to the office staff and waited for the time to go by. Rita and Bill Clements soon entered the governor's office. It was a very pleasant surprise and very thoughtful of him to come by before the inauguration.

We had a good visit, and at the appointed time, Bill and Rita, the other state office holders, and their legislative staff all gathered in the outer office and went down in front of the Capitol. Janey and I waited until the clock struck twelve and then walked out of the back of the Capitol where Bill Williamson was waiting with a car to take us to the airport. We flew from Austin to Dallas in our plane and spent the night at the Adolphus Hotel. We flew to London the next morning. Janey had made reservations right after the primary election at the Connaught Hotel on Carlos Square. I had tried to make reservations there in previous years but always waited too long. The Connaught is what I would call a typical English hotel of the Victorian era, with a "stiff upper lip." We arrived there the next day. We had a nice room, with a small fireplace. Of course, it was a very cold and damp winter.

We thought we would probably stay about two months, but after six weeks my partner, Red Nunley, called me and said, "Dolph, you

Fellow former governors Preston Smith, John Connally, and Price Daniel Sr. join me for a picture at our reunion with Bill Clements when he was governor of Texas. *Texas State Library and Archives Commission Prints and Photographs Collection.*

have got to come back, we've got a deal to buy the Valdina Ranch from Bob Woodward, and you've got to come home and close that deal for us with him." I protested and said, "Red, you can take care of that, you don't need me." He said, "Nope, can't do it, you've got to come back and do it, we don't want to lose the deal." So Janey and I packed up and flew back to Dallas.

Without any problem, we closed the deal on the Valdina. It became very obvious that Red didn't need me, but he had determined in his mind that it was time for us to come home, and that was what we did. And he was right.

We returned to Austin in March to attend the official swearing-in ceremony of the three individuals whom I had appointed to the University of Texas Board of Regents at the end of my term: Howard Richards, James Powell, and Jon Newton.

Some months later Janey became ill. She suffered from a headache from which she could get no relief. It also affected her balance while walking or standing. The doctors could not determine the cause. Our local friend, Dr. Sterling Fly, researched the situation and said there were two clinics that specialized in diagnosing and treating the type of symptoms Janey had. One clinic was in California and the other was the Baylor School of Medicine at Methodist Hospital in Houston. We wanted to stay as close to home as possible, so Sterling made an appointment for Janey to see Dr. Bobby Alford, head of the Neurosensory Department at Baylor in Houston. Dr. Alford discovered a tumor in her inner ear that was life-threatening. The whole family traveled to Houston, and Janey went through ten and a half hours of surgery to remove the tumor. The good Lord answered our prayers, and it was benign. Janey soon had her good health back.

We then began a project that dominated our time for the next few years. We had, some years earlier, bought a ranch south of Uvalde on the Leona River from the W. E. Lee Estate. W. E. Lee was a well-known, successful Houston oilman and a partner in the Yount Lee Oil Company. Reading Black, the founder of Uvalde, built a house on the land many years before it became the Lee Ranch. During the time the Lee family owned the house they added four rooms downstairs and a second floor.

I decided to move this house down to Catarina for additional sleeping space when we had a large crowd. In the early years of the twentieth century, David Sinton had owned the Catarina Ranch, which is some 240,000 acres in size. Sinton's only child married Charles Phelps Taft, the older half-brother of William Howard Taft, who later became president of the United States. Sinton had all the lumber brought by wagon from Cotulla to the hilltop at the middle of the ranch. In the days of the Catarina subdivision of the 1920s this house was the headquarters of the Catarina Farms Company, and the town of Catarina was built around it. Janey and I purchased this house. We got a mover, Earl Bradford, to cut it into three sections and move them about fifteen miles out to our headquarters on the old

Catarina Ranch. After Bradford moved the sections, he set them up on a foundation that he had built. Moving this large historic house was just the beginning of our work.

About that time, we had not only a drought, but also a major drop in cattle prices, so the Taft House sat there for several years before we could refurbish it. Janey often referred to it as "the bag lady" because it looked so bad. The house is a three-story frame structure with columns and balconies and a widow's walk on top. When we began the project to refurbish the place, it turned out to be much more of a project than I had anticipated. We added a family room and an elevator.

A friend of mine from my legislative days, former senator Don Kennard of Fort Worth, called me and said there was going to be an auction at Piedmont, which was the old Briscoe Home built in 1732. Piedmont is located in the Shenandoah Valley near Charles Town, West Virginia, and close to the homes of two of George Washington's brothers. Don suggested that we come up and take a look at the furniture that was going to be sold. We did so, and we ended up buying quite a few pieces, four beds, several sofas, and several large mirrors. The furniture from Piedmont is now in the Taft House.

Briscoe Ranches and the Cattle Business Today

The ranching business has changed radically in my lifetime. Some of those changes have been beneficial. We used to do our ranch work exclusively with horses, for example. Now my son, Chip, uses a helicopter for rounding up his livestock. Helicopters are much more efficient than horses for rounding up cattle in the heavy brush. Fewer people are needed on a ranch now because we have modern equipment and better fencing. We make much more use of screen fencing instead of barbed wire. The eradication of the screwworm also has resulted in a reduction in the number of cowhands that we employ. We don't have to spend so much time just taking care of sick animals.

There have been other changes, however, that have not been so positive. Historically, the cattle rancher and the cowboy have been among the most enduring symbols of American life. For a period of well over 125 years, they have represented two basic American values:

freedom and self-reliance. One of the saddest developments in my lifetime, however, has been the steady decline of American ranching. That decline has accelerated rapidly during the past two decades. I have been shocked, but not surprised, by reports documenting that more than half a million ranchers have been forced out of the business since 1980. Currently, there are approximately 800,000 ranchers, and the economic conditions and trends that prevail today threaten the existences of nearly all. More ranchers than you can imagine are barely hanging on, selling their cattle at cost or at a loss. Many have had to find second jobs to survive. The truth is that the independent cattleman has become an endangered species.

As a cattle rancher, I know of several factors that are contributing to the demise of our industry. They include vast increases in land prices, much of it the result of suburban sprawl, which makes it nearly impossible to start new operations or to expand old ones. High inheritance tax rates force families to sell off their ranch land to pay tax bills. A large increase in the shipment of live cattle from Mexico and Canada has helped to stagnate beef prices. Sensational stories in the news media, often based on unfounded or scientifically disputed allegations, have caused health scares in the general public about beef that have resulted in a steep decline in beef consumption.

In my opinion, however, the most significant cause for the demise of the independent cattle rancher has been the transformation of the meatpacking business into something close to an industrial monopoly. There is a natural adversarial relationship between beef producers and meat packers; the former always want to sell their cattle at the highest price possible, and the latter always want to buy cattle at the lowest price possible. That is a natural process in a balanced free market system. As long as there are plenty of cattle-producing sources as well as many different competing meatpacking companies, there is a free market. If one side becomes so powerful that it eliminates the business options of the other, however, the market is no longer balanced or even free. The sad truth is that cattle raisers no longer operate in a truly free market.

For more than sixty years, a federal agency called the Packers and Stockyards Administration (P&SA) regulated the beef industry to prevent price-fixing among the meatpacking companies and to guard against the creation of a meatpacking monopoly. Under the P&SA, the meatpacking industry was highly competitive. Small and independent local meatpackers comprised a major portion of the industry. Cattle prices were determined in fair and open auction markets in which typically there were numerous competitors making bids. In the early 1980s President Reagan's administration deregulated the industry, which led to a series of mergers and acquisitions in the meatpacking business. The result, ultimately, was the consolidation of the meatpacking industry into four enormous companies, which now dominate the market. These companies now process nearly 85 percent of the beef in the United States.

The meatpacking monopoly now engages in unfair business practices to keep cattle prices artificially low. They own about 20 percent of the nation's cattle, many of which are held in company feedlots. When cattle prices start to rise, cattle are released from these feedlots to increase the supply and control prices. The meatpacking conglomerates also purchase large numbers of cattle through confidential agreements in which the prices are kept secret. When you don't know how much the buyers are paying for a major part of the supply, it is difficult to determine what the fair price should be. These and other practices allow the meatpacking monopoly to control prices, especially in the fed cattle segment of the business.

The meatpackers claim that the real cause of low cattle prices is oversupply, but that is a misleading statement, because they base their argument on statistics from the domestic market. The fact is that we have a world market that thrives on our beef exports. If seen from the perspective of the export market, there actually is less production per capita today than has ever been the case in the past. Oversupply is simply a useful myth encouraged by the meatpackers.

It is important to point out that although the independent cattle raiser is a vanishing breed nationally, Texas cattle raisers do have a major advantage over their colleagues in the rest of the country. Texas cattle raisers benefit greatly from the terms of the state's annexation in 1846 in which Texas was allowed to enter the union without having to give its public land to the federal government. That means that many

Texas cattle raisers operate largely on land they own, while a large percentage of cattle raisers in other states, especially in the West, lease their grazing land from the state or federal government. Obviously, when you own your cattle land, you normally build up equity in that property, which allows you to use that increase in value as collateral for loans to finance your operation. If most of your business is on leased land, you don't have that critical financial option, and it can be the difference in failure or success.

Having an operation on their private land also allows cattle raisers in Texas to generate income from hunting leases. Currently, hunting leases produce four times more income per acre than raising cattle. In addition, landowners in Texas usually own the mineral rights to their land. The lease of those mineral rights to an energy company can produce substantial amounts of bonus income even when there is no oil or gas production. Natural gas production on my land has provided my cattle business with a significant safety net during especially difficult times. The ownership of mineral rights and the income it produces have preserved many of the old family cattle ranches in this state.

I don't want to give the impression that I'm a defeatist when it comes to what kind of future we face as cattle raisers. The advantages we enjoy in Texas, as I have mentioned above, are substantial. If the cattle raising industry can get regulatory help from the federal government to restore effective competition in the meatpacking industry, I am somewhat optimistic about the future. I sincerely believe there is tremendous potential for the Texas beef industry in the world market. Cattle raisers simply need a fair market in which to operate.

Despite these very real problems, I wouldn't discourage a young person in Texas from trying the ranching business. Ranching is a way of life that helps develop independence and strength of character. It can be a very hard life, but it can also be extremely satisfying. As a rancher, you have to be able to do a lot of things on your own, and much of that can only come from experience. But I would advise anyone wanting to be a rancher to go to college and major in business administration. A successful rancher has to understand accounting, for example. It is critical to have a current and accurate financial record at all times. If you don't know what you are doing financially, you probably won't make it in ranching. Agricultural courses are important as well. But the people who succeed in ranching are the ones who best know how to handle money.

I am delighted that my children have continued to be involved in ranching. My oldest daughter, Janey, and her husband, Jim Marmion, own a ranch in South Texas. Janey has one daughter, Janey Katherine (Kate) Marmion. My youngest daughter, Cele, is married to John Carpenter III of Dallas, whose family has land development and cattle operations in North Texas. The famous Las Colinas office complex was developed on the Carpenter family ranch land. Cele and John have three kids, Benjamin H. Carpenter II, Austin Williams Carpenter, and Bonner Briscoe Carpenter. My son, Chip, always wanted to be a rancher like Red Nunley, who was his role model. When he was kid, he told me that when he grew up, he wanted to be a working rancher, "just like Mr. Nunley." Chip earned his degree from the University of Texas at Austin. He now operates the Catarina and our other cattle operations in South Texas with great skill and dedication. He is never happier than when he is on horseback cutting cattle. Chip sometimes buys cattle in Mexico, and he brings them out just as my father and Red and I did for many years. He and his wife, Jill, have two sons, Dolph Briscoe IV, who we call "D. B.," and James Leigh Briscoe.

Catarina now is all cattle, mostly dark Santa Gertrudis, which is a hardy breed developed by the King Ranch. Santa Gertrudis cattle are ideal for the climate and land conditions of the area. My father began the Santa Gertrudis breeding program on the Catarina Ranch with stock from the King Ranch, and I have continued that program. As years passed, we replaced our other breeds at Catarina with red Santa Gertrudis cattle. I was a charter member of the Santa Gertrudis Breeders International organization. Today, deer and bird hunting leases produce a significant portion of the ranch's income. In the off-season, we have numerous hunters who enjoy stalking the large number of feral hogs that have populated the ranch in recent years.

Besides the Catarina and the 40,000 acre Chupadera, we own the Carla Ranch, which is adjacent to the Catarina. A few years ago, we purchased 33,000 acres in Marathon that were once part of the historic

Iron Mountain Ranch. We also still own the Rio Frio Ranch, north of Uvalde; several farms in the Uvalde area; and ranches in La Salle, McMullen, and Culberson counties. Briscoe Ranches now operates in nine counties with a total of 660,000 acres. We also lease about 100,000 acres at several ranches around Uvalde and in West Texas.

In addition to my ranching and other related businesses, I have had a majority interest in the First State Bank of Uvalde since 1959. When the bank came up for sale that year, I was very fortunate in that Clyde Shannon, president of the old Alamo National Bank in San Antonio, loaned me the money to make the purchase. I was a director of Alamo National at the time. It has been a very good investment. When I bought the bank, it had a value of about $8 million. Today the bank's value exceeds $300 million. I later also acquired the Security State Bank in Pearsall and the Zavala County Bank in Crystal City. I continue to serve as chairman of the board of each of these banks.

JANEY

Throughout the years after we left the Governor's Mansion in Austin, Janey and I led an extremely busy life. We were active together in our ranching and banking businesses, and we each had community service work that meant much to us. Janey served six exciting and fulfilling years as a regent of the University of Texas and she worked hard as a member of the Development Board of the UT-San Antonio Health Science Center. In the latter capacity, she raised $5.1 million to build a children's wing, which the university named for her. The children's center meant more to Janey than anything else she had done in her career of giving. Her efforts helped to save the lives of many children who would not have had a chance otherwise.

My beloved Janey died of heart disease in San Antonio on October 12, 2000. I have tried to make it clear in this book that Janey was my absolute full partner in everything, including the ranching business, politics, and in every other part of our lives. We had fifty-eight years together, and every single day of those years was wonderful. I just wanted more. I wanted fifty-eight more years, but, of course, it didn't work out that way.

PAST AND FUTURE

On the Chupadera there is a place on a high bluff above the Rio Grande where Janey and I liked to picnic with our grandchildren. The grandkids call that spot the "edge of Texas." It is a beautiful and remote location. It is a place where one can escape the drone of daily life and take a few precious moments to recall the past, take stock of the present, and contemplate the future. This memoir has been my attempt to recall some of my past and to take stock of the present.

In doing so, I can say honestly that for Janey and me, it has been a great ride. I can't imagine anything more wonderful than to be able to live here in the greatest state there has ever been, and to live our lives among and with the best and finest people to be found anywhere.

It is such a privilege to be a Texan. It is no surprise that so many people from other states move to Texas. It basically shows their good judgment. Texans are unique and different from the people of other states. That is because of many factors that truly make the Lone Star State the best.

One of those factors is our heritage as an independent nation with unlimited opportunity for those who were willing to work. Those who migrated to Texas in the early part of the 1800s came looking for an opportunity to create a better, more rewarding life for their family and themselves. Despite extreme hardship, deprivations, and dangers, they persevered. The result has been that their children, their grandchildren, and their descendents have had the privileges and opportunities that those original settlers dreamed of and wanted for them.

Any way you look at it, the history of our state is an example of determination, hard work, and dedication, and, through all that, achievement of a better way of life, a life of greater opportunity. I firmly believe that we cannot really understand the present without knowledge of the past. And, as we look to the past, I think we can better and more accurately see the future of the state that we all love.

As I hope that you can tell from this memoir, I believe in the great value of historical knowledge. Learning about the history of our state and nation has enriched my life in so many ways. And I want others to have their lives enriched as well. That is one of the reasons why I

In my Uvalde office with Rick Eason, UT-Austin vice president for development, left, and Dr. Don Carleton, executive director of UT-Austin's Center for American History, right. Don has been my steadfast partner in writing this memoir. *Briscoe Papers; di_03302.*

have established the Dolph and Janey Briscoe Endowment for Texas History at the University of Texas Center for American History. The center is an amazing treasure house of valuable documents, maps, books, and other items that are essential to the study of Texas history, as well as other aspects of the story of our country. The center's work to preserve the historical record and to facilitate teaching and research in American history deserves the support of all Texans. I am proud that Janey and I have been able to enhance that work with our own support.

I don't see how any one of us could look to the future and be anything but enthused, challenged, and truly, as some like to say, "pumped up." It is true that we have the problems of an expanding economy and a rapidly growing population. In the past, the people of Texas have always risen to the challenge and, at the same time, created new and better opportunities for all Texans. I have no doubt that that will be the Texas of the future. We will meet our challenges and turn them into opportunities for building an even greater state, a stronger economy, and an educational system, both primary and higher education, that is second to none.

I believe the future of Texas could not be brighter. The best is yet to come for our great state. *Photograph by Wade Carpenter, Uvalde.*

To maintain momentum and remain competitive with other states, we must be determined to continue down the path of being the greatest state of all, in every sense of the word. That, of course, means that we will have to excel in many different ways.

Perhaps the most critical thing we could do for the future is to make certain that we have the very best educational system possible. We must continue our efforts to improve the effectiveness of our public schools. And certainly our institutions of higher learning must not only be competitive, but must be the very best in the nation. That has to be our goal. It is essential to our future.

To maintain and enhance our strong economy, we must continue to run an effective state government at the lowest cost possible. We must maintain an economic environment that encourages investment in existing businesses and allows us to compete for new businesses, all of which will create more and better job opportunities.

We must maintain a tax system that encourages investment and growth, and to me that depends on the continuation of our distinction as a state that has no income tax.

This is a great time to be alive and an even greater time to enjoy the privilege of being a Texan. I think the young people of our state have the greatest future available to them ever in the history of our state, of any other state, or any other nation. To the younger generation of today, I would like to say this: think about the past, think about those who came here seeking a better way of life, and how, through hard work, they achieved it for themselves and their children, and then think about the opportunities that exist today that they didn't have. You can truly say that we have a great history and heritage, as unique as it is, but I also firmly and unequivocally believe that the best is yet to come.

INDEX